A Civil War Marine at Sea

Miles M. Oviatt

A Civil War Marine at Sea

The Diary of Medal of Honor Recipient Miles M. Oviatt

Edited By

Mary P. Livingston

White Mane Books

Any illustrations not otherwise credited are from the editor's collection.

This White Mane Books publication
was printed by
Beidel Printing House, Inc.
63 West Burd Street
Shippensburg, PA 17257-0152 USA

In respect for the scholarship contained herein, the acid-free paper used in this book meets the guidelines for permanence and durability of the Committee on Production Guidelines for Book Longevity of the Council on Library Resources.

For a complete list of available publications
please write
White Mane Books
Division of White Mane Publishing Company, Inc.
P.O. Box 152
Shippensburg, PA 17257-0152 USA

Library of Congress Cataloging-in-Publication Data

Oviatt, Miles M. (Miles Mason), 1840-1880
    A Civil War marine at sea : the diary of Medal of Honor recipient
Miles M. Oviatt / edited by Mary P. Livingston.
        p.   cm.
    Includes bibliographical references and index.
    ISBN 1-57249-076-4 (alk. paper)
    1. Oviatt, Miles M. (Miles Mason). 1840-1880--Diaries. 2. United
States--History--Civil War, 1861-1865--Naval operations. 3. United
States--History--Civil War, 1861-1865--Personal narratives.
4. United States. Marine Corps--History--Civil War, 1861-1865.
5. United States. Marine Corps Biography. 6. Vanderbilt (Ship)
7. Brooklyn (Ship) 8. Olean (N.Y.)--Biography. I. Livingston,
Mary P. , 1932-   . II. Title
E601.09   1998
973.7'58'092--dc21
[B]   97-50177
                                                           CIP

PRINTED IN THE UNITED STATES OF AMERICA

To the Memory of the Marines and
Sailors Who Gallantly Defended the
Union at Home and in Far off Seas
during the Civil War. May They
Never be Forgotten.

Table of Contents

List of Illustrations

List of Maps

Acknowledgements

The production of this manuscript was made possible by many private individuals and institutions. The Indiana University Library in Bloomington, containing the complete Official Naval Records of the Civil War, helped me round out and detail the historic events lived by Miles Oviatt. The efforts of the Naval Historical Foundation, the National Archives in Washington, D.C., and Miss Alice S. Creighton of the Nimitz Library at the U.S. Naval Academy, Annapolis, Maryland, produced many of the officer and ship images herein. My relatives in Olean and elsewhere, who put up with my persistent inquiries and searches into their attics and basements, are given my undying gratitude. Their cooperation was always fruitful. Special thanks goes to David M. Sullivan of Rutland, Massachusetts, a recognized expert on the Marine Corps in the Civil War, who guided me through the maze of image collections and steered me on the proper course needed to publish this work. His help and encouragement have been invaluable. To Dr. Martin K. Gordon whose vision started the book toward publication. The constant rewrites and corrections would have taken years longer if it had not been for my computer and printer kept running in good repair by my faithful husband and friend, Julian. This manuscript would never have been written if it had not been for providence that placed these diaries in my hands, and membership in the Daughters of the American Revolution sparking my interest in genealogy and American History. My gratitude to all of you.

Introduction

BY MARY P. LIVINGSTON

Many stories and accounts of the Civil War have been written, published, and depicted in paintings, movies and television about armies and famous battles of Gettysburg, Chancellorsville, Charleston and others. One would almost believe that the War of the Rebellion was fought only on land. We read mostly about the great generals and their deeds and are less aware of the countless men—privates, corporals, volunteers—who came from farms, small towns and obscure families to fight for the cause they believed in. These men on both sides—the Blue and the Gray—are what make up the stirring story of the Civil War.

While both Union and Confederate generals were leading their troops on the battlefield, there was another group waging battles of their own. The Union Navy and Marine Corps, aboard fine sailing ships armed with guns and fighting gear, were transversing the Atlantic Ocean from the Northern to the Southern hemisphere. As far east as Africa and Mauritius in the Indian Ocean, those steam frigates searched out, captured or destroyed blockade runners bringing goods to the Confederacy. The South also relied on the sale of its cotton crop to European countries for money to support its army. Conditions on the high seas were as perilous and unsanitary as those on the battlefields at home. The threat of illness, drowning, and the danger of fire were part of the sailors' everyday life, as they sailed from port to port looking for contraband and the whereabouts of enemy vessels. The wooden ships needed a constant supply of coal and had to rely on foreign governments to supply it. Repairs were difficult and often could not be done at all. Large sums of money were required to keep these ships in service. Many countries were forced to take sides in an action that resulted in a homeland scarred by battles, ravaged cities, and loss of many lives.

This story is about one such young Marine from a small farm village in western New York State, assigned to, first, the U.S.S. *Vanderbilt*, and then the U.S.S. *Brooklyn*, two ships that made their mark in the naval battles of the Civil War. Miles M. Oviatt, at twenty-one years, left the safety of his home to face an unknown voyage into history. As we read his words, we feel the anxiety with which he starts his naval career, his longing for the sights and sounds of home, his regret at taking such a bold step. We are alongside him as he learns the jargon of the sailor, as he tries out his newly found skills and strengths. His words flow more easily as time goes by. Through his eyes we see the Bahama Islands, the Caribbean Islands, the Azores, the ports of South America and South Africa. We are on board as enemy ships are captured and prisoners taken. We learn how long one must wait for news of the progress of the war at home; newspapers and word passed from other friendly ships were the only source. We wait with him as days turn into weeks, finding nothing but another island, another load of coal, another holy stoning of the deck. Dates are recorded incorrectly, occasionally, as time has no meaning on the high seas. Each day is like the last.

Then we experience the excitement of battles alongside important men such as Admirals Farragut, Wilkes, and Porter, facing enemy gunfire and torpedoes. We learn how little these men were paid for taking such a dangerous mission; the sparse meals available on shipboard. A stop at a tropical island meant fresh fruit paid for out of the men's pockets. An occasional liberty was greeted with delight for just a few hours off from the hard life on board a frigate.

Not much is known about Miles Oviatt's life beyond what has been included here. He proved to be a reliable, brave Marine, capable of staying at his battle station, doing his duty as he had agreed on. The majority of his compatriots were of the same caliber, and were rewarded at the end of the war with prize money for capturing enemy ships. His diaries have made it possible to learn a lesson in honor and dedication to duty. His memory is well served by this careful transcription of his words.

Biography of Miles M. Oviatt

The wilderness of western New York State was slowly being settled by hardy pioneer men and women during the first half of the nineteenth century. Thomas Van Rensselaer Oviatt, a log raft pilot on the Allegany River, and his wife, Lydia Jane Rice, had established a home in Boardmanville, a section of Olean, New York, purchasing large acreage from the Holland Land Company. In 1849 Thomas had turned to farming as a better vocation now that he had a family to support. Their three children had been born earlier in neighboring Allegany County, where Thomas and Lydia had begun their courtship in the mid 1830s, while Thomas was still working at his trade on the river. Helen Elizabeth Oviatt was born in 1838 soon after the couple's marriage; Miles Mason Oviatt, born December 1, 1840, in Little Genesee; and Milo Allison Oviatt in 1845.

The mark of the Oviatt family on the history of this country is indeed important enough to include a story of the people who provided the strong fibers that gave life to the future Miles Oviatt. The family has its roots in Connecticut with the first immigrant, Thomas Oviatt, a soapmaker, arriving in 1664 from England. Settling finally in Milford, Connecticut, he produced eight children, naming one after himself. That son, Thomas, moved to New Milford, Connecticut, in 1723, where he and his wife, Lydia Kellogg, became active in the Congregational Church. Their first son, Thomas, born in 1706, fought in the French and Indian Wars as a private in both the Third and Fourth Regiments of Connecticut in 1758 and 1759, respectively. He and wife, Margaret Brownson, had nine children, one naturally named Thomas. That name, Thomas, was to continue down through each generation until 1840 when Miles Oviatt was born.

Thomas Oviatt, born in 1736 of Thomas and Margaret, was the pioneering Oviatt that started his family branch westward. While in New Milford, he married Elizabeth Botsford, and together they produced four children. Their lives were quite stable in this quaint village until the arrival of Jemima

Wilkinson, the religious fanatic from Rhode Island. Elizabeth Oviatt became caught up in the fervor that enveloped the town. She and others left their homes and families on the advice of the Universal Friend, as Jemima was known, to follow her to the New Jerusalem to be located in central New York State. Elizabeth's desertion is recorded as December 5, 1785, leaving four young children and a bewildered husband. Elizabeth and her brothers, Abel, Jonathan, and Elnathan Botsford, moved to Yates County, then Ontario County, settling in the religious community formed by the Jemimakins, where Elizabeth Oviatt died about 1802. Her husband, Thomas, had divorced her on January 31, 1793, and moved with his sister, Anna and her husband, Job Camp, to Wyalusing, Luzerne County, Pennsylvania. The Connecticut Company owned the northeastern section of Pennsylvania and was deeding land to families who wanted to move westward. Thomas' daughters, Lydia and Elizabeth, eventually moved there, inheriting his possessions upon his death in 1810.

His sons, Joseph and Thomas, had taken up residence in New York State earlier. Son Thomas set up his household in Steuben County adjoining the land where his mother, Elizabeth, lived. He and his wife, Cynthia, gave birth to Thomas Van Rensselaer in 1809, Cyrus in 1817, and Luther in 1819. The family farmed and lived well off the lush land of the Finger Lakes. Disaster struck when Thomas died shortly after the birth of Luther, leaving Cynthia with three small children. Cynthia soon married widower Simeon Trim, a local farmer, and combined their small children into one large household, adding several children of their own.

Thomas Van Rensselaer Oviatt accompanied this newly formed family to Allegany County where he learned the trade of rafting on the Allegany River. Working for a local lumber company, he spent many months each spring floating logs to market as far away as Cincinnati, Ohio. He met his future bride in Portville, New York, but had to pursue her to Trumbull County, Ohio, where she had gone to keep house for her uncle. They were married there in 1838, eventually moving to Olean to farm and settle down to a more permanent way of life.

The southern tier of western New York State was a fertile area nourished by rivers and streams. In 1797, the Big Tree Treaty defined tracts of land exclusively for the Indians' use, creating reservations, thus opening the rest for occupation by the whites. The next year, a company of Holland Merchants purchased from Robert Morris his title to four large tracts he had bought from the State of Massachusetts. The Holland Land Company had no trouble selling this land to the eager pioneers who were moving west. Adam Hoops, in 1804, purchased twenty thousand acres on the Allegany River, believing it would become a large commercial depot. He laid out a village which he named Hamilton after his compatriot, Alexander Hamilton, in the Revolution. In 1807 Hoops led a band of pioneers to the area, dedicating the public square. His brother, Robert, built the first log dwelling. But unable to meet the purchase payments, most of Hoops' land reverted back to the Holland Land Company. They sold tracts to individuals who wanted to farm. By 1809, Hamilton was known as Olean Point. Saw mills were abundant, and eleven tanneries called Olean their home. Logs were floated down the Allegany and Ohio Rivers to markets at Warren, Pennsylvania, and Cincinnati, Ohio. Thomas Van Rensselaer Oviatt was one of the early customers of the Holland Land Company, establishing his farm next to Jeheil Boardman and the Olean Creek.

The peaceful life of the Oviatt family continued until the sectional controversies of the 1840s and 1850s led to the outbreak of war in April, 1861. Patriotic enthusiasm led Luther, an uncle of Miles Oviatt, and Luther's son, Thomas V., to sign up to fight for the Union. Luther named one of his sons after his brother, Thomas Van Rensselaer Oviatt. Records of the two men could be confused if it were not for the thirty-year gap between them. Luther enrolled October 21, 1862, in the 14th Pennsylvania but died a year later in Point Lookout, Maryland, of severe diarrhea. His son, Thomas V., enlisted August 9, 1862, in the Pennsylvania Militia Infantry for nine months. He reenlisted September 14, 1864, for one year in the New Cavalry Company K, 199th Regiment of Pennsylvania Volunteers.

From census data we learn that Miles Oviatt had more than one occupation in his youth. The 1860 census for Cattaraugus County records him as a tinner's apprentice at age nineteen and living in a hotel. In those days, a few hotels lined Union Street near the train tracks and perhaps the tinsmith was also centrally located. One can imagine Miles trudging through the dirt streets kicking up dust on his way to his job at the tin shop, perhaps carrying a quickly prepared lunch from the hotel in his handkerchief. No evidence has been uncovered as to why he was not living at home, helping his father on the farm. Brother Milo was fifteen at the time and on the farm, as well as sister Helen, so that may have given Miles the opportunity to try his hand at another trade.

The 1865 census lists Miles at twenty-four years in the household of his father, even though he was still in the Marine Corps. An affidavit issued from the Marine Corps Adjutant and Inspector's Office concerning Oviatt's enlistment states his occupation as clerk. When enlisted on August 19, 1862, in New York by Captain Charles Heywood, later to become commandant, Oviatt was described as 21 years old, five feet, eleven and one-half inches tall, with blue eyes, brown hair, and a fresh complexion.

Shortly after joining the Marine Corps Volunteers, Company M, 5th Regiment, Oviatt was assigned to the U.S.S. *Vanderbilt* for a lengthy period through March 1864. He was promoted to full corporal on June 6, 1863. He must have been quite proud of his ship and his service because he sent to the family at home a photograph of a painting of the *Vanderbilt* on a carte de visite. On completion of the *Vanderbilt*'s assignment to search for blockade runners in the South Atlantic, that ship was moored at the

Brooklyn Navy Yard where Oviatt was hospitalized suffering from a severe cold. He was absent from duty for some time. Concurrently, the bloody battle at Chancellorsville under General Joseph Hooker, Army of the Potomac, and General Robert E. Lee, the Army of Northern Virginia, stained the rolling farmland and forever changed the landscape of Virginia. Vicksburg and Port Hudson's fall to the Union forces opened the Mississippi, and changed operations focus to Admiral David Farragut and the Gulf.

Having recovered sufficiently to resume his duties, Oviatt was then transferred to the U.S.S. *Brooklyn* on April 14, 1864, two days after the Capture of Fort Pillow, Tennessee, a station that tried in vain to guard the Mississippi River from invasion by the Union army. Farragut was formulating his plans for the capture of Mobile Bay that spring, observing and noting the South's strength in that area. He asked the Navy Department for iron-clad vessels as well as five thousand men to wage a battle against Forts Morgan and Gaines. The *Brooklyn* was assigned to that fleet and Oviatt was on his way. He, once again, showed his pride of service by sending home three carte de visites of the *Brooklyn*. One was the original, inscribed on the back by J. Hansen, Marine Painter, 173 South Street, N.Y. Oviatt had penned "U.S.S. Sloop of War Brooklyn, Capt. Jas. Alden, Commander, M.M. Oviatt" and had added the date "Aprl. 30th 1864." He used his time before sailing on May 10 to secure these and to write home. His family carefully stored the pictures in an album where they survived in excellent condition for one-hundred and thirty years. Miles' diaries give the details of the *Brooklyn*'s service during the following year.

After the campaign of Mobile Bay, while the crippled U.S.S. *Brooklyn* lay in Pensacola Harbor waiting to sail home to Boston for repairs, Oviatt, as he casually mentions in his diary, was promoted to sergeant on September 1, 1864. News arrived that two months earlier, the long awaited destruction of the C.S.S. *Alabama*, sought by the Union fleet, had occurred off the coast of France through action of the U.S.S. *Kearsarge*. The South's position on the high seas was permanently damaged. The crew of the *Brooklyn*, which had also searched for the *Alabama*, was overjoyed at the news.

The *Brooklyn*'s crew transferred to the Charlestown Barracks where they received a well deserved liberty for two nights. When the *Brooklyn* had been repaired enough to resume her sea duties, the crew reboarded and started for Hampton Roads to join Admiral Porter's squadron and operations in Wilmington for the Battle of Fort Fisher. The *Brooklyn* returned to Hampton Roads in January 1865, proud of her role in that victory.

Oviatt was assigned to the Marine Barracks in Brooklyn, New York, on January 31, and finally to the Marine Barracks in Washington, D.C., where he was stationed at the time of his acceptance of the Medal of Honor on June 17, 1865. He was assigned to the guard of the *Marion*, a 566-ton screw steamer, where he had duties of 1st sergeant. It was during the spring of 1866 that Oviatt was again hospitalized with chronic diarrhea, and severe head pain. It was fortunate that his discharge after four years' service was coming up as he might not have been able to carry out his duties much longer. He was honorably discharged on August 20, 1866, and returned to Olean where he resumed his metal working trade. This assertion is based on the evidence in a photograph which shows Miles, after the Civil War, driving a team of horses pulling a boiler through the streets of Olean.

During the last days of Miles' service, his mother wrote him a letter that gave a few homespun sentiments. His brother Allison had bought light pants, vest and fine boots and returned home to await the spring floods so he could rejoin the crews of the river log rafts. Thomas had plowed the pasture for fall wheat, and they were down to two cows for the summer. A neighbor had sent a servant girl over to work for the Oviatts but Lydia didn't think she was worth the money it took to feed her. His mother also reflected on the Methodist Church and its plea for one thousand dollars to support Genesee College at Lima, New York, and the surprising fact that it had been raised. The letter closed with a recipe for a cholera remedy, supposedly to help Miles with his cure at the hospital.

We get a clearer picture of Miles' life prior to his enlisting in the Marines in 1862 from his diaries. He makes many statements about his hasty decision to enlist and how much he regretted it. Olean was very small in those days and it would seem reasonable for a youth of nineteen to live at home, even though he might be pursuing a different vocation than his father. However, he was living in a hotel, and one can only assume he was trying to break away from his parents' home. He joined the Marine Corps in haste, swept along by the fever of war and the excitement of many of his friends doing the same. A good friend, Willard Moon Smith, enlisted with Miles and was also cited for his part in the Battle of Mobile Bay. Both men received the Congressional Medal of Honor. Two others, George W. Kelsey and George H. Bandfield, mentioned many times in these diaries, were also from Olean. They had teamed up with Oviatt and Smith on their way to Brooklyn to enlist. During the four years of service, Oviatt grew to love the military life, its disciplines, its excitement. His pride of service to his country was evident for the rest of his life.

On July 19, 1868, Miles married Lucetta Alzina Crandall of Ceres, Allegany County, New York. She was born March 19, 1847, in Genesee, New York, the daughter of George Spencer Crandall and Corintha M. Hamilton, well-known farmers of Ceres. By 1875 he and Lucetta had established their own household in Pleasant Valley, just north of Boardmanville. They are listed as farmers in the county census of 1875. There is some discrepancy as to Oviatt's correct middle name. Census records list "Allen," "Mason," and at one time Miles himself even wrote "Mortimer." His tombstone reads Miles M.A. Oviatt.

A single child, Frances Emily Oviatt, was born to Miles and Lucetta on November 26, 1876, in Olean. Frances eventually became an important business woman in Olean, owning a partnership in the W.H. Mandeville Insurance Company, founded in the middle 1800s. She also was appointed by New York Governor Franklin D. Roosevelt as a delegate to the Conference of the National Tax Association in 1929 and 1930.

The sequence of events leading to Miles' returning to service as a member of the Pleasant Valley Cavalry unit was as follows. After the close of the Civil War in 1865, the army turned its attention to the continuing Indian unrest that was affecting all areas of the country. Bloody battles continued to rage until 1891, resulting in the slaughter of thousands of U.S. soldiers and Native Americans. The Indians were fighting to retain their lands, and their killing methods were a horror to the white man. Many grisly accounts have been documented in the history books. The army had been using old muzzle-loader small arms, relics of the Civil War, which were finally replaced in 1867 by new, improved Springfield .50-Caliber rifles, the first of its type ever issued to troops in Indian country. This gave the army a welcome advantage.

Major General Philip Sheridan was appointed commander in chief of the army in 1868. His Indian policy was one of extermination. A significant event in the later years of the Indian Wars was the Treaty of 1868 with the Sioux which was broken by General George A. Custer. He and the 7th Cavalry discovered gold in the Black Hills, Sioux territory covered by the treaty, and disregarded the agreement by promoting mining. The Sioux Campaign of 1876, and the ultimate surrender of Chief Crazy Horse that year, demonstrated the Indians' desire to keep the lands marked out for them by the treaty, which had been violated. This was followed by the capture of the Cheyenne in 1878 by Sheridan and the entire division of Missouri; and the Northern Cheyenne "Dull Knife" outbreak at Fort Robinson, Nebraska, in 1879. Miles Oviatt wanted to support this policy; he was again being swept up in the popular fever.

His obituary from a local newspaper states that Captain Miles M. Oviatt, after drilling and preparing his men to join the battles, was taken ill and died, at the young age of 39, on November 1, 1880. On his widow's Declaration for Original Pension, the immediate cause of death was stated as Congestion of Brain and Inflammation of Lungs due to Exposure. This was probably a result of the chronic diarrhea that plagued him for many years and which may have been a result of exposure to diseases in the course of his ocean voyages during the Civil War.

Oviatt's Pension File No. 18756, obtained from the National Archives in Washington, D.C., contains many documents supporting Lucetta's claim for pension benefits. Several affidavits are from his fellow-Marines, Willard Moon Smith, George H. Bandfield, and George W. Kelsey, which describe their visits to Oviatt while he was confined to the Brooklyn Navy Yard

Hospital following his service on the U.S.S. *Vanderbilt*, and again in the spring of 1866 at the Marine Barracks Hospital in Washington, D.C. His friends described him as "a healthy, strong able-bodied man" at the beginning of his enlistment and, as they all lived in Olean, they were able to see how his health had deteriorated after the war. Smith stated in his affidavit that Oviatt was "seriously ill with a severe attack of Chronic Diarrhea, so diagnosed by his surgeons. The pain was very hard in the stomach and bowels." Smith believed that some blackberry cordial which he brought to the hospital gave Oviatt some relief. Pains in the head and lung trouble added to his discomfort. Therefore, it seems curious that he would resume a military career in the face of many ailments and having a wife and young child to care for at home.

His young widow, Lucetta, married Charles A. Turner on November 19, 1890, providing a new father for her young daughter. Lucetta did receive pension benefits in the amount of $20.00 per month and was raised to $25.00 by the end of 1917. Upon her death on November 11, 1925, she was receiving $30.00 per month.

Miles M. Oviatt is buried in the Pleasant Valley Cemetery on Route 16 north of Olean. He lies beside his father and mother, marked by a tall monument in a grove of trees at the rear of the cemetery. In 1989, nearly 110 years after his death, the United States Government provided a bronze marker for his grave, noting his Civil War service and his Congressional Medal of Honor. Only after this was done did a flag appear on the grave, probably put there by the local American Legion. During the research for this book, it was distressing to find very little about him in the Olean historical records. The Federal and County Census for 1850, 1855, and 1880 located him in Olean, and the Child's Gazeteer and Business Directory of 1874–75 records him owning 47 1/2 acres on Route 4 which would be the area north of Olean in Pleasant Valley. No file in the Olean Historical Preservation Society provided any record of Miles' Civil War service, his Medal of Honor, or any other details of his life. In fact, his obituary is very short, with no mention of his four years in the Marine Corps nor any other admirable aspect that should have been known in the hometown of a hero. Only the most recent events concerning Miles' work with the Pleasant Valley Cavalry Unit were noted. The Garfield and Arthur Club, active in Olean when Miles died is not known to the Historical Society. The local Civil War Round Table organization is proud of the local sons of the Civil War but did not know of Miles Oviatt nor Willard Moon Smith and their heroic service.

The History of Cattauragus County, New York, mentions briefly the arrival of Thomas Van Rensselaer Oviatt as one of the first settlers, and the First Methodist Church records have a few sketchy remarks about Thomas as an elected trustee in 1851. A small obituary for Thomas appeared in 1881, mentioning only the immediate circumstances of his death and his church affiliation. Another surprising discovery during the research period was at Friedsam Memorial Library at St. Bonaventure University, just west of Olean. Their microfilm newspaper files of the Olean papers of the nineteenth century are missing the years 1861 through 1865. The librarian had no explanation for this.

One of several conclusions can be reached in an effort to understand this lack of information. Miles did not live long enough to join the Grand Army of the Republic (G.A.R.) or to figure into the Civil War-interested era of the early 1900s. Willard Smith had moved to Buffalo, and the focus may have been on the weary soldiers of Gettysburg, New Market, and the surrender at Appomattox Court House. Miles did not receive his discharge until August of 1866, over a year past the date of the surrender by the South on April 10, 1865. He undoubtedly returned to his hometown after the excitement of the end of the war had passed.

The following photograph shows Miles seated at the reins of a team pulling a wagon through a dirt street of Olean in 1868. It is, incidentally, a historical record of the now missing buildings on Union Street of that year. The boiler must have been quite heavy to require eight horses. This picture was taken two years after his discharge and suggests a man capable of doing a day's work, not the sickly soldier described in the application for pension. Perhaps he was able to work from time to time as his infirmity would allow. As Miles and Lucetta were married in that year, he had to provide a home and amenities for his new bride.

The search for a good closeup photograph of Miles Oviatt looked hopeless. After many visits to distant cousins in Olean, digging through boxes in attics, leafing through albums, it seemed painfully clear that none existed. One person recalled a tintype of Miles in uniform but it had disappeared half a century ago. His diaries were going to be published without an image of the man who had set down his thoughts so well on paper. But fates smiled down at the last moment. An album, long forgotten in a closet, was brought forth. Among its tattered, yellowing pages, containing many images of long dead men and women, sprang forth the face of Miles Oviatt. Labeled with his name, the sepia carte de visite clearly shows the head and shoulders of a man dressed in a dark suit jacket, collared vest, white pleated-front shirt and tie tucked under the shirt collar. His slim face, with strangely sad eyes, sports a small moustache under a long straight nose. His dark hair is tightly curled at the ends, and his wide chin shows a slight crease and dimple. High cheekbones seem to be inherited from his mother as seen in her carte de visite. Nestled close by were the pictures of his beloved ships, *Vanderbilt* and *Brooklyn*, all hidden together for over a century. The story now seems complete. But will it ever be? How many other hidden wisps of Miles' life are still waiting to be found? Will we ever know?

"Union St. at the corner of Laurens St., 1868. First team, my Father's, Miles M. Oviatt. He is driving sitting on front of boiler. In back ground is the M.E. Church, the building now owned by Hastings Est. and the old Pierce Residence"— Written by Frances E. Oviatt, daughter of Miles Oviatt

Olean, May 27, 1866

My Dear Son Miles

It is with pleasure I sit down to write you a few lines, as it is the only way at present we can converse. but I anticipate much greater pleasure when a few more weeks have passed. You enlisted the 12th of August I think if so you have 11 weeks from the day when your time is expired. I have been wishing they would give you a discharge when the fleet leaves I do not see why they need you longer; we have a very cold backward spring it froze several nights last week we have not had but few days that we did not kneed a fire to sit by

Allison is home again and wishing for another flood he bought him a pair of light pants and vest

Unsent letter to Miles Oviatt from his mother

These three pages show an unsent letter to Miles Oviatt from his mother, Lydia Jane Rice, during his enlistment period.

down the river and a pair of fine boots
since he came home. The new Tannery
is adding greatly to the groth of this
place. They are building now 12 dwelling
houses in the pine grove in the rear ground
Pa has got this spring work done and a
piece of pasture plowed for fall wheat
Moore's folks got hard of their Duch girl
and sent her to me. She can do a goodmany
chores by being told, every time it costs
but little do pay her or I would not keep
her. three shillings a week is the price
but it costs something to feed her and
the patience of Job to learn her to work
My house work is not much I could do
without help as we have only two cows
this summer i neat have got any house
cleaned

This is the hundredth year of
Methodism in the United States
a centenary meeting was held this month

in the church at Clean. at the
close the Presiding elder said to the
congregation that they wanted one
thousan dollars from Clean for the
purpose of endowing Genesee College
at Lima. I did not think he would
get half but the whole amount was
soon subscribed. but it was the Big
men and not the Church

Mrs Mulling has married an Irishman
whiles I am hard up for something
to write but there is a receipt for Cholery
that Edward G. Price wrote me with a request
I should send it you

One part Laudalum
One part Spirits Camphor
Two parts Tincture of ginger
Two parts Capsican

Dose one tea spoonfull in a glass of warm
water. if the case is obstinate repeat in
three or four hours

An Unsent Letter

Unsent letter to Miles Oviatt from his mother, Lydia Jane Rice, during his enlistment period.

Olean May 27, 1866—My Dear Son Miles, Its with pleasure I sit down to write you a few lines, as it is the only way at present we can converse. But I anticipate much greater pleasure when a few more weeks have passed. You enlisted the 12th of August, I think, if so, you have 11 weeks from today when your time is up but I have been wishing they would give you a discharge when the fleet leaves. I do not see why they need you longer. We have a very cold backward spring. It froze several nights last week. We have not had but few days that we did not kneed a fire to sit by.

Allison is home again and wishing for another flood. He bought him a pair of light pants and vest down the river and a pair of fine boots since he came home. The new Tannery is adding greatly to the groth of this place. They are building now 12 dwelling houses in the pine grove in the rear ground. Pa has got his spring work done and a piece of paster plowed for fall wheat. Shrooves folks got tiard of there Duch girl and sent her to me. She can do a good many chores by being told every time. It costs but little to pay her or I would not keep her. Three shillings a week is the price but it costs something to feed her and the patience of Job to learn her to work. My house work is not much. I could do without help as we have only two cows this sumer and have got my house cleaned.

This is the hundredth year of Methodistsm in the United States. A centenary meeting was held this month in the church at Olean. At the close the Presiding elder said to the congregation that they wanted one thousan dollars from Olean for the purpose of endowing Genesee College at Lima. I did not think he would get half but the whole amount was soon subscribed. But it was the Big men and not the Church.

Mrs Nutting has married an Irishman. Miles I am hard up for something to write but here is a receipt for Cholery that Aunt S. Price wrote me with a request I should send it you.

One part laudulam

One part spirits camphor

Two parts tincture of ginger

Two parts Caprican

Dose one teaspoonfull in a glass of warm water. If the case is obstinate repeat in three or four hours.

[This letter ended at this point, no signature]

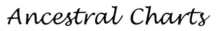

Ancestral Charts

ANCESTOR CHART for MARY PATTERSON HELIKER LIVINGSTON
4-digit dates are a guess; final 4 zeros indicate month and day unknown.

BD:=Birth Date
MD:=Marriage Date
DD:=Death Date
BP:=Birth Place
LR:=Last Residence

HELIKER CLARK RICE

BD:18320000 MD: 0
DD:19120000
BP:NY STATE (STEUBEN CO?)
LR:INDIANAPOLIS IN

BUEL(L) SARAH C. HELIKER

BD:18501229
DD:18870314
BP:ROME TWNSP CRAWFORD CO PA
LR:ROME TWNSP CRAWFORD CO PA

OVIATT MILES MASON ALIO

BD:18401201 MD:18680719
DD:18801101
BP:GENESEE TWP, NY
LR:OLEAN NY

CRANDALL LUCETTA ALZINA OVIATT

BD:18470319
DD:19251104
BP:GENESEE NY
LR:OLEAN NY

HELIKER ALBERT JOHN

BD:18730601 MD:18970629
DD:19370418
BP:TITUSVILLE PA
LR:GREEN COVE SPR FL

OVIATT FRANCES EMILY HELIKER LARKIN

BD:18761126
DD:19350526
BP:OLEAN NY
LR:OLEAN NY

HELIKER OVIATT VAN RENSSELAER

BD:18990107 MD:19280908
DD:1978 0317
BP:OLEAN NY
LR:CUBA LAKE CUBA NY (NEAR OLEAN)

HELIKER MARY PATTERSON LIVINGSTON

BD:19320622 MD:19530808
DD: 0
BP:OLEAN NY
LR:BLOOMINGTON, IN

xxviii

ANCESTOR CHART for MARY PATTERSON HELIKER LIVINGSTON (*Continued*)

PATTERSON JULIAN S

BD:18560000 MD:18800000
DD:18960000
BP:CARMICHAELS GREEN CO PA
LR:PHILADELPHIA PA

EATON MARY GILLAND PATTERSON

BD:18590202
DD:18830619
BP:PA
LR:CARMICHAELS PA

PATTERSON JAMES CLARENCE

BD:18810121 MD:19071226
DD:19450218
BP:CARMICHAELS PA
LR:EAST ORANGE NJ

WALTON ABNER BRINTON

BD:18531106 MD:18740311
DD:19280430
BP:WEST FALLOW FLD CHESTER CO PA
LR:COATESVILLE PA

HARTSHORNE ELIZABETH CROSLEY WALTON

BD:18510913
DD:19360731
BP:WEST FALLOWFIELD PA
LR:COATESVILLE PA

WALTON ELIZABETH VIRGINIA PATTERSON

BD:18880525
DD:19510426
BP:COCHRANVILLE CHESTER CO PA
LR:408 LAURENS ST OLEAN NY

PATTERSON DOROTHY ELIZABETH HELIKER

BD:19081023
DD:19620608
BP:COATESVILLE PA
LR:OLEAN NY

ANCESTOR CHART for MILES M. OVIATT
4-digit dates are a guess; final 4 zeros indicate month and day unknown.

BD:=Birth Date
MD:=Marriage Date
DD:=Death Date
BP:=Birth Place
LR:=Last Residence

OVIATT THOMAS

BD:17360929 MD:17690126
DD:18100402
BP:NEW MILFORD, CT
LR:WYALUSING, BRADFORD CO, PA

BOTSFORD ELIZABETH OVIATT

BD:17400922
DD:1802
BP:NEW MILFORD, CT
LR:YATES CO, NY

SHUMWAY REUBEN

BD:17591228 MD:1785
DD:18271220
BP:OXFORD, MASS
LR:STEUBEN CO, NY

TOWNE MIRIAM SHUMWAY

BD:17560713
DD: 18190403
BP:BELCHERTOWN, MASS
LR:STEUBEN CO, NY

OVIATT THOMAS

BD:17811104 MD: 1809
DD: 1819
BP:NEW MILFORD, CT
LR:STEUBEN OR ALLEG CO NY

OVIATT THOMAS VAN RENSSELAER

BD:18091231 MD:18380215
DD:18810525
BP:TOMPKINS CO,STEUBEN CO, NY?
LR:OLEAN NY

SHUMWAY CYNTHIA OVIATT TRIMM

BD:17790700
DD:18610113
BP:NEW YORK STATE
LR:EAST BRANCH, WARREN CO. PA

OVIATT MILES MASON ALIO

BD:18401201 MD:18680719
DD:18801101
BP:GENESEE TWP, NY
LR:OLEAN NY

ANCESTOR CHART for MILES M. OVIATT (Continued)

RICE LYDIA JANE OVIATT

BD:18180115
DD:18851214
BP:CORTLAND CO NY
LR:OLEAN NY

RICE GROVE

BD:17890503 MD:18121017
DD:18400605
BP:GLASTONBURY HARTFORD CO CT
LR:ALLEG OR CATT CO, NY

BRIGGS TRYPHENA

BD:17900516
DD:18640321
BP:
LR:OLEAN CATT CO, NY

RICE ELIPHALET LUMAN

BD:17461024 MD:17720205
DD:18191110
BP:ASHFORD, WINDHAM CO, CT
LR:HOMER, CORTLAND CO, NY

NICHOLS MARY RICE

BD:17520000
DD:18170303
BP:GLASTONBURY, CT.
LR:HOMER, CORTLAND CO, NY

?

BD: 0 MD: 0
DD: 0
BP:
LR:

?

BD: 0
DD: 0
BP:
LR

ANCESTOR CHART for THOMAS OVIATT
4-digit dates are a guess; final 4 zeros indicate month and day unknown.

BD:=Birth Date
MD:=Marriage Date
DD:=Death Date
BP:=Birth Place
LR:=Last Residence

OVIATT THOMAS
BD:17360929 MD:17690126
DD:18100402
BP:NEW MILFORD, CT
LR:WYALUSING, BRADFORD CO, PA

OVIATT THOMAS
BD:17060428 MD:17320118
DD:17821200
BP:MILFORD, CT
LR:NEW MILFORD, CT

OVIATT THOMAS
BD:16770830 MD:17050607
DD:17410113
BP:MILFORD, CT
LR:NEW MILFORD, CT

OVIATT THOMAS
BD: 1611 MD: 1663
DD:16910528
BP:MENDIPPI HILLS TRING, ENGLAND
LR:MILFORD, CONN

BRYAN FRANCES
BD: 1634
DD: 0
BP:WENDOVER, BUCKS CO, ENGLAND
LR:MILFORD, CT.

KELLOGG LYDIA (CLARK) OVIATT
BD:16760400
DD:17420704
BP:NORWALK, CT
LR:NEW MILFORD, CT

KELLOGG DANIEL
BD:16290000 MD:16550000
DD:16880000
BP:ENGLAND GREAT LEIGHS ESSEX CO
LR:NORWALK, CONN

BOUTON BRIDGET KELLOGG
BD:16370000
DD: 1690
BP:CONN
LR:NORWALK,CONN

ANCESTOR CHART for THOMAS OVIATT (*Continued*)

BROWNSON (BRONSON) MARGARET OVIATT

BD:17151003
DD: 1790
BP:NEW MILFORD, CONN
LR:NEW MILFORD, CT

BRONSON SAMUEL

BD:16750000 MD:17000000
DD:17331027
BP:FARMINGTON, CONN
LR:NEW MILFORD, CONN

WARNER LYDIA BRONSON

BD: 0
DD: 1745
BP:FARMINGTON, CONN
LR:DERBY, CONN

BRONSON JACOB

BD:16410000 MD: 0
DD:17070300
BP:HARTFORD, CONN
LR:FARMINGTON, CONN

?

BD: 0
DD: 0
BP:
LR:

WARNER JOHN

BD: 0 MD: 0
DD:17060301
BP:PROB FARMINGTON, CONN
LR:FARMINGTON, CONN

?

BD: 0
DD: 0
BP:
LR:

Family Group Sheet for: OVIATT MILES MASON ALIO
(4-digit dates are a guess; final 4 zeros indicate month and day unknown.)
(unmarried surname is first, followed by first and middle names)

Born: 18401201 - GENESEE TWP, NY
Christened: 0 Occupation: TINNER'S APPRENTICE
Married: 18680719 - OLEAN NY
Died: 18801101 Last Residence: OLEAN NY
Buried: PLEASANT VALLEY CEM OLEAN NY   Cause of death: COMPLICATION
FROM SEVERE COLD
Father: OVIATT THOMAS VAN RENSSELAER Mother: RICE LYDIA JANE OVIATT
Comment: SEE BIOG.IN DIARIES/BRONZE PLAQUE, GAR MARKER, FLAG ON
GRAVE

Memo:
Cited for Personal Valor-Battle of Mobile Bay 5Aug1865 Congr Medal of Honor;
Diaries kept during Civil War service published; enlisted Aug 19, 1862 USMC
Brooklyn, NY-U.S.S. Vanderbilt & U.S.S. Brooklyn; Battle of Fort Fisher; discharged
Aug 20, 1866; farmer in Pleasant Valley; prior to death trained cavalry unit there;
Pension request by widow Lucetta A.Crandall Oviatt Turner;affidavits of Willard Moon
Smith, George W. Kelsey, George H. Banfield, all fellow Marines, as to Miles' health;
W.O. No18758 sworn statements by friends & neighbors as to his history. Congressional
Medal of Honor Society Natl Hdqtrs Mt, Pleasant,SC has all Medal recipients engraved
on 100 ft silver wall.

Name of Mate: CRANDALL LUCETTA ALZINA OVIATT
Born: 18470319 - GENESEE NY
Christened: 0 Occupation: HOUSEWIFE
Married: 18680719 - CERES, NY
Died: 19251104 Last Residence: OLEAN NY
Buried: PLEASANT VALLEY? OLEAN NY   Cause of death:
Father: CRANDALL GEORGE SPENCER Mother: HAMILTON CORINTHA M.
CRANDALL
Comment: MARRIED CHARLES A. TURNER AFTER MILES DIED

Memo:
In 1900 Lucetta applied for Miles' serv. pension, receiving $20 per mo./photos available
in grandson O.V. Heliker's album/sever arthrts/Olean Daily Herald 27Sep1881 Tues:
"Mrs M. Oviatt, member of a choir singing 'Asleep in Jesus'in a service in Olean for
Pres. Garfield- Micro film Friedsam Lib, St Bonas/See Miles' Pens Papers for details
of pension appli-last payments were $30 per mo/

KNOWN CHILDREN OF THE ABOVE COUPLE: (Format: Name, Birth, Brthplc,
Marr, Death, Husband)
OVIATT FRANCES EMILY HELIKER LARKIN 18761126 OLEAN NY 18970629
19350526 A. J. HELIKER

Family Group Sheet for: OVIATT THOMAS VAN RENSSELAER
(4-digit dates are a guess; final 4 zeros indicate month and day unknown.)
(unmarried surname is first, followed by first and middle name)

Born: 18091231 - TOMPKINS CO, STEUBEN CO, NY?
Christened: 0 Occupation: PILOT/FARM
Married: 18380215 - GREENE, TRUMBLE CO, OH
Died: 18810525 Last Residence: OLEAN NY
Buried: PLEASANT VALLEY CEM OLEAN NY   Cause of death: HEART FAILURE
Father: OVIATT THOMAS Mother: XXX CYNTHIA OVIATT TRIMM
Comment: NEW CONNECTIONS IN YATES & STEUBEN CO NY

Memo:
Hist Annals of SW NY Vol 11 Chapt XLI Hist of Olean Pge 661 "24May1851 TV
Oviatt elected one of the trustees; pge 658-other prominent settlers who arrived in
Olean between 1810-1820 were: twelve names, and during the next decade came 7
other names, one was Thomas Oviatt"/Oviatt St. in Boardmanville (Olean) named for
the Oviatt fam who resided on that prop/Meth E church org 25May1836/Christ Meth,
Main & Oviatt Sts./Tompkins Co,NY Hist & Biog/Tompkins, Tioga, Chemung &
Schuyler Co. Hist./Steuben Co,NY History (Clayton)/Steuben Co,NY Hist (McMaster)/
Steuben Co, NY Reg-Births, etc (Martin)/1934 ltr from Western Res His Lib Cleveland
links TVO with Cyrus & Luther in Angelica, NY-father was Thomas-2, half-bros
Simeon & Ezra Trim, mother Cynthia.

Name of Mate: RICE LYDIA JANE OVIATT
Born: 18180115 - CORTLAND CO NY   Christened: 0   Occupation: HOUSEWIFE
Married: 18380215 - GREENE TWP TRUMBLE OH
Died: 18851214 Last Residence: OLEAN NY
Buried: PLEASANT VALLEY CEM OLEAN NY   Cause of death:
Father: RICE GROVE Mother: BRIGGS TRYPHENA
Comment: HIST CATT CO ERRORS:FV OVIATT,GEORGE SHD BE TV & GROVE

Memo:
See Catt Cens 1850/55/60/80/Olean Meth Church records/possible move to Trumbull
Co. OH with Uncle Allen Rice to keep house/Little Valley,NY wills Box 610 Vol 10 pg9
Probate 5-3-86/

KNOWN CHILDREN OF THE ABOVE COUPLE: (Format: Name, Birth, Brthplc,
Marr, Death, Mate
OVIATT HELEN ELIZA MOORE   18381116 OLEAN, NY   18600000
19090427 Lovell Moore
OVIATT MILES MASON ALIO   18401201 GENESEE TWP, NY   18680719
18801101 Crandall Lucetta
OVIATT MILO ALLISON   18450306 OLEAN, NY?   0 19051030

Editing Techniques

In order to make these originally handwritten diaries more readable and to enhance the modern reader's enjoyment of the story therein, the following methods have been used to make minor legibility changes in the text. These changes have not changed the author's intent or his mode of relating events:

{brackets}...used for illegible words, the editor's interpretation of the word.

[enclosure]...used to complete thoughts or spelling, editor additions.

{?}...used after a questionable word or spelling.

Punctuation has been added where needed to break up run-on sentences.

Misspelling of regular words has been left so as not to detract from the author's personality.

Misspelling of places has also been left untouched (correct spellings have been placed in brackets).

Grammar has also been left exactly as written by the author.

(parens)...these are Miles Oviatt's own marks left intact as he wrote them.

Sail Terms Referred to in Diary Text

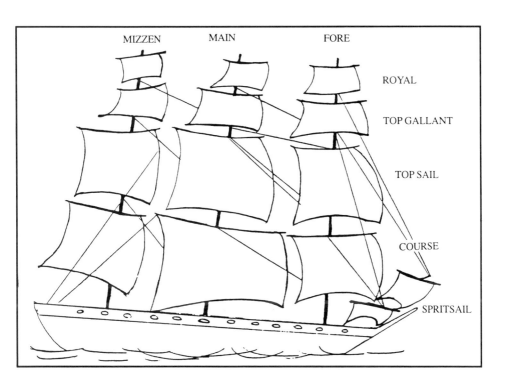

Thomas Van Rensselaer Oviatt
Father of Miles M. Oviatt.

Lydia Jane Rice Oviatt
Mother of Miles M. Oviatt.

Helen E. Oviatt Moore
Sister of Miles M. Oviatt.

Milo Allison Oviatt
Brother of Miles M. Oviatt.

Lucetta Crandall Oviatt
Wife of Miles M. Oviatt.

Frances E. Oviatt
Daughter of Miles M. Oviatt.

Diary Book One — [Part A]

THE VOYAGES OF THE U.S.S. VANDERBILT

EDITOR'S NOTE —Miles Oviatt wrote a second account of this trip, some-times adding and expanding events of the original account. These second writings have been inserted as [2] entry on the same date. Only additional words and new events have been included.

Aug 19th 1862 Enlisted in the U.S. Marine Corp—*[2] Written by M. M. Oviatt of Olean, NYork on board the U. S. Steamer Vanderbilt—Came on board the Vanderbilt Nov 4th, of the same year.
[MARGIN NOTES and LISTS OF ACCOUNTS IN FRONT OF DIARY]—
US Steamer Vanderbilt; MM Oviatt, Olean N York, Catt. Co.; Lackawanna; Colorado Crew left Marine Barracks Brooklyn Oct 1st 40 Privates 2 Sergts & 2 Corps.; knapsack inspection every morning; Mankido; copied Olean, N York; Oct I Pr Boots Shoe Maker 5.00 Vest Send clothes home Daggerreotype Wattermellon Apples Peaches

Jan 10th 1863
I Signed account today for the bal due Me since Oct 1st 1862 after deduct-ing clothes drawn from Purser. [Suspect this was added later]
Miles M Oviatt Olean NYork 1862—Amt. of Clothing Recd from Gov—
Pants Blue Aug 19,62 1
White Pants Sep 10,62 2
Coats Uniform Sept 6,62 1
   "   Relief Aug 19,62 1
   "   Watch Sept 6 1
Drawers Sep 6 2
Shirts Sept 10 2
Stockins " 2 pr
Shoes Aug 19 1

Caps Relief Aug 19 1
Dr Parade Sep 6 1
Knapsack Aug 19 1
Blankets Aug 19 1
Oct 11 Rec'd pay't of Gov. from Aug 19 up to Oct 1st 1862—15.47
Dec 29 Recd of Pamt 5.00
Aug 19th 1862 Enlisted in the US Marine Corps this day M.M. Oviatt

Nov Drew	I Matrass	9.13
	1 Doub Blanket	5.04
	1 Bottle Peper	.16
	1 Dr Mustard	.16
	1 Bar Soap	.31
Dec	1 Pr Kip Shoes	1.65
	2 " Drawers 1W	3.13
	1 Rd Silk Hectkf	1.00
		$20.58 [END OF MARGIN NOTES]

Monday Oct 27th 1862

Marine Barracks Brooklyn - Twelve Privates, one Sergeant & two Corporals left for Portsmouth N.H. Was on Liberty in the afternoon. Sent my Valices home Via US Express.

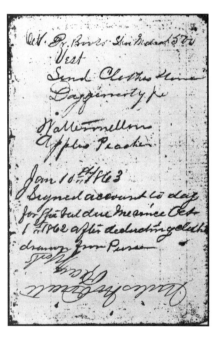

Notes concerning Oviatt's personal affairs

Tuesday 28

Was a ready man today but did not have to stand guard. Wrote a letter home & one to Frank. Cleaned my musket.

Wed. 29th

Stood guard today under Lieut McKeen, Sergt. Mann.

Marine Barracks Thurs Oct 30

Came off guard this morning. Went on liberty in the afternoon. Went over to york in the evening to the Cooper Institute Mass Meeting.[1] Saw Gen Wadsworth & Lyman Tremain & herd them speak. Then went to 39 Sispendor St. with Ed McKee to See Nillie.

Friday Oct 31

Readyman this morning. Did not stand guard, did not feel very well. Drilled at 11 o'clock. Lieut Corp officer [of] Day.

Willard Moon Smith
Courtesy of Allegany, N.Y. Area Historical
Association

Captain Charles Heywood,
U.S.M.C.
Enlisting officer of Miles M. Oviatt. Later
commandant of Marine Corps.
Courtesy of David M. Sullivan

Sat Nov 1

Stood guard today 1 Lieut Kirt Officer [of] Day.

Sunday Nov 2

Came off guard this morning. Went to church today.

Monday Nov 3rd

Got up at Reville this morning. Went through Dress Parade & Knapsack inspection at 11 o'clock. After dinner went on Liberty over to York with Will S.

Tuesday [Nov 4]

After dress parade packed up things & went on board the U.S.S.G.R. Vanderbilt. Stood guard on her for the first time next morning. We formed in line on the starboard side & at 1 1/2 o'clock the flag was run up & she was declared to be in commission.

[2]...we who had volunteered for the Vanderbilt wer[e] ordered to pack up our things & be ready accordingly. At 12 M. fell out for inspection and at one was on our way. About two hundred blue jackets came aboard at the same time from the receiving ship, North Carolina. At two we wer[e] formed in on the starboard side and the penant was sent up at the main. We gave a present arms & three rolls and she was declared to be in commission. The whole scene was rather imposing & solemn. The whole company took off their hats.

U.S.S. Vanderbilt
Copy of carte de visite Miles Oviatt sent home to his family.

U.S.S. Vanderbilt
Department of the Navy photograph, U.S. Naval Academy Library

[2] The Vanderbilt at this time was lying at the navy dock, coaling, filling up and coaling. Her officers are as follows:

Chas. H. Baldwin, Act. Lieut. Commander
Jos. P. Daniels, Act[ing] 1st Lieut, Ex. Officer
E. M. Keith, Acting Master
E. S. Kiser,   "   "
McGloin   "   "
H. C. Lewis   "   "
Alexander, Ensign Act. Sail[ing] Master
Mathew, Sailing Master
Germain, Chief Engineer
Golden, 1st Assistant [Engineer]
Hamilton, 1st Surgeon
Williard, Act. Assistant [Surgeon]
Jas. Tollfree, Paymaster
L. H. Parker, Lieut. Marines
Crew is about 200, but had an increase of 80 sinse.

Wednesday Nov 5

Stood guard at 4 this morning. Raining like Blazes. At 5 o'clock pm tryed to run out into the stream but found we wer[e] stuck 3 ft in mud & 2 tugs & one of her engines could not move her.

Captain Charles H. Baldwin

A later photograph of Captain Charles H. Baldwin, *center*, as admiral aboard the U.S.S. *Lancaster*, 1883.

[2]...on the wharf from 4 to 6...had no shelter...could not start her. We found by soundings that she was beded three feet in the mud.

Thursday Nov 6

Got up for post at 6 this morn. Stood guard in the Brig. Went out afterward & found we were anchored off the Battery for the Purpose of taking in powder. Snowing very hard. Sea runs high, wind blowing a gale, could not go after the powder. Several vessels got loose & drifted past us and one struck us.

[2]...imagine my surprise when at 8, I went on deck & found we wer[e] lying in the stream...several vessels dragged their anchor past us & one loaded with hay ran into us but did no very serious damage.

Friday 7

Raining very hard, wind blowing hard but we took in powder this day & made preparations for starting Sat Morning.

Sat 8th

Did not leave our anchorage today as the storm increases. The large passenger Steamer Scorio passed us this afternoon with Ex. Sec. Cameron & Lord Russell for New York.

Sunday 9

Got up at 8 Bells M. Raining like the devil. Stood two hours. Holy Stoned[2] the gun deck.

[2] Stood post on the fore-cassel, it raining as usual at 4 A.M...had Articles of War at 10.

Monday Morning 10th

This is a very beautiful Morn. Sun shines brightly—expect to leave for sea today. We are anchored in the upper N.Y. Bay at the junction of the East & North Rivers in View of Gov. Island, Staten Island, NY City & Castle Garden,[3] the same that Layfaette[4] landed on his last visit to this country & where Jenny Lind[5] sang first in America. Which is now converted into an Immigrant Landing. This was the first night I ever saw the sun [sink] into the watter. Run East all day. Started at sea at 12 1/2 o'clock.

[2] The morning sun was shining brightly when I arose this morning and have a better chance of contemplating our present situation...

Tuesday 11

Was divided into watches today & have to stand watch of 4 hours off & 4 on. Saw a sail at 8 Bells [A.M.] Did not hail it. Continued East all day. We wer[e] formed into a guns crew & manned the pivot gun aft. I am first loader.

[2]...four on and four off, day and night...at the one hundred lbs...pivot rifle, pivot aft...

Wednesday 12

Sailed South of East. Sea begins to get rough. I feel Very sick. Oh, if I was only at home I would be content. Saw several Vessels today. Signaled one, an Amer. Merchant.

Thursday 13 1862

Are in the Gulf Stream, sea quite rough. I am still sick at my stomach with a severe headache. Saw two Schooners today. Boarded one which proved to be a Spanish fishing vessel. Did not get near enough to board the other. Continuing South of East running about 8 nots average. Drill twice at our gun. Fired the first shot today.

Friday 14th

Saw a sail at daylight this morning at our port. Overtook her about 9 o'clock & spoke her which was the Adrien from St. Johns to Plymouth, Eng. Ran about an hour. Sent to quarters & shut down. Fired at a target but could not tell whith what effect on ac't of fog & smoke. Sea very calm, misting a little but very fogy. Suppose we are off the Grand Banks, N.B. Saw a light at 6 Bells. Supposed to be a lighthouse off the G. Banks.

Saturday 15

Scrubbed decks this morning. Weather clear but commenced raining at 11 o'clock & very foggy. Heared a whistle & returned the same then stopped running to find out where it was. Started at 6 Bells ev. morning West by North.

Sunday 16th

Wind blowing allmost a gale. Sea runs very high, water comes in the ports. We must stand on the gun deck aft to hear the Articles of War read. Wind went down with the sun.

[2]...mustered on the half deck for Articles of War...

Monday 17th Nov

Weather moderate this morning. Had quarters at 10 o'clock. Practised at the guns. Fired at the target & made the best shot fired. Afternoon had musket inspection, and fired at the target with muskets. Beat the Sailors & made the Second best Shot.

[2] Mild and pleasant...I came off second best, Pope 1st.

Tuesday 18th

Stormy this morning & roughf Sea. Saw a whale spout water. Running West by North. Saw 2 Sails but did not overtake them.

Wednesday 18th Nov

Very warm this morn. Saw a sail at 7 Bells. Overtook it about 9 o'clock & stopped. She ran into us.[6] Went on board her. She refused to show her papers but said she belonged in England. It took till afternoon to repair the damages done by the collision. We then started again sailing east by south.

[2] Wednesday Nov 19...Very warm and pleasant...Stove her Gib boom in and took till afternoon to repair her. Ch'd to west by south.

Thursday 19th 1862

Weather very warm indeed so warm as to be quite uncomfortable. Sun rose very beautifully. Are in the Gulf Stream running south by 1/4 East. Sea very calm, not a ripple on the wave or a breath of air is stirring. Oh, how I long to [be] home once more. That name seems dearer than ever. I would that I had not been so head strong & left in such a haste. Perhaps I would have thought again & remained there. Home. Home. Oh, shall I ever, ever to thee return. God only knows. Sailing East by South.

[2] Thursday Nov. 20...the Gulf Stream which is generally pleasanter than on other side...all is calm but the gentle heavings of the never motionless deep. I am homesick and tired of this new life and begin to wish sincerely that I never had left home. Home, home, name how endearing. Shall I e'ver to thy joys return.

Friday 20th 1862

Weather getting warmer. Changed our course to due East. Saw land for the first time since we left York. At 2 o'clock came along side and Anchored at 6 o'clock. It was the Isle of Bermuda. I should think it was probably 20 or 30 miles in length as we ran along side two or three hours. It is a very barren, wild, grown up strickly with bay orange which looked very beautiful. It belongs to the English. I counted 6 Forts or Fortifications on the East and within 1/2 mile from another with guns arranged to bear on every port. I would judge by the looks that the Fortifications cost more than the value of the Island. The captain went ashore in the evening & the [U] S Con[sul] came aboard. I counted 9 or ten houses opposite our anchorage. There is quite a town farther up the harbor. There is an English Steamer lying in the harbor loaded with Arms & Ammunition for the Rebels, but there is a debt of 18000 Dollars due on her and has got to be paid befor she leaves. So she will not leave immediately.

[2] Friday Nov 21...land on the port side or bow. Took on a pilot at 4...by the side of one of the Bermuda islands...The scene was very beautiful in the setting sun. The island grown up thick with bay orange, shrubs & trees, while here and there could be seen whitewashed huts intercepting the wild monotony...I counted 5 or 6 forts within a mile of each other on the west end of the island...the Amer. Consol came off...

Saturday 22nd

Three boats went ashore, two came back loaded with sand, the Consol & Pilot in the other. We raised anchor & got under way at 10 AM as we were informed that we could not remain but 24 hours where we were. Saw [sails] about 1/2 hours after starting. Overtook & signaled her. She hoisted the Stars & Stripes. This is the second vessel we have seen since we started that sailed under that flag. Saw three more, boarded 2 of them, both Eng.

Sunday 23

Getting cooler, sea runs big. Stearing most West, expect we are going to Charleston, S.C. Nothing important has passed today. Went to guard at the usual time. We have all been talking about home. Read a few chapters in the Bible for we have been taken with scripture reading since we came to sea. As a natural consequence when a fellow is homesick.

[2] Inspection at the usual time. Sea very roughf agen. Homesick as usual.

Monday 24th 1862

Sea rough, weather getting cooler & mists a little. Drilled at quarters after washing down deck after dinner. Stood guard on the Brig & write this while on post. Saw a sail before coming down, reported as a steamer. Was an English trader. At dusk saw two more. Boarded one was English, the other was Amer[ican].

[2]...Overtook her before I came off. She was an Eng. Merchantman...

Tuesday 25th 1862

Warm this morning. Running east of North, saw two Vessels today & boarded both. The last hoisted the Star & Stripes but not till we had ordered her to show her colors. Then boarded her, said she saw the Alabama one hundred & eighty miles South. Was chased by her four hours then boarded her. We did not start to look for her, however. Drilled at quarters & fired at a target with all the guns except ours.

Wednesday 26th 1862

Washed down decks this morning. Heared six sails reported before 8 Bells. Ran along side of a bark at 3 Bells which was from N.Y. bound to San Francisco 2 days from York. Drilled at quarters & came near letting our gun go overboard in a surge of the sea. The vessel was owned in Providence & said the last account of the 290 she was off Cape Goodhope.

[2]...Providence, R. I.

Thursday 27th 1862

Cold & stormy this morning, do not feel well. Was reported for not having my hammock up in time & expect will have to do extra duty. Oh, ye gods, forgive the wish that I have to get out of this most detestable of all services. One year spent here will be the death of me with this longing desire to go back home burning in my bosom.

[2]...I am still so homesick, I feel as though one year with this desire to be free burning in my breast, would be the death of me.

Friday Nov. 28th 1862

Scrubbed hammock this morning at 4 1/2 o'clock till day light then washed down decks. Drilled at quarters at the usual hour.

[2]...weather freezing cold, made it rather unpleasant.

Saturday Nov. 29th 1862

Cold & Stormy. Holy Stoned decks this morning. Running east till 10 then changed to west. Sounded at noon 65 fath[oms], 2 o'clock, 60 fath[oms], midnight 10 fath[oms].

Sunday Nov 30th

Very pleasant this morning. Sighted land at daylight. Took on Pilot at 8 o'clock. Saw the harbor of NYork & cast anchor at 10.

[2]...The old Illinois lay at anchor off the battery loaded with volunteers for Washington. As we came in, the band played Hail Columbia.

Monday Dec 1

Clear & cold. Sunshine very bright. Was twenty one today. Had bean soup for dinner. Geo Kelsey counted one Hundred vessels in sight.

Tuesday Dec 2nd

Cold & disagreeable. Wrote....

Wednesday Dec 3rd 1862

Very cold & cloudy. Prayers on deck. Three Transports with volunteers came down the river and anchored along side of us. They were the M. Sandford, Eastern Queen, & Salvira. The Illinois lay at anchor when we came in loaded with volunteers for Washington. Saw the Persia go out for Sea at 1 1/2 o'clock while on post. Purdy recd the appointment of Ass. Paymaster today of the U. S. Navy. Johnson went ashore with him about one o'clock.

[2]...three transports from Albany loaded with troops...The English Mail Steamer, Persia, left for Liverpool...One of our Marines by the name of Purdy rec'd his appointment....

Thursday Dec 4th

Very pleasant but sting cold air. The Sandford and Illinois left this morning for Burnsides expedition.[7]

Friday 5th 1862

Stormy snowing in morning. Cleared up about {noon}. Lieutenant told us today we could not get anymore liberty.

[2] Very stormy and unpleasant in the forenoon. Mr Parker told us we could not have more liberty because OS Morgan broke his.

Saturday 6th

Clear & cold. Nothing new transpired today only Mrs Vanderbilt came aboard.

[2]...Mrs C. Vanderbilt...

Sunday 7th Dec 1862

Pleasant with sting cold wind. Stood orderly from 2 to 4. Saw the Soldiers at the Battery break up their encampment & go on board the Transport while on post.

[2] Clear with strong cold wind. Stood Capt's orderly...

Monday 8th 1862

Severly cold this morning. Wind has died away some. The Lieutenant told us when cleaning the gun that we were going up the Mediteranean{?} this cruise. Wrote a letter home to Helen today.

[2]...Mr. Parker told us that we would probably go up the Straits this cruise...

Tuesday 9th 1862

Finished loading coal today. Weather getting warmer. There was another Transport loaded with Volunteers sailed today at 1 o'clock. Three more Marines came aboard today at 2 pm.

[2]...Got three Marines in place of Purdy, Remington & Cameron. They were Kimerle 1st, 2d Somace...

Wednesday Dec 10 1862

Weigh anchor and started to sea at ten 1/2 o'clock. Passed two more Transports with volunteers while on our way to sea. Oh, how I wished I had been with them.

Thursday Dec 11

Ten o'clock, weather moderately. Just came down into the Brig to stand Gard. John Murdock came down and hid when ought to be on deck. Wants to be waked at 4 Bells. Stearing East by South. Weather warm in morning but got cool toward evening.

Friday Dec 12 1862

Weather pleasant. Holy stoned deck this morn. Running East by South 1/2 South. Saw one sail. Sailors thought would have quarters last night so they cast loose their lashings.

[2]...We had all had the promise, in case of quarters, the first gun fired, the crew should receive a barrell of slush.[8] The Blue Jackets cast loose their guns.

Saturday Dec 13th 1862

Made up my mind to stop swearing for one month at least - M M Oviatt Stearing East saw a light last [night]. We stopped the Engines and ran with sail till daylight but did not make out anything. Had quarters at the usual time this morning.

[2]...running East by South.

Sunday Dec 14th 1862

Cool and cloudy. Continue stearing East. Assembled on the Gundeck at 5 Bells for Articles of War by the first Lieutenant Mr. Daniels. 2 1/2 o'clock Feeling rather homesick agin. Oh, Home, Name how endearing. Oh, May I to thy joys agin return safely with plenty of soup {soap}.

[2]...Continue East by South. Began to get homesick.

Monday Dec 15th 1862

Weather very mild & warm. Sea has gone down so that not a wave is rolling over it's surface. Drilled at quarters this forenoon at ten o'clock. Fired one shot at target with our gun which fell well within 20 feet of it. Boarded a ship in the mean time with the Stars & Stripes run up Thirty days from Liverpool loaded with Irish to join Gen Corcoran's Legion.[9] Oh, I am tired of this aimless life. I wish I wer[e] out of this. Stearing East by South.

Tuesday Dec 16th 1862

Stearing East by South. Very rough sea this morn but calmed down toward night. Signaled an Eng Merchant Ship at 12 o'clock today.

Wednesday Dec 17

Saw a sail at daylight. Ran along side of it all day but did not get close enough to make it out. Lost sight at night. It appears to be running the same way we are. Weather quite pleasant.

Thursday Dec 18th 1862

Warm but cloudy. Steared East by South till night then changed & ran South by 1/4 East. Nothing transpiring to mar the monotony of sea life. Darling found his blanket in possession of a darkey.

[2] Clear and pleasant...V.P. Darling found his blanket which had been confiscated by one of the darks. They punished the offender by putting a tall canvass hat, White-washed, on his head with this inscription—"I am one of the Thieves."

Friday 19th 1862

Four months today since I Enlisted a Marine. The sea rolls very bad but not so much but that we had quarters and drilled at the guns.

Saturday Dec 20th 1862

We have got so accustomed to the same routine of life that sea life, it comes almost second nature, and live in kind of lethargy. Our minds almost a machine only when we begin the subject of home. At five bells the creaking of pumps and the splashing water on deck may be heard. After this, sand is thrown over, then the Musical notes of the Holy Stone greets the ear for about an hour. Then the deck is washed down & dried. We are indeed in a favored vessel maned by highly intelligent officers who regard fine coats more than the lives of the men. The sea is the roughest today that it has been since we have been to sea.

[2]...Our minds are not occupied enoughf to keep off the lethargy which is brought on by inaction...then pump, hose, buckets, squeegees, swabs, & scrub brooms are used promiscusly for an hour more. When the deck is said to have been washed. We are said to be on a favored vessel. I think we must indeed be, for the width and length to Holy Stone and wash down.

Sunday Dec 21st 1862

Weather growing calmer. Sun shone but quite pleasant agen this morn. The first time for several days time. 8 Nots yesterday 2 & 3 was all we made. Did not go to quarters this morning for inspection. Was centry over the prisoner that was confined yestarday for insolence to the paymaster.

[2] Weather pleasant agen. Making 9 Nots yestarday...

Monday Dec 22 1862

Sail Reported this forenoon but did not run to it. Land reported about 2 o'clock afternoon, but owing to the fog, could not see it from the deck. Lay still last night from 8 bells till daylight next morning. Weather cloudy & misty, wind blowing directly from South East the same direction we are sailing.

Tuesday Dec 23rd 1862

Saw land this morning about 8 o'clock. Came along side of an Island while at quarters. This lays in sight of the Flores island.[10] It is a rocky, barren mountain of a brownish color rising abruptly from the water. The top was not visible on account of the fog. After dinner ran along side of the Flores & boarded an English Schooner. There was also a boat come along side with the Pourtigese {Portuguese} Flag. Said the 290 had not been in this vicinity since Sept 15 when she destroyed to {two} of three whalers. The Tuscarora was here the 8 of Dec and another Man of War also about the same time. This is a fertile looking Island although hilly. It is destitute of timber but is grown up with underbrush and the fields are seperated by Hedges the same as at Bermudas. The fields looked quite green. Weather warm and pleasant as an Indian Summer in NYork.

Wednesday Dec 24 1862

Saw a light at 12 last night. Supposed that it was land at first but found afterward that it was a vessel running accross our bow. Sighted land at daylight but was reported at 12 M that we were only Thirty Miles from it; consequently we lay still till morning. When first seen looked like a little rock of[f] standing alone in the distance. But as we came closer we could see two or three rocks seperated from the Maineland. The principle Island lay back of these. Fayal [Faial-Azores] is the name given to this land &

belongs to Portugal. It presents a fruitful appearance at the distance which we ran from it being two or three miles. Grapes, Figs & Oranges are Abundant. They grow two crops of the latter a year. The land is mostly cultivated except on the highest Mount which are thickly grown of Orange & Fig trees. One of the highest peaks has been a volcano judging from the ravines & channels cut down its sides, although we could not see the summit on account of the fog. We ran into the harbor of Horta and dropped anchor at two o'clock. This place contains about two thousand Inhabitants. They are Catholicks {Islands?} judge from the number of their Institutions there. Three churches, a convent, nunnery etc. The buildings are mostly one story without chimneys, are all whitewashed constructed of clay & Bamboo.

[2] As we wer[e] only thirty miles from Fayal [Faial] last night, we lay still and started up and ran into the harbor of Horta and anchored at 12 M. When first we saw the island, which we afterwards found to be the Peak of Pico, it looked like a mere rock standing alone from the depths of the sea...two or three thousand inh's. Their religion is Catholic...four churches...covered with tile.

Wednesday [Thursday] Dec 25 1862

The churches wer[e] lighted up last night & ringing their bells every half hour. I saw a very large crowd gathered togather in their Amusement grounds today. Supose they have some great doings. Vesper bells ring about 5 o'clock in the evening which sound very solemn. We fired a salute of 21 guns with the Portages {Portuguese} flag hoisted & was returned at their fort but without the colors up. The consol came aboard this afternoon with a number of natives. There is a Bark lying up on the rocks in the West side of this harbor where she was blown in a gale. The Harbor is not very good because it is not protected enough on the sea side. The Island of Pico lies about two miles South East of us. The Mountain of the same name is full view from here. It is not burning now although has been lately. One of the natives informed me it is 7613 feet above the level of the sea. About 5 thousand feet it is timbered with Palms and orange trees but above this it [is] nothing but dry sand looking rocks, almost perpendicular. The top comes off to a point. When the Alabama was here, she distroyed one Whaling Vessel belonging to Manay, a native, with Nine Hundred Brls of Oil. The fields on these islands are divided up into lots containing about an acher {acre} each by Hedges of Bamboo to break the wind off from the crops. It is said to be fourteen miles from base to the top of Pico. The weather today was a nice October day for Cattaraugus. We have not worn our Watch coats since we landed, not even at night. The Natives wear summer clothes & straw hats.

[2]...There was quite a crowd gathered on the square in front of one of the public buildings to enjoy their hallowday...all that it has is formed by Pico

which lays about 2 1/2 miles South East...The peak of Pico...covered with trees but the balance is a barren rock of a brownish color. It is said to be fourteen miles to the top. The Alabama destroyed three whalers in this vicinity...

Thursday [Friday] Dec 26

It clouded up and rained this morning but cleared off before noon. One of our boats went aboard the vessel of rice to see if they need any assistance as they are flying a yellow flag from her main mast. We fired a salute of twenty one guns which was returned from the island.

[2] Weather very beautiful, smoky like our Indian Summers. The natives dress in white clothes...

Friday [Saturday] 27th 1862

Warm & pleasant. Was a large vessel ran between the islands today. Wrote a letter home & sent it with out paying postage. Have had but 9 cts since came aboard the ship. Heared some of us we[re] going to be transfered to the Tuscarora.[11] Commence to wash down ship to paint. Wrote to our Folks today.

Saturday Dec 27th 1862

Commenced to coal & paint ship with coal brought off in lighters which resemble our small Boats. Weather pleasant with occasional showers. Wrote to Allison.

[2] Saturday [Sunday] Dec 28...Pleasant with occasional showers.

Sunday 28th

The News Boy from Boston the 15 inst[ant] brought news of the defeat of Burnside with five thousand killed. Also of the Alabama at St. Thomas when we was at NYork. The news was at Halifax while we lay in NY but was not sent there till we left.

[2] Sunday [Monday] Dec 29—The schooner News Boy...

Monday 29th

A Spanish Transport came to anchor here yesterday directly from the West Indies. It also brings news of the 290 there & destroyed two American Vessels. Weather very warm. Nothing very important transpired only the Amer. Consol came aboard. Monday Dec 29 1862.

[2]...the Alabama then also had destroyed two of our vessels. Rec'd five Dollars Green Backs to buy Oranges with.

Tuesday 30

Recd Five Dollars from the purser. Bought One Hundred Oranges and divided with Ed McKee. Besides I gave him one dollar. Also gave Towle two. [See Margin Notes Pg 1, also end of Part 1B.]

Wednesday 31st

The Gov. of the Island came aboard today with Several other Military officers. His daughter with other ladies accompanied him. We fired a salute of Fifteen Guns which was replied to from the Fort. We were assembled on the Spar Deck Aft and gave them {him} a present when he came aboard. The Young ladies went into the Ward Room & played & sung several tunes in Portage {Portuguese} so we had a chance to hear some Portuese {Portuguese} sing. Bought a drum of Figs for a green Back, One.

Got ready this morning, hoisted signal for all to return at 8 o'clock. Weighed anchor at 10 1/2 & left the Island of Fayal {Faial} after taking on 350 tons coal.[12] A propeler came in last night & commenced to coal this Morning. This is three besides us that are taking on coal. Stearing South West making 10 Nots. Ship rocks very bad. Had quarters at 6 Bells and such confusion may better be imagined than described. No [one] fired the shot & won the b[ar]rel of slush. Did not make the attempt to fire the aft Pivot on ac't of just being newly painted.

New Years Jan 1st 1863

Arose at 4 o'clock this morning with new resolutions. Holy Stoned deck then cleaned guns. While at this the fire Bells rang & such going to quarters I never saw. It was enough to make ones hair stand. Just the thought of being two Hundred Miles from land and the ship on fire. But the fire did not prove to be very serious. Although the solemn faces showed that it was not all Humbug. How unlike my other New Years day that I ever spent before Heretofore. I have usually [spent] them in some pleasant diversement & today am learning the Arts of destruction to destroy me both with the 100# Rifled & Musket. Many wer[e] the wishes of the Happy New Year to you at twelve last night when our watch turned in. Saw a sail at 4 Bells. & have ran along side & stopped to board her at 2 Bells this afternoon while I am on Watch in the Brig. She was a French Schooner. Also Boarded an English Bark at 4 Bells from Guam by Three Months & 6 days out. We have been running East by South till 4 this afternoon. Then we changed to North by qtr West & continued this course. It is surmised that we are Homeward bound.

[2]....only to think of a fire on the ocean, it is enough to make ones blood curdle. But fortunately it was not very serious but sober faces at quarters showed themselves.

Friday 2nd 1863

Cloudy in the morning & did not get very pleasant through the day. We drilled twice with Small Arms today. The second time we fired at a target & did some splendid firing. As good, the Lieut. says, as he ever saw, putting several shots apiece through the Target. Appears like a storm tonight. They ran down the Galant yards for the Capt. says we will see rough weather before many days. We climb{ed} riging last night. I believe we all guards went aloft but 4 of the{m}. I went up 3 times as far as the main yard & came down the stays twice. This is the best to teach one what a small speck such a vessel is compared with the Mighty Atlantic. From the yard the ship did not look larger than a skiff.

[2]...and did some splendid shooting, as Mr Parker says...Most of Marines had a turn up the rigging...

Saturday Jan 3rd

Weather getting cooler than yesterday. Wind allmost directly ahead. Making 8 or Nine Nots. Running North West Quarter West. Sea considerably rough at night with cold wind. Saw a Bark at 3 o'clock. Ran across our port Bow. It was going South West. We are probably going north to get a supply of ice out of an Iceburg as I understand the Captain has run short.

Sunday Jan 4th 1863

Still we continue our course North by quarter West. Many are the conjectures as to the land we will make for. Appearances indicate that will see land before long. As they have made a letterbag and hung out for the reception of them.

Monday 5th 1863

Weather getting roughf. Wind directly ahead & blowing very hard. Are making 8 or Nine Nots.

Tuesday Jan 6th 1863

Rainy, wind blowing harder, sea getting roughfer than yestarday. Did not drill at the gun today nor have not since Sat on account of bad weather. The sea ran so high & roughf that it was difficult to stand up. I think we have not seen anything like it before. Continued on the same course till 8 o'clock then changed to North West by 3/4 West. Heard say that we [are] now off the Grand Banks of Newfoundland.

Wednesday Jan 7th 1863

Cleared up and sea went down last night so that waves did not roll at all. This morning Sun came out, very pleasant. Drilled at quarters & with small arms. Also cleaned gun in the afternoon. Wind blew up very cold agen. The sea is getting roughf.

Thursday Jan 8th 1863

The weather clears up in the day time, & clouds up and rains invariably at night. Changed our course to West last night. The wind Shifted to North about the same time & made the ship roll & pitch tremendious for two or three hours. Saw a Vessel about Nine this morning. Changed our course to

North and run for her & overtook her about two hours afterward. Hailed & then boarded her. It was the American Packet, Hudson of Bath, ME, seven days from NYork. Got several NY papers from her. & then we learned that a bill was before the House to transfer the Marines to the land service.

[2]...to transfer Marines into the Army or land service.

Friday Jan 9th 1863

Rained & snowed a kind of sleet. Wind shifted to East. Ran with Fore & Aft Sails & Top Sails. Made from 10 to 13 Nots. Signed our accounts today. I signed for 13.70 Thirteen Seventy.

[2]...making 9 + 10 Nots...

Saturday Jan 10th 1863

[See Margin Notes Pg 1 for a notation for this date.] Cleared up this morning & was a most beautiful day with a nice cool North East wind. Ran with full sail and made as high a[s] 13 Nots. We seldom see the sea a[s] smooth as it has been today. We saw a light at 8 o'clock this eve. When first saw was two points to the Port Bow but we ran past with out going nearer. Supposed to be a steamer goin in the opposite direction. We are running directly West by quarter North 9 Nots.

[2]...8 o'clock running West by North qr North.

Sunday Jan 11th 1863

The weather has changed a little since yesterday. A[t] 7 Bells all hands wer[e] called to run down T. Galant Yard which we only ran up yesterday & close scaf sail. The wind at this time was blowing very hard by squalls which has been increasing all the while since. Have been lightening the upper part of ship by sending down coal in bags which was piled up to protect the boilers. One o'clock at night the sea is roughfer than it was at dark. (Running North qr West). We are making about one Not now. We do not run strait toward the wind but obliquely or catering across the waves which makes the ship roll worse but do not ship so much sea. Several pieces of timber & boxes drifted past us. The Tompion[13] came out of one of the guns & washed up onto the guard & was recovered.

[2]...T. Gallant yards...protect the engines. At dark was making about one Not...across the waves with wind on Star. bow...does not ship the sea as bad as though we ran direct toward the wind...

Monday 12th 1863

Soon the sea went down so that we ch[ange]d about ship this morning & are running West qr South. Saw a square rigged ship about 8 Bells running before the wind with close scafed sails, & two Barks & a schooner since at Noon. Also saw one about dark. At 8 Bells that night the alarm of Fire was given which created a great deal of excitement. More than would but the

Sailors and Marines relaxing on the deck of gunboat Mendota

National Archives #111-B-129 (Brady)

fire was supposed to be in close proximity to the Magazine. The night was awful, the wind blowing almost a gale & was raining very hard. The very thoughts of a fire was enough to strike terror to the calmest heart. When they thought that we wer[e] on the restless deep. But thank Providence we escaped the awful death of burning or drowning & our fears wer[e] with any very serious cause.

[2]...as the smoke was coming out in great quantities...nothing serious was the result as the smoke came from the cabin stove in which was building a fire.

Tuesday Jan 13th 1863

Another day has dawned upon us and brings with it the same troubles & trials that the day previous did or perhaps some new one. Thus, day by day we are getting nearer our last home. And as we sit down at night we ask ourselves if we have improved the time as we ought. Then we form new resolutions and as we lay our heads down, our thoughts wander back to the scenes of childhood. & we see our fond parents and friends and Oh, how we long to quit this unfriendly world & return agen to our dear home. The day has been quite pleasant quite a change from yesterday. I think we are in the Gulf Stream. The watter stood at 68° at 12 M. Wer[e] going 8 to 9 with Fore Main Trisails, both Gib sails & aft anker{sp}. Stearing West by South qr South. We have heared that the Cap. got Scared in the Storm of the Eleventh and is going South to keep out of any more.

Wednesday Jan 14th 1863

The day has been very beautiful with a warm breeze blowing from the South. We came out with our Blouses on agen today & drilled at one o'clock with Muskets. Drilled at quarters agen this morning for the first time in several days. We made 18 Nots last night till 4 this morning, and was making 12 Nots at 12 M today. Then stopped the engines for repairs. Since have been running with sail at 1 1/2 Nots.

Our T Gallant Yards are down, consequently we have not full sails. Some of the boys went up the Main Top and the Sailors tied some up there.

Thursday Jan 15 - 63

Cloudy this morning & looked very much like storm agen. The wind raising & Sea getting roughf. Saw a sail this morning running across our Port Bow. Ran so as to cross her bow till could see what she was. She was supposed to be an English line of Battleship. We run close enoughf to see two row of Ports. She was sq'r Rigged Propellor. We then ch[ange]d to our old course and about Ten stopped to board a Brig with Breman colors flying. Hailed her 4 or 5 times & ordered her to heave to, but she did not do so. Then fired a blank shot but still she kept on her course. We then about ship and started after her. Then fired a rifle shot and she hove to. Boarded her and

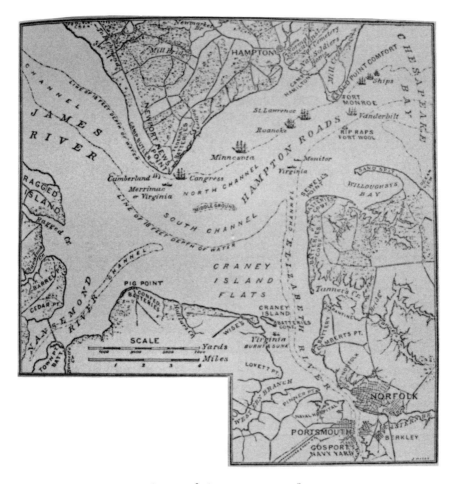

Map of Hampton Roads

See Diary January 18, 1863.

Battles and Leaders

gave us N.Y. papers containing the capture of the Ariel by the Alabama with all of her Marines & Crew. We have coal for only 4 days left.

Friday Jan 16th 1863

Commenced to blow a gale this morning about 4 o'clock & continued to increase till 12 M. & kept up till about Mid Watch. Then died away. It commenced to blow North East but ch[ange]d to North West & was very cold. Are running West by North making 4 Nots.

[2]...a NE gale...

Saturday Jan 17th 1863

This is the Seventeenth day from Fajal {Faial} & the first land we have seen since. We saw about Two o'clock today. The first indication we saw was a very dense smoke like camp fires rising in the distance. This was about Ten. As we came closer could distinguish trees rising out of the watter. This I suppose is the sacred soil of Old Virginia. We took on a pilot about 5 o'clock & came to anchor at 6 with land in view on each side in Hampdon Rodes {Hampton Roads}. It probably being to[o] late to proceed farther till daylight. Have made 18 Nots since 2 M.

[2]...We made 22 Nots running in.

Sunday Jan 18th 63

At anchor off Old Fort Monroe. Commenced to take on coal this forenoon about 9 o'clock. Three Schooners loaded with coal came alongside with about Nine Hundred Tons. This is all we are going to take on here. The Captain went over to Norfolk in the forenoon & this afternoon went to Washington for Orders.[14] Thought the weather is very cold. Thermometer 33° Several important points can be seen from here. Fort Monroe, Rip Raps, Sewals {Sewall's} Point, New Port News. We can also see the Minesota[15] which lies at anchor off New Port News. This is the Flag Ship of the squadron stationed here. The Brandywine[16] lies within a few yards of us. She is used [as] a store ship for the Army. She brought Lafayette to this country. The transport, New York, went up the Jas {James} River with a flag of truce. Several Hudson River sound steamers & Ferries are used as transports & Gunboats here now.

[2]...Thermometer 35 deg...Minesota flag ship...

Monday 19th 1863

Wrote a letter to send Helen today but did not have a chance to send it, it being to[o] [late] before I finished it. Saw another transport come in loaded with troops. Three scows loaded with stone came in tonight.

Thursday Jan 22nd 1863

Nothing unusual has transpired during the past few days only it was to[o] roughf to coal a couple of days. Yesterday the Paymaster went to NYork.

Today the Iroquois and a Monitor came into this port. Some of the boys have been on liberty.

[2]...The Monitor Nahant came in today...

Friday Jan 23rd 1863

There has been quite an excitement over to the rip raps on account of hanging a man there for shooting a donkey. Last [night] About Ten O'clock, the Monitor Weehawken[17] and the Iroquois ran in here & came to anchor.

[2]...hanging a soldier...

Saturday Jan 24

The Weehawken and Iroquois left last night. It is supposed they went up the James River as there was signal Rockets sent up from Newport News or the Minesota which lays at anchor there, and firing of Musketry. Have not heared of anything serious happening there. Sent a letter home.

[2]...firing of muskets in that direction...

Sunday 25th

Three Steamers with prisoners to be exchanged went up the Jas {James} River with a flag of Truce. Another Monitor came last night & went away after this evening under cover of the darkness. We were employed as wood passers most all day. Quite a number of volunteer officers we[re] aboard today from the Fortress. The Captain went to Washington agen this evening.[18]

[2]...rebel prisoners to be exchanged...

Monday Jan 26

For the last two days it has been very calm without wind enough to riffle the water. This morning a slight breeze is blowing and the entire Schooner fleet is on the move to sea which consists of over a Hundred. The Lac[k]awanna came in this morning and the transport Illinois with troops also. Another of the Monitors is to be seen at anchor here but wheather it came from NYork or down the Jas {James} River, cant say. The Illinois left for New Orleans this afternoon & The British Frigate left also. (Cadmus).

Tuesday Jan 27th

The Monitor went up the Jas {James} Riv[er] today. Was the Weehawken. The Lac[k]awanna came in this morning.

Wed 28th

Raining this morning. Cap. came back this forenoon. One and a half o'clock the Jack is flying at the fore top for a pilot. A Jack at the Foretop is signal for a Pilot at Maintop. The Pres. of the U.S.S. Atis[19] is aboard. Weighed anchor and ran down to the mouth of the Harbor but did not run out on account of the high sea. Mr Mathews, the sailing master, refused to come aboard although there was two bo[a]ts sent for him, 3 Cutter & Gig. We also lost 4 Contrabands while in Hampton Rodes {Roads}.

[2]...the jack is flying at the fore for a pilot. When flying at the main, the Pres is on board...Lost 4 Darks here by liberty.

29 [Jan]

Weighed anchor and got under way about half past ten. The weather is severely cold. Mr Alexander is acting in place of Mr Mathews. Running South East by South. Think are bound for Havana.[20]

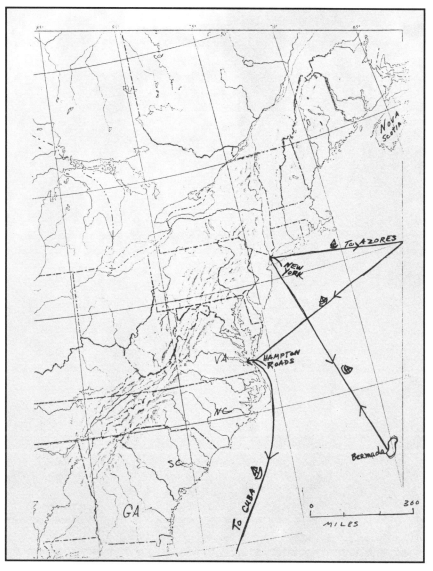

Routes followed by the Vanderbilt in Book One. Part A

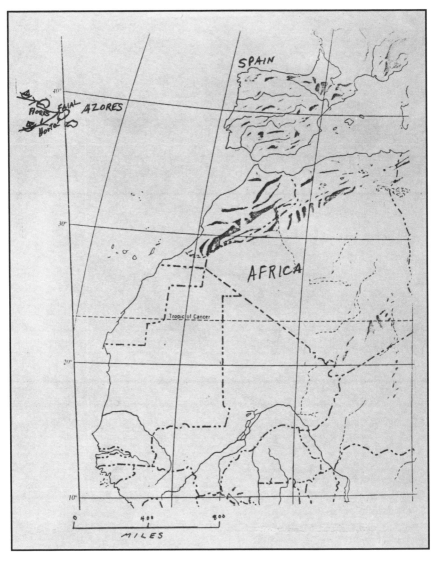

Ports visited in the Azores

Diary Book One — [Part B]

THE CONTINUING VOYAGES OF THE U.S.S. VANDERBILT

*EDITOR'S NOTE—[2] Entries continue in this second part of the diary. Only additional words and new events have been included.

Friday Jan 30 1863

Saw the light at Cape Hattros {Hatteras} at 11 O'clock last night. Very roughf sea this morning. Saw a sail about 3 Bells. Went to quarters at 5 Bells and trained our guns on her. But found it was the British Frigate Cadmus which left Hampton Rodes {Roads} on the Twenty Sixth.

Saturday Jan 31

Growing warmer, sea calmed down. Fires in both furnaces, making 12 to 15 Nots.

Sunday Feb 1st 1863

Very warm & pleasant, hot as June in York. Saw land about 1 o'clock today. The Island of Abaco. Saw what is named the Hole in the Wall as we past opposite the light house. Very pleasant tonight. Wrote this after 8 Bells by Moon light while on the Port Guard Aft.

*[2]...it was Great Abaco...

Monday Feb 2nd 1863

Saw land this morning about Half past six to our Port side with what looked like a lighthouse to port. Went to quarters at Three Bells & drilled at 10. Saw a vessel. Went to quarters to board her about Half Past Twelve. Fired a shot to fetch her too. Was an English Mail Steamer ladened with French troops for Mexico. Saw another Vessel ahead at 5 o'clock. Went to quarters. Cast loose and prepared for an action but she ran away so we left them agen till 8. Then came along side of her and had our guns ready to fire til we past her. Did not signal her or try to find out what kind of ship it was. Only could see she was another steamer. We rec'd our Grog Money today $3.00 or $2.85.

[2]...and all thought one of the Privateers as she tried every possible way to avoid us as we passed. She opened her ports to let us know what she was.

Tuesday Feb 3rd 1863

Weather awful hot. Saw land at daylight on our Port Bow also several light houses. And at Ten saw the Island of Cuba and run into the Harbor at Havana. Droped anchor at 12 M. At the entrance on the left is a fort of solid masonry which almost overhangs the vessel as we enter which is of considerable extent. Castel of Moro {Morro} is the name.

[2]...strong forts* cut out of the rocks...Castle Moro {Morro} which stands up very high and over hangs vessels as they enter, which makes ones hair feel rather loose, especially if it was an enemy's country. Havanna.
*Two 16th Century fortresses

Wednesday Feb 4

Got up anchor and started for sea at 4 o'clock PM. Strong wind blowing outside of the Harbor. The British Ship, Trent, that started with Mason & Slidell[1] for Eng., came in this afternoon. A small boat with Secession flag ran directly under our bow today. The Amer[ican] Consol was aboard at 11

Confederate steamer Alabama ("290")
Department of the Navy Photograph, Neg No. 1430, U.S. Naval Academy Library

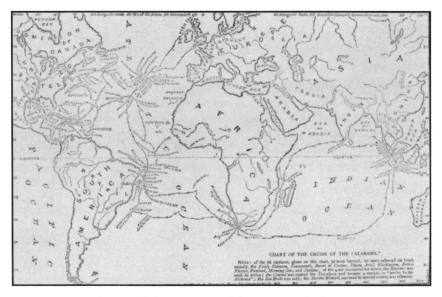

Chart of the cruise of the C.S.S. Alabama

Battles and Leaders

A.M. with several other persons of distinction. A vessel or Schooner loaded with Cotton that had run the blockade ran into Port 24 hours ahead of us. We heared that the San Jacinto[2] was lost running into St. Thomas. Also the 290 was sunk or had run into Jamaca {Jamaica} for repairs. Green Backs 50 pr ct Discount here. Several Amer. Vessels run into this harbor today so there is about as many flying that flag as any other kind. Several f[er]ry boats run from one part of the City to the [other] some of which are Isabella M. A'Francisia, Bota Feuego, [and] Tug Union.

[2]...Mail Steamer, Trent...heared that the 290 was in Kingston, Ja[maica], repairing...Greenbacks 50 cts discount. There is about as many vessels with Stars and Stripes flying as any other in the harbor. There is several ferries from NY that run across the harbor...

Thursday Feb 5

Running South West by West. About ten o'clock, Two sails hove in sight. Came up with them at Twelve & fired a shot for them to heave too. One a Hamburg, the other flying the Stars & Stripes. Boarded both at the same time. We heared from the Alabama. Sat outside of Jama[i]ca getting repairs as she is not allowed inside. But it is thought by the Officers that the Rinaldo[3] Which left Havana as we went in, or another Eng. Man of War which left two hours after, went to carry the News of our Arrival to Cap Simmese {Semmes}. The Rinaldo carried Mason & Slidell to Eng. from Boston. About three in the afternoon boarded another Yankee Bark. Run down the T. Gallant Yds. Looked like heavy weather. Saw a light at dark

Three points to our port bow. When we left Havana we ran West by South up by New Orleans and at dark was only Six hours steam from Havana. Should not think that the 290 was in any immediate danger.

[2] Running South West by South...fired a blank...Heared the Alabama was at Kingston, Ja., getting repairs last Saturday...the Brit Frigate, Rinaldo, which left Havanna, we went in, or the one that left a few hours afterward, went to carry the news of our arrival to Cap. Simmes {Semmes}...left Havana, we ran west by South and took a circuit up through the Gulf of Mexico, and at dark saw the light house which is only six hours steam from there...Sent down T Gallant Yds as it looked like heavy weather.

Friday Feb 6 1863

About noon commenced running a little faster as the Cap probably thinks he will have to burn a little more coal if we ever get to Jama[i]ca. Got my fatigue coat out of the lucky bag. The weather is a little cooler today for it lightened so much last night.

Sat 7th 1863

Making about the same time as yestarday. Weather getting hot again.

Sunday Morning [Feb 8]

Saw land at two last night. Have been running along side of it since. Think it is the Island of Jama[i]ca. Ran to the mouth of the harbor and took on a pilot. At ten stopped at Port Royal & took on the American Consol and then went up to Kingston and anchored at one. Intended to coal here but the watter was to[o] shallow that we could not get up to the wharf and they have no lightens. Then thought of coaling at Port Royal[4] but some say that we wer[e] forbidden to stay in the harbor over twenty four hours unless it was actually necessary to get coal to leave with. But thank Providence we had enoughf.

Monday Feb 9

Accordingly on Monday morning at 7 o'clock we weighed anchor & got under way. Stopped at Port Royal as we went out and left the consol. We left the Pilot about Ten o'clock. Ran East by South. Saw the last of the Island of Jama[i]ca, the Pt. of Morant, at dark but passed it at Two o'clock. We passed several vessels on the way and boarded a schooner, but I was on post and did not learn what it was. Also saw two at anchor in a little cove along the Island. They wer[e] large full rigged vessels. The Island of Jama[i]ca is like all the other land we have seen in the warm climates. Hilly and baren but is covered with green trees and shrubs in the val[l]eys. The inhabitants pass for white allthough sunburnt very much.

[2]...The distance between Port Royal and Kingston is about 7 miles. The channel is very crooked and marked with spikes on each side...Saw the last of Ja., Point (Morant) at dark but passed it at Noon...schooner but got

no news. The 290 left Kingston two weeks before we went in. We learned from some Amer. sailors she had lain there five days repairing & when she left, was in a very bad condition...

Tuesday Feb 10th 1863

Saw land on both sides today about noon. Towards evening we ran close to the Island of St. Domingo. The wind has been blowing strait against us since we left Kingston. The 290 left Kingston just two weeks before we went in. She lay there 2 days to repair without being molested and I think it looks as though the sympathy there was for the south as they would not allow us there but 24 h[rs]. I forgot a little incident which happened while there Sunday evening. A party of half a dozen of both sex came out to serenade us with Dixie. When we turned the steam hoes {hose} onto them giving them a good soaking which I have no doubt will be quite beneficial to them.

[2]...St. Domingo or Hati...Sunday at Kingston...good shower bath which they, no doubt, could appreciate, and will probably [be] beneficial to their health.

Wednesday Feb 11th 1863

Saw four or Five vessels today but did not overhall any as they were not exactly in our course. Sent down our y[ar]ds & top masts this morning because the ship was getting light & was afraid of storms. Saw land at four o'clock on our Starboard. Suppose a portion of Haiti. Went to quarters at 4 & fired at a target 16 Shots but none of them hit the mark.

[2] Saw five or six vessels...

Thurday Feb 12 1863

Had a little exercise with the Holy Stone, the first in some time. Had target firing with Muskets after quarters. Fired 56 shots and about 50 hit the Target. 5 went through the bulls eye. While the Sailors had one the other day and out of 70 hit the mark 7 times. Passed a brig while at quarters but did not speak [to] her. She showed English colors. Yesterday at Twelve o'clock was 500 Miles from Kingston Ja[maica]. Passed five sails in sight but did not hail any of them.

Friday Feb 13th 1863

Saw several sails this morning also saw land about 9 o'clock. About two saw St. Thomas. When within 6 or 7 miles of the island, I counted 7 islands all within 10 miles of each other. One on the Port side the shape of a Hay stack which looked very green. We ran into St. Thomas and anchored before dark. The City of St. Thomas is the most beautiful we have seen from the sea being situated on three hills. The Castel of the Sea Pirate, Blue Beard,[5] stands on the first, that of Gen Santeanna {Santa Anna},[6] the Pres. of Mexico, on the second. The harbor is the most perfect natural one

I ever saw. Our ship swung across the mouth would allmost effectively blockade the entrance.

[2]...is like a haystack. It is only a small island and looked very green and beautiful...Blk Beard's[7] and Gen Santainna of Mexico house on the second [hill]. There is probably two or three thousand people here. Back of the City and on all but the front side, are high hills. The harbor is a good one & afford good anchorage free from sea at 15 fathoms or 5 fathoms deep.

Saturday [Feb 14]

Commenced painting ship black. At twelve M. fired a salute of Twenty one Guns with the Danish flag at our formast, which was immediately returned from the fort in front of the town. The fort at the mouth of the Harbor has three guns, the largest not over 68" & bothe the others smaller. Anyone would think by the looks that a Mick with a Shelalah could take it on top of the skull. On the West side of the harbor is a lookout with a telegraph so they can tell them at the fort all that is going on outside. The English Mail Steamer, Clyde of London was in here. Also our Man of War, Alabama. She took the Univ. of Watterford as a prize. There is vessels of most every nation in this harbor.

[2]...On top of the hill, the same side, is a fort with telegraph station so they can tell at the town when a vessel is coming in...also our Side Wheel Str, Alabama...

Sunday Feb 15th 1863

Ships company dressed in white for inspection. The Cap. went ashore and got permission of the Gov. for the crew to go ashore. Accordingly 25 Sailors and 5 Marines went on liberty & got drunk & made such a row that it was likely to spoil the Bal[ance] of our liberty. But they concluded to try this once more, so on Monday Ed McKee, G Bandfield, Angus Potts & myself with some sailors went & came back all right. Went up to Blue Beards Castle and all the most important places. Commenced to coal ship & fin[ish] painting.

[2] Monday Feb 16...Twenty five Blue Jackets, Ed McKee, Geo. Bandfield, myself and several others went today...

Tuesday Feb 17

Came aboard at 9 this morning satisfied that I have had liberty enoughf for the present. The Shepard (Napp)(Knap), an American Man of War Sail Vessel formerly a packet between N.Y. [and] Liverpool, came in this morning. They had a reception on the Danish Man of War for our Captain in the evening & keep it up to another late hour.

[2]...There is 8 guns mounted there [Blue Beards Castle], and a lot of shot which they dug out of the fort. The place is now owned by a French Gentleman who is fiting it up agen. Took a walk out on the beech at daylight and

saw Gen Santa Anna's two daughters...Danish Sloop for our officers which kept till rather late.

Wednesday Feb 18th 1863

The British Mail Packet Clyde of London left about noon. Several other Mail Steamers of the same kind have left since we came in.

Thursday Feb 19th 1863

The Shepard Knap fired a salute today. We learned today that the crew from the Jacob Bell of New York came in on a Danish Brig being taken as a prize by the Privateer, Oreto.[8] Also that they wer[e] on her at the time of our chasing her on the 2d inst[ant] and expected we would fire into their every missed {midst}. They say the crew of the Oreto is not disciplined at all & could not done anything had we given them battle.

[2]...cliper ship, "Jacob Bell"...She was taken by the Florida and was homeward bound from the East Indies loaded with tea (6000 chests)...They say her crew is destitute of discipline.

Friday Feb 20

The Captain & Mate of the Jacob Bell wer[e] aboard today. They say the Oreto was only 200 Miles from here Wednesday. Finished coaling or taking on Six Hundred tons & made preparations for leaving.[9] Weighed anchor at 7 o'clock and started to sea after procuring a pilot to act as Sailing Master. Nothing important transpired the first night except we saw two or three sails & several islands.

[2]...a pilot to guide us around the island.

Saturday Feb 21st 1863

Did a good job of Holy Stoning this morning. In the morning, Will Smith was quite unwell and I took his place to act as cook. Had quarters at the usual time and did some drilling. Three men ran away at St. Thomas & we shipped three. About two o'clock passed the Island of Dominica. At Seven saw the Isle of Guadaloop {Guadeloupe} and saw a steamer at the same time. Half Past nine went to quarters but passed without any signal.

Sunday Feb 22 1863

This morning at five o'clock off Martineake {Martinique} saw our gunboat, Alabama, which left St. thomas two days before us. We signaled her but did not pay any attention to that, but came after us to within hailing distance. Capt. Baldwin then went aboard her. After he returned we lay still, and the Alabama went into Martineake {Martinique} and returned to us agen. After this we both started back the same way we came, the Alabama taking the lead. But we soon passed her at nine. Passed Gaudaloop {Guadeloupe} and at one o'clock saw the last of Dominica. At two, land on both sides and ahead. Several sails are also in sight. About five o'clock we anchored in the harbor of Point Peters {Pointe-a-Pitre} on the island of Gaudaloop {Guadeloupe}. Lay here all night and in the morning weighed anchor and left. Ran around the island and found out the Alabama laying outside of a Harbor waiting for us. Went along side. The Capt went aboard her afterward. She ran into the harbor then came back & started off to sea. We lay still all day. At night left with covered lights. Went to quarters at Nine O'clock to pass a vessel. We passed several islands some of which I could not learn the name.

[2]...off Bassa Terra, Martinique saw the U.S. Gunboat, Alabama. She came down in full speed after us. We knew her and signaled her. But the fog was so dense, I suppose she did not know or make us out. And we really thought she would run into us. She finally made us out and stopped but not any too soon to prevent a smash...she ran into Bassa Terra & we lay off and waited her return.

[2] Monday Feb 23—Weighed anchor and left. Ran around the island and found our Alabama lying off the land wating for us. Ran along side & the Captain went aboard her. Afterwards she ran into the harbor. We lay still all day, but she came back and went to sea.

[2] Tuesday Feb 24—Started up at dark last night with covered lights. At Nine this forenoon went to qrs. to pass a vessel...[Bird Key] there is no inhabitant except a man & family to tend the lighthouse...

Wednesday 25th

Yestarday we stopped at Bird Key to get sand. They brought off many curiosities. There is a man & family living on this island that has been here 16 yrs. At 10 last night went to quarters and past a vessel with out signaling her or making any sign[al] to know what or who she was. Lieut Parker swore he knew twas either the Oreto or 290. They say twas an Engl. Man of War for an excuse! We have been running in the direction of St. Thomas. Pass Santa Cruz at Ten and ran to the mouth of the Harbor of St. Thomas. At 2 o'clock, just as we came to the entrance, a steamer left. We sent a boat off to go ashore but was met by a boat from one of our vessels that said the steamer that left was bound to run the blockade. We then immediately left in persuit {pursuit} and overtook

Captain Charles Wilkes, U.S.N.
U.S. Naval Historical Center

her about five miles out. Sent a boat off to her. After it returned we sent two boats crew under Mr. Alexander with orders to take possession of her in the name of the United States of America. Then went back and reported to Com. Wilkes. About Ten o'clock ran out agen. Put a crew & four Marines under Mr. Lewis on her & started her for Key West. Her name was PeterHoff.[10] We took of[f] Twentyfour men, her crews, but left the pas[s]engers. The crew value her at 750,000. She had on twenty tons of wine, ten of it was taken on the night before. She was bound to Matamoras, Mexico.

[2]...The Wachusetts flagship lay in the harbor and we sent a boat off to see what to do, but it was met by one of his boats telling us the Str. which left was a blockader...sent two Armed boats crews...put 25 Sailors and four Marines under H.C. Lewis & sent her to Key West. Her name was Peterhoff...twenty tons of wine which she took in St. Tho's. Was from Liverpool to Matamoras, Mexico...

Thursday 26

We ship[p]ed 6 men today & got back one that ran away when we was here before. Com. Wilkes wanted to attach the Vanderbilt to his fleet but Capt. Baldwin did not think proper. However he is to go to Havana with us. He came aboard about 8 o'clock in the eve.[11] And we started to sea agen before ten. This is the fourth time out of St. Thomas. The Sailors on Wachusetts say the men on the Peterhoff made faces & all that they could to agravate them telling them "here goes a prize—come and take us" as they passed that ship. Little did they expect the Vanderbilt was coming round the point so soon.

[2]...six men today off the Jacob Bell's crew...I hear that Ad. Wilks is going to attach this vessel to his fleet. This does not please Cap. Baldwin...The crew of the Peterhoff made up at Ad. Wilks when they passed...also showed a Cesesh flag. They knew the boilers of the Wachusetts wer[e] out of repair and...

27 Friday Feb 27

Ran along side of [Gaudaloop scratched out] Porto Rico {Puerto Rico} all the forenoon. About 11 o'clock we hailed a schooner & told them to heave too which they did immediately and waited till we had also. When they about ship & started off for land. But a shell made them lay up agen. We then sent a boat off to her. She was the Francis bound to Halifax with Molases. She flew the Eng. flag. At six we came along side of Mona Island. Ran around it to the south and sounded to find a place to anchor. After several attempts at Ninety Fathoms did not find bottom. So we lay off & drifted all night. The cause I think was they either expected to see some vessel or was afraid to run the pass in the night. Jas Murphy was sentenced to 30 Ds {days} Bread & Water—sol[itary] confinement Doub[le] irons &

Ninety Dollars pay stop[p]ed for assault to the 3 Assist Engineers while on shore at St. Thomas.

Sat Feb 28

We ran past Mona Island in the morn. Saw several sails. Passed quite a number of small islands. Came to the island of Porto Rico {Puerto Rico} and ran by the side of it till 1 1/2 o'clock. Stopped & took soundings. Turned about & ran back. It appears to be well cultivated from us, a distance of 4 or 5 miles. They are having another court martial today having three prisoners to try. Sent all the yds down this forenoon. About 5 o'clock ran into the town of Aguadilla and anchored. This is a very old spanish town. The most prominent feature of the Place is the Cemetery which looked very beautiful. The town is small, there not being room for much of a place on account of the hills which come down most to the watters edge. They being rocky & uncultivated. We left at Nine o'clock & ran south of East. Aguadilla is situated on Porto Rico isle.

[2]...[Aguadilla] This is a very pretty Spanish town although very old...cemetry which must have cost quite a sum as it is walled around with a high wall with a large Arched gaitway. It is filled with shade trees... Porto Rico is well cultivated in places...

Sunday March 1st 1863

Still continue south East. The weather is warm with frequent showers. Wind blows a stiff Breaze from the east. About one o'clock saw an American

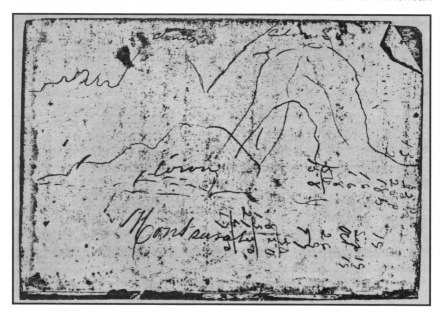

View of Montserrat from the ship

Man of War Bark. Signaled her. She* came off towards us & sent a boat along side with their captain. We passed St. Thomas at 4 o'clock P.M. Did not stop. Was not out sight of land after we left Porto Rico till dark tonight.

[2]...She was the Gems Bock*...{Gemsbok}

Monday March 2

Pleasant with heavy head winds. Passed a small island on our port side this morning and at two o'clock are about the island of Montsurat {Montserrat}. The top at the highest points cannot be seen. Came abrest of Point Pertre {Point-a-Pitre} on the island of Guadeloupe and lay outside all night. This is the same place where we lay all day the....

[2]...the top of the highest peak on account of the fog...

Tuesday March 3rd 1863

Started this morning at five and ran along the isle till we came to Point St Peters {Point-a-Pitre} and ran into the Harbor. Droped anchor, ran up the Yds & fired a salute of Twenty one guns with the French flag at the fore top, and one of the Seven with the American for the Amer. consol. We had this done by two o'clock. Immediately there was scores of boats with visitors came along and once more the old Vanderbilt was the wonder of many Frenchmen, especially her guns. One of the men fell out of the fore top while sending up the yds.

[2]...water swarmed with boats with visitors who wer[e] all anxious to see the Yankee Man of War and...

Wednesday March 4 1863

Still we lay at the Port of St Peters and still the polite Frenchmen continue to visit our ship by scores. This now beautiful harbor was once a thickly populated city so say the inhabitants. But was sunk by an earthquake[12] a great many years ago. Quite a number of pretty little Mademoiselles have passed us their respects today. Weighed anchor and started to sea at six P.M. The mouth of the harbor is the narrowest we have run into. We could step off on shallow watters on either side. On the rocks there is buoys that mark the channel all the way out to sea. We started South and lay off Dominica all night from dark till five in the morning.

[2]...the polite Frenchmen continue to pay us their visits by hundreds... The harbor was made by an earthquake.

5th 1863

Then started and came to Martinique at Eleven and lay off the harbor. This is the most beautiful place I have ever seen. The beautiful sloping hills covered with such a beautiful carpet of green encircled with green lawns of Mangolia {Magnolia} trees. While here and there can be seen groves of CoCoa trees from which hang clusters of CoCo Nuts, all present a pleasant & charming view to the beholder. Some parts of the isle is very roughf

& mountainous, but it does not compare with Dominica for its de[e]p dark ravines & gorges & such frightful chasms. Where the soil will perit, it is highly cultibated, & beautiful fields of sugar cane about a foot high are seen. We left St. Pierre[13] about six o'clock and ran south passed Fort Royal. At dark saw a Frigate going in as we came past.

[2]...lay off Bassaterra...the valleys which look as though they wer[e] hollowed out to suit the taste of man and covered with such a beautiful green carpet at this season of the year...and behind which peeps out the little white cottage of the industrious tiler of the soil. All have a tendency to inspire the beholder with a love for the romantic...roughf & wild with high uncultivated hills & deep gorges down which torrents of watter flow. This is an advantage this island has over others—it is well watered...Eng. Frigate...

Friday March 6th 1863

Saw the island of Barbados a little after daylight. Came in sight of the town of Bridgeport {Bridgetown} about half past nine. When about three Miles out a whale boat from an Amer. Brig came out and harpooned a whale. They passed close along side of us going at a speed not at all to be envied, but did not run a great distance before they brought him too after throwing half a dozen lances. But before doing so the quantity of blood which he spouted up and such struggles made one pity him. After he was dead, some more boats went to their assistance and they towed him to the Brig where they have been busy cutting up and hoysting aboard all day. We fired a salute of Nine guns for the Comedore {Commodore} at one and Twenty one at two [o'clock] for a National salute which was returned from the fort. The Oreto was here one week ago today & coaled up here. We have heared that the 290 had gone up the straits. Saw N.Y. Papers of the Tenth & Eleventh of Feb. Some of the Aristocracy came aboard. Quite good looking, some of them Feminine. They played and sang several songs which in the states would be called quite out of date.

[2]...quantities of blood which he blew up was frightful to behold...where the operations of cutting him up immediately commenced. We fired a salute of twenty-one guns for the Eng. flag at the fore...some of the Barbadoes Aristocracy came aboard in the evening. Some of the "Femme Solo" wer[e] quite good looking. They favored us with some music & singing such as "Nellie Bly, Wate for the Wagon" and several other "popular" tunes.

(The island of Barbados is the livliest and best tilled island we have seen.[14] It belongs to England & most of the inhabitants speak Engl.)

Saturday M 7th 1863

Weighed anchor at ten o'clock as our Twenty four hours were up about this time. Sent off a Mail from here by the consol. Then started to the southard and ran around the island and started back to Gaudaloop {Guadeloupe}.

Ran with fore & aft Main & top sails set. The wind blows from one way, or South East for six Mos & then changes around. Shipped a boy and also a Man in Bridgetown.

Sunday March 8th '63

Running North West passed between several islands, several small islands during the forenoon with Gaudaloop {Guadeloupe} on the port side. (The Island of Gaudiloop {Guadeloupe} is cultivated on the beach but back it is hil[l]ey or rough and untillable.) Had inspection & muster in the forenoon. Ran around Gaudaloop to Point a Petre and dropped anchor at two o'clock. This is the third time we have been in this port. I believe we are going to coal ship here.

Monday March 9th 1863

The officers wer[e] ashore to a Theater and returned about two feeling rather jolly. The Comidore was with them. Commenced to coal ship this morning. Are going to take 250 tons on. The gunboats Alabama & Oneida came in this afternoon, also a French Man of War. The Oneida was at St Thomas when we wer[e] there with the Wachusetts. The Eng Bark load[ed] with coal came in & we are coaling from her. The weather is very hot. All hands went in a-bathing this evening.

[2]...on shore to a French Theater last evening and returned merry enoughf. The Admiral was with them...

Tuesday March 10 '63

Rains every forenoon & clears up in the afternoon & the sun fairly scalds. Visitors continue to flock to the ship. Some of the ships crew have had liberty. The Orderly Sergt. went today. He reported me for telling the prisoner go out of the Brig with the Master of Arms. I went in a-bathing in the evening. Watter very warm, got about my fill of salt watter which did not sit very well on my stomach.

[2]...Morgan reported me for letting the prisoners leave without the M.A...

Wednesday March 11/63

The French Man of War left this morning. Our boats went off and brought 5 or 6 loads of visitors of both sex. They sang & danced for the amusement of the Officers. Some of the females wer[e] very pretty.
(Saw the town of Basse-terre at Ten.)

Friday March 13th/63

Rained like blazes yesterday. Sergt. Pope put up his revolver last night and I drew for it but lost-ticket 8 p. Weighed anchor at 6 Bells this morning and started to sea. We must have taken on a thousand tons of coal a[t] Point a Pitre. The Consol came aboard and went off with the Pilot. Ran sout[h] till got clear of land. Then ch'd to north west. We have a colored pilot to go with us around the Islands.

Saturday March 14/63

Saw several small islands and also Santa Cruz just before going into St Thomas. Our crew went to quarters and we fired our gun off at Pilot Rock which stands just out side of St. Thomas. The charge had been in ever since we fired at a target & was rusted very bad. The gun recoiled with great force the whole length of the carriage. We did not hit the rock because we had not elevation enough. But fired the Tompion away & blowed part of the stern away with the wind. Ran into St. Thomas a little before noon. As we went in, the Engl. Frigate, Phaeton, which lay in the harbor, fired a salute of 13 Guns. Directly after, the Danish sloop of war fired the same. Then the 1 & 2 Divisions went to quarters and returned, each of them dressed in uniforms and stood on the quarter deck all the afternoon. At Three, the Govinor of the isle came aboard & we fired another salute of 15 Guns with the Danish Flag at the foretop. This was immediately returned from the fort. There was three Blockade runners laying here, and about 5 o'clock one of them got up anchor and ran outside. The Wachusetts then made preparations to leave in persuit. But she came back and anchored at the mouth of the harbor. It was thought she calculated to leave in the night so our third cutter went out to watch them. The Wachusetts chased her from Charleston here and came in 10 hours late. There was five Eng. Mail Steamers in the Harbor today.

[2]...at "Sail Rocks" but did not hit it for want of elevation. On looking around, we saw quite a quantity of rope on deck, yarn, on looking to see the cause, found to our surprise we had fired our Tompion away & blew part of the stern away...Danish Sloop of War with the Amer. Flag flying at the fore. We answered both...one of them got up anchor and ran outside and came to anchor agen. I suppose it was for the purpose of leaving in the night...

Sunday March 15 '63

Dressed in uniform for inspection after which got up anchor and left this miserable place. Saw the island of Porto Rico at dark and also the town of San Juan. Have been running with sails all set and more steam than usual. Should think was making 15 Nots.

Monday March 16 '63

Drilled at quarters & trained the gun different so if we should fire would not blow the stern out. Saw the island of Haty {Haiti} at 8 o'clock. Are running along the North side of it. Saw a steamer at 7 Bells M. Went to quarters & made every preparation for an action but did not have any occasion for fight as she was only a Spanish Mail Steamer, "Mejico" {Mexico}, from Havana to St Thomas. At 7 o'clock in the evening went to quarters with another steamer ahead. She was a Spanish transport.

Tuesday March 17th '63

Are still along side of Haty {Haiti} or St. Domingo. This part seems to be barren except that it is covered with small stunted shrubry that looks as though it was scorched by the heat of the sun. About 4 o'clock saw two men of war. One on the port, the other on the Starbo[a]rd bow. Soon we saw they wer[e] American Men of War. Then we sent up a signal for them to follow us which they did. & then we started for land which was only a short distance off & ran into a kind of Harbor where we all came to anchor. We ran out 35 fathoms of chain but dragged, drifted and had to get up anchor and ran in nearer to shore & drop it agen. This time let out 45 fathoms. The R[h]od[e] Island fired a salute of 9 guns for the Comidore which we attempted to return but failed firing three guns at one time & two at another. We weighed anchor agen at half past Nine & went to sea. The Rhode Island & San Jago D'Cuba stayed in the Harbor all morn. There was several forts that looked as though they wer[e] abandoned & one was partly washed away.[15] [Margin Note] St Nichlas Mole

Tuesday [March 18th '63]

Wednesday {corrected in ink} scrub this morn. Saw the Island of Cuba about 10. Are running in sight of land now with all the fires going and sails set making about as fast time as the Vanderbilt is able to. Saw a steamer flying the spanish flag and boarded. After she started, gave us three dips with her flag for a salute. We anchored at 11 o'clock in the evening on the Great Bahama banks in sight of the lighthouse on Lopez island which is 275 feet high.[16](Senomas)

[2]...running North west are in sight of land...12 Nots...

Thursday March 19 1863

Weighed anchor at 4 this morning and went after a steamer which just passed us. Chased her about 4 hours, fired two shots to make her heave too, then boarded her. She was a spanish mail steamer. At this time we wer[e] 60 miles out of our course. Then ch'd about and ran back to the lighthouse. Sent a boat off with Lieut. Todd. Then started on our course. Saw quite a number of other steamers and sail vessels.

Friday, March 20th '63

Saw lights all night. At 6 this morning, saw a French Frigate going in the opposite course. Did not stop. About 11 o'clock an American Man of War Steamer, the Seminole. She came along [side] & sent a boat off to us. She chased the Oreto and tryed her best to overtake her but her Engines broke down just as she was going to open fire upon her. Came in to the harbor of Havana about Two o'clock & came to anchor and fired a salute for the Amer. Consol of Nine Guns. The Seminole came in about two hours after. The weather is very hot, fairly scalds. They still continue to fortify the island. At the present time there is centries {sentrys} within hailing distance of each other all over the island. Can see several extensive Sugar houses. Got 4 hours extra duty for taking the tins out of my Cartridge box.

Saturday, March 21st 63

Mr. Griswold,[17] a Masters Mate acting, left today and did not return. Mr. Pierce is to be sent home and dischgd from service for a letter which he wrote to the Editor of the NY Times.

[2]..went ashore on liberty and forgot to return. Since, I have heard that he joined Rivers & Duroyce's Circus. Mr. Pierce, Act. M. M., is to be sent home. He has since been appointed Consul to Nassau, N.P. He was sent off on account of a letter which he sent to the NY Times which did not commend our acts very highly.

Sunday March 22d 63

Weighed anchor at 8 o'clock and ran over to Key West & came to anchor off Fort Taylor at 4 P.M. The wind was on the Starboard almost direct ahead as we came in. The Band was upon the Battlements playing National Airs. When we came out of Havanna, there was 3 Ceseshe {Secession} flags flying on ves[s]els in the harbor. There was one the day before descharging cotton all day. She had run the blockade.

[2]...The Pheaton Eng. Man of War played Hail Columbia...As we came past Fort Taylor, the band played National Airs, and I must say, I felt delighted to see the American flag float over her own soil once more. Key West is a small island, very low. Nothing more in fact than a Military Station. Very dry & nearly barren. The rock comes to the surface. Fresh water is scarce this time a year. We paid 2 1/2 cts pr gall. The way they collect it is by building a wall around a level piece of ground near the house & when it rains, they run the watter from the building into it. The beach is covered with white sand which gives it a dazzling appearance in the sun.

Thursday March 26th, '63

After coaling two or three days off of the Frank Boult, we ran along side of the dock & commenced to coal here yestarday, and are taking it on very fast. There is several Men of War lying in this place. The St Lawrance, Octorora, Magnolia togather with several small ones. The 90 NYork, 49 PA Regiments are here in the fort. There has quite a number came aboard to see the old V. Have got a Vessel along side to coal out of....

[2]...Frank Bolton to lighten her...We hoist it in by steem...Frigate St. Lawrence, Gunboats Octorora, Magnolia...

[2] Friday Mar 27 '63—Rec'd a letter from Frank & N. and wrote an answer. Weather is very pleasant & hot.

Sunday March 29

Friday rec'd a letter from Frank & Nell. & wrote home & ans. Nells. Last night at 1 1/2 while on Post, gave the alarm of fire. Afterwards Smith and

Myself went over. Was a house, Blk Smith Shop & Barn burned. Watter being very scarce, all the fresh watter they have is rain watter which the[y] catch in Cisterns built on top of the ground for the purpose. They can't dig down for the rock comes to the top of the ground. Watter at present is two & a half cts pr Gall[on]. Has not rained for a Mo[nth]. Went ashore to church today and went all round the isle. The shores are covered with snow white sand which dazzles the eye.

[2]...The fire caught in a Blacksmith shop & burned it down togather with a barn & probably would not have stoped here, had not they sent off a lot of men & pails to put it out from the ship...

Monday March 30

The PeterHoff's crew went away on the Fair Haven bound to NYork, also the Retrobution men. Read Jim Henry's Paper which was sent to Geo. about the New Fleet which was comprised of the Lackawanna, Ticonderoga, Iroquois & etc., where he says the Iroquois had never been to sea.[18]

[2]...Retribution men which we took on in St. Thomas.[19] Finished coaling at night.

Aprl 1st Wednesday 1863

Finished coaling last night.[20] Commenced fixing to weigh anchor in the morning. The transport Eastern Queen came in this [morning] and ran up to the Dock to coal. She came from New Orleans with sick & wounded soldiers bound to NYork. We got up anchor at 5 o'clock and found we wer[e] aground forward, drawing 21 ft 6. Got under way about 6.

[2]...Got ready to leave but found we wer[e] aground as the tide was out. Waited till 6 when the tide came in, and left.

Thursday Aprl 2nd '63

A little after daylight saw land. Ran into the Harbor of Havana at 7 o'clock & anchored at 8. The flags wer[e] all flying half mast & all the Spanish ships had their Yds Cockbilled. They are keeping some Religious days, being Catholics.[21] Saw a steamer outside which they say was a Block-ader. There was 3 Secession flags flying when we came in. Painted the ship agen today.

Friday Aprl 3rd '63

We are flying our flags at half Mast. So is all the flags in the Harbor. There is four Secession flags, 3 on Schooners & one on a steamer. Ex-pect the Comidore off all the while. The Guard is all dressed in Uniform to present Arms to him when he comes. The English Frigate ——{?}—— came in and fired a salute both for the French & Spanish flag of 13 Gns. Then sent a boat to us & would have fired one for us but it was to[o] late. The Admiral came aboard at five o'clock P.M.

Saturday Aprl 4th 63

To commence with, the Eng. Frig. saluted our flag with 13 Guns which we immediately returned with the Eng. Ensign at our fore top. At Ten all the bells commenced ringing. They began to fire at the Forts, on the Men of War an[d] squared all the yds. We the[n] fired Twenty One with the Spanish flag at the fore top and left it up all day. At Two the French Admiral came aboard. We presented Arms to him & when he left fired 13 Guns which was responded to by the French Man. A Schooner loaded with cotton came in early this morning soon after the Octorora came in. She passed one as she came in that had been flying the Secess. flag in here, but had none up when she left. There are 8 ships on sight loading with sugar besides the schooners which are lying at the wharf. There are immense sugar store houses on the sides & end of the harbor. 28 on one all connected under one awning.

Sunday Aprl 5th '63

The Octorora got up anchor and went out but Met the Semona & came back. In the afternoon some of us went aboard the Oct. She carries 1 9in. one 100th Rifle, 4 32#, 4 24 Howitzers. There was two steamers came in loaded with cotton flying the Eng. Ensign. Talked with one of the Cumberland's crew, J. Gardner. Was well acquainted with Chas. Lenhard's Brother. Was the last man that spoke with him before she went down.[22]

Monday Aprl 6th 63

The Octorora left this forenoon. We fired a salute for the Amer. Consol of 7 Guns at One o'clock. Took on fifty Tons more coal today to cap off Painting with. Oh dear, Ye Gods, when will this Humbugging End. We have to dress in Uniform all the time. The weather is very warm in the day time but cool at Night. Drew our Grog Money today. 4.25.

Tuesday, Aprl 7th 63

Another steamer loaded with cotton came in. And one of the Blockade Runners has been getting up steam & we have been expecting her to leave. An Eng. sloop Man of War came in which caused a good deel of excitement as she was taken for the Oreto. She is a low black Propellor with Raking Masts & Bark Rig. Her Smoke Stacks (2) just forward of the Main Mast, a perfect Picture of the Oreto. Grisswold, the Masters Mate, has joined a circus which he belonged to before he joined the service. One of the Jacob Bell men told me that we passed the Florida off Abaco. She lay too with her smoke stacks, top masts down knowing who we wer[e] as we passed. Scrubed Hammocks this Morning, all Hands. The Mail Steamer, Columbia, from New Orleans came in about Sundown. The French & English Frigates left in the Afternoon.

Wednesday Aprl 8th 63

Marine Guard is getting very indignant at having to dress in uniform & remain on the quarter deck. The weather is intensely hot and we have seen enoughf of this detestable service to appreciate freedom. Although one can stand a considerable bondage for the sake of seeing all that we have seen. If we could only leave when we had seen enoughf before it became a bore. Havana. We enter the harbor from the west through a Narrow Entrance of a quarter to a half of a mile in length which is not as wide as twice the length of the ship. On the left at the Mouth stands Castle Moro {Morro} on which stands a lighthouse tower, on which is inscribed (ODonel 1844).[23] With this is connected forts of solid masonry half a mile long with only one short vally between. These walls allmost ov'rhang the Entrance & would be impossible to assend the hill from the watter. The other side is strongly fortified. On the Right stands the City of Havana. The Harbor is surrounded by hills on which are forts closely connected. They say this is next to Gibraltor.

[2]...but it is all in ones lifetime. The principle part of Havana stands on the right side of the entrance with Moro {Morro} Castle on the left... (ODonel 1844) in large letters inscribed on it. The dry docks are floating. They fill them with water to run the vessel in, then pump it out.

Saturday Aprl 11th 63

Are Making preparations for another voyage to sea. Thursday the Columbia left for NYork. & the Northern Star bound to Panama came in out of watter with Thirteen Hundred Passengers bound to Oregon, probably to avoid the draft. Yesterday Two French Line of Battle ships, 74 Guns each, with a Yellow flag at the fore. Also a Spanish sailing vessel loaded with passengers. I was Made Acting Corporal Yes[terday] in Carbery's place, he having slept on his watch, by order of Lieut. Parker. Got up anchor at Two & started to sea having taken on a darky for Pilot. Since we went in, two schooners went ashore on the right of the harbor.

[2]...[Northern Star] She was out of water...passengers bound to California and Oregon...At two o'clock, seen two schooners on the right as we came out, which ran on while we lay inside.

Sunday had inspection in uniform and Muster afterward. Went to quarters twice last night. The last time for a little schooner.

Monday saw land on the Port side about two. Ran abreast of an island for an hour or two. Had Target practice in the morning at quarters when we fired 42 shots or 3 apiece. We had the credit of doing the best shooting. We came to anchor at Night in 30 fathoms of water and sent a boat off to an Island. Weighed at 12 M.

Tuesday Aprl 14 '63

At daylight saw 4 or 5 sails in sight which wer[e] all small except one. This let go but chaised up two till could see what they wer[e]. At Nine Boarded a steamer from NY to Nassau. They got some late papers from her. Boarded several schooners afterwards, one which was the Victoria of Nassau loaded with cotton. We boarded her agen at two o'clock in the Night.

[2]...but run after a schooner till could see what it was...

Wednesday Aprl 15 '63

Ran south of Abaco in the forenoon. Boarded several schooners and a propelor from New York to Nassau. At noon saw two Steamers but they ran under cover of the land. About four o'clock we came to the Mouth of Nassau Harbor (New Providence) & dropped anchor immediately. Three Gov. Officers came off & said that American Vessels wer[e] not allowed in the harbor without a pass. If they wer[e] he would be glad to extend their hospitality to us. When at the time there was a dozen secesh flags flying in the harbor. This is English Neutrality. A steamer which ran the Blockade with cotton came in two days ago & was discharging her cargo. She brings news of the Bombardment of Charleston.[24]

[2]...not be allowed to go in the harbor. I suppose because Ad. Wilks was with us and they had issued a proclamation not to allow the Notorous Wilks in any Eng. port. Although they pretend to be neutral, there is quite a display of cesesh flags inside. A Blockade runner came in today with a load of cotton.

Thursday Aprl 16 '63

Left Nassau at dark last eve. Ran North & 1/4 East. At daylight saw a steamer ahead. (Schooner Rig. which could see on the star[board]). Chased her, she making directly for land after she discovered us. When 4 Miles off, fired a shot to Make her heave too. But she did not pay any attention to it. Afterwards fired 3 more. The third shot went between her two Masts and exploded right ahead. Half an hour afterwards was along side. All hands to quarters & would have blown her out of the watter if she had not stopped. Sent two fiting boats crews off to her with Kiser & McGloin. The Cap. came aboard & took Breakfast in the Ward Room. The Vessel was the Gertrude[25] Cleared from Nassau. Had been to Charleston to run the Blockade but our vessels wer[e] too thick so returned on her way to Nassau. She is an iron screw lead color schooner rig vessel loaded with Powder (150 Kegs) & other things for secesh. While chasing her they threw a keg of Powder overboard to see if it would sink. If it had the whole lot would have followed suit. The remainder of the day was spent in put[t]ing coal & crew aboard & taking her crew off. Some of the {crew} wer[e] recently discharged from the Alabama. One had run the Blockade on the Peterhoff. She had two Pilots, one from Nassau & the other from Charleston. The Cap. Made him (the latter) take the Oath before he released him.

[2]...the third went between her mast & funnel & exploded just ahead of her...she was still going. Wilks on deck saying heave too or I will blow you. All hands to quarters with the guns trained on her. After she hove too, sent two fiting boats crews off to her armed to the teeth with Act. Masters Kiser and McGloin...had been to Charleston but failed to effect an entrance. Her

Capt. did not deny her being a blockader but said we had got a valuable prize...lead colored propelor of about 600 tons...spent in putting coal, prov., and men aboard of her. At dark, sent her off with McGloin as Capt. of her with 25 men. We took her crew off...

Friday Aprl 17 '63

Lay still a part of the night as usual. Started at 6 o'clock after a Bark. When about 3 Miles off, she hove too & sent a boat off to us for watter, they having been on short allowance for the past weak. Sent a boat off to see if she was all right. Supplied her with watter & sent the Gertrude prisoners aboard her as she was bound to Nassau. While doing so, the Octorora came along. The Cap. came aboard. Then we both started off agen in opposite direction, we after what was reported to be a smoke from a steamer, but was only a watter spout.

[2]...a Bark with Eng. colors...

Saturday Aprl 18 '63

Started up about daylight with land in view astern. Saw several Islands through the day. At Noon saw the Island of St Salvador or Cat Island. Ran to the Southard & came to an anchor off the place called Baily Town. The Natives showed us the place Where Columbus landed nearly 400 years ago.[26] This is the first land discovered by him. Weighed anchor at 5 o'clock & lay too till after dark, then started off in SoutherlyxEast.

[2]...south E. direction with covered lights which is a common thing with us. Anchored in 14 fathoms of water. Could see the bottom very plain.

Sunday Morning saw land agen Port side. Fortune Island. Stopped about one o'clock. Sent a boat off. Heared from the 290. She run two Amer. Barks ashore last week and is at Turks Island coaling now, where we lay yestarday in 14 fathoms. Could see the bottom very plain.

Monday Aprl 20 63

Eight Mos ago today enlisted a Marine. Stood orderly over a court martial. We ran from daylight till about nine o'clock. Came off the East end of Cuba where lay too all day wating for the San Jago D'Cuba.

Tuesday Aprl 21

Lay off Cuba till 1 o'clock today. Saw a vessel on our Star[board] & made for her. She was coming toward us till we started after her when she turned & run away. 2 1/2 o'clock are running with sails set. Wheels making 12 Rev. pr Miniut {minute}, 42 Revolutions pr Mile. The vessel did not happen to be a prize so we returned agen & boarded a Spanish Mail Steamer. Just dark Wednesday, another Mail came along today, Mejaco {Mexico}. After boarding, we left Cape Maysi. Four o'clock found us at anchor in St Nichalos harbor. The Senomas was at anchor when we went in. All Hammocks wer[e] piped down last night but at Ten our ears wer[e] greeted with a pleasant musical sound like drawing a Stone boat over a bridge with gravel under it. On looking up to see the cause what did Greet our vission but the Ships Corporal calling all hands to up anchor. We made out to say excused when after considerable growling, he left us.

[2]...turned and ran away at the same [time] making for land. She caused a considerable excitement and we made sail and ran with steam...giving her a good overhauling, we returned...the 1st was Eng.

Wednesday Aprl 22

Came to the east end of Cuba and ran south till came to St Jago {Santiago} harbor and ran in & anchored at Two o'clock P.M. Fired a salute of 7 guns. It is six or seven miles from the mouth to the city. & there is no place till we get this distance that to s[w]ing the ship arround but would almost fill the channel. It bounded by high rocky bluffs on each side.

[2] Thursday Apl 23—Ran to the East end of Cuba & then South till we came to St. Jago d'Cuba {Santiago de Cuba}...mouth of the entrance to the harbor. The channel is very winding and narrow. Scarcely wide enoughf for two vessels to pass. On the right stands a high bluff. 8 + 10 hundred feet high on this rock is a solid fort.[27] There are also casemated guns put in the solid rock.

Saturday Aprl 25 '63

Nothing has transpired since we arrived worthy of note. Everything is quiet except a few visitors which usually visit us in such places. We have taken 200 tons of coal. Got up anchor and left a little after four P.M. About 11 o'clock ran across the Senoma. Sent Capt. Wyman aboard her.[28]

Sunday Aprl 26 '63

Mustered at ten on the Half Deck & Mr. Daniels read the sentence of Maliry who was Court Martialed for insolence to the Pay Master in Havanna. We are stearing due east. Sighted Hayti {Haiti} about noon. Ran to the north of it. And then ch'd to east agen. Probably are going to St. Thomas. We passed through the Tortuga Pass in the afternoon. Here is the place to see scenery. The Mountains on each side are covered with a luxurient growth of trees which seem to move "En Mase," sway back & forth with the breeze like fields of grain. Haty {Haiti} is on the south side & Tortuga on the North of this passageway.

[2]...on the half deck for Malory's sentence and articles of war for the better gov. of the Navy...Fortune island on the North of this pass.

Monday Aprl 27 '63

Saw a steamer ahead at 5 A.M. Immediately got up more motion and over-took her at noon. Pass the Mona pass at 12 M. This is between Haty {Haiti} and Porto Rico. Is not more than 5 or 6 miles wide where we passed it.

Tuesday April 28 '63

Ran in the harbor of St. Juan {San Juan}, Porto Rico towards night. The American Brig, Frances Jane of Baltimore, was at anchor there. St. Juan is situated on a Peninsula on the North East end of Porto Rico. Is surrounded by a high wall on which are spaces for Guns to be planted. It contains two or three Thousands inhabitants. It is the best built & most Americanized of any place we have entered.

[2]...San Juan d'Porto Rico stands on the Eastern end of the island of the same name on a peninsula...The Capt. and Ad. both went ashore. They say Wilks has a lady love here.[29]

Wednesday Aprl 29 '63

The Frances Jane of Baltimore left at Two o'clock with our mail. I sent one home on her. Had a good shower this forenoon. Fired a salute of Twenty One Guns for the Spanish Flag & afterwards 9 for Spanish Ad[miral]. Weighed anchor & left just before dark & ran East.

[2]...fine shower this forenoon. Something we have not seen for some time before...

Thursday April 30th '63

Ran into St. Thomas this forenoon & came to anchor. Heared the 290 was in a little harbor on Martinique coaling, & according, got up anchor & left at One P.M. The Amer. consol [Edgar] came aboard & we fired a salute of 9 Guns for in honor to him. Expect the Oneida & Juneetta have the 290 Blockaded. Heard the Cap. say would be back to St. Thomas in 5 or 6 Dys. The Schooner, Herald of Nassau, left while we was here. She is said to be engaged in carrying rebel communications between St. Thomas & Nassau, & has run the Blockade.

[2]...Heared the Alabama was in a small port[30] on Martinique coaling by the American Consul. It appears that the Consul at Bassa Terra had heared that she was coaling on the isl[and], and had chartered a schooner & sent it with all haste to St. Thomas with the news, hoping to find some Man of War...then up anchor & left...[Herald of Nassau] she has run the blockade but has regular papers now. The Capt. says will be back in 5 or 6 ds.

Friday May 1st 1863

On our way from St. Juan to Martinique, Passed the island of——{?}—— at nine. At ten was off Gaudiloop {Guadeloupe}. Passed Basse-Terre about One. At 6 o'clock had pass[ed] Dominica with Martinique in sight. Stoped & boarded the Eng. Schooner, May Queen, from Berbades {Barbados} to Nov Sc. Trained our guns on her before she hove too, & the Cap. Sayd he thought we might bee in better business than boarding Schooners.

[2]...May Queen from Barbadoes bound to St. Johns. Her Captain said...

Saturday May 2nd '63

Came to the point off Tampa Bay at Ten last night. Lay there till this morning. Sent up several Rockets which wer[e] not answered. This was rather a dampner on our faith in the 290s being here. In the morning ran past & boarded an Eng. Bark which gave coal to the 290 & then ch'd about & ran over to Point Pier, the other side of the island. Here found the Alabama & Oneida. They say that a darky came across the island & told them the 290 was coaling on the other side. After 6 or 8 hours got up steam & went around the[re]. [The] 290 had been gone 3 hours. They sailed around but did not see anything of her. We left Point-a-Pitre & went to Fort Royal, a distance of 15 Miles, & fired a salute of 21 Guns with the French Ensign at our fore. Which they returned from shore without any flag up.

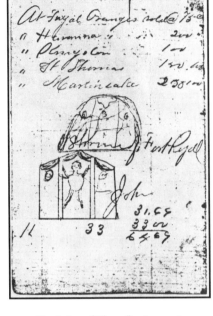

Sketch of the shrine at Fort Royal

Also comparison of prices for oranges at the different ports.

[2]...After this ran around to Bassa Terra.

Fort Royal is an old French town of about a Thousand inhabitants. It takes its name from the extensive forts which are here. The houses are all two story, very narrow & joined together. They are all catholics & have several sacred relics, one called a shrine built in an oval shape with Christ & the two thieves nailed to the cross, one each side of him.

[2]...a schrine with the image of Christ and the two thieves as they wer[e] crucified, situated on a hill. They are mostly ceseshonists. They helped the Alabama to escape the San Jacinto here.

Sunday May 3rd '63

To begin the day at Nine, went up and gave the Cap. & Adm. a present as they went off, & agen on return. At ten, inspection. At Half Past Ten, the Gov. of the island came aboard. In the afternoon, gave him a present & a salute of 17 guns when he left which was answered from shore. There is a reservoor the end of which is arched over with a large white stone arch, also a sugar refinery here.

[2]...Fort Christian ans[wered] it.

Monday May 4 '63

Got up anchor at 6 this morning & went over to Point St. Pier[re] and came to anchor agen. The Adm. went ashore at Ten with the consol. We gave him (Consol) a salute of 7 guns. Many aples, Mango, & oranges. Bananas are quite abundant here also.

Tuesday Aprl {May} 5 '63

We left St. Pier, yes[terday] at two P.M. Ran south at dark. Saw the last of Martinique & daylight. Saw Barbados. Ran into Bridgetown at 10 A.M. Did not come to anchor. Lay off the harbor & sent for the Consol who came aboard. Lay still till two without any news, & then started back but ran around the island. The Phaeton lays here. Ran up to St. Lucia Is. & lay still the balance of the night. Sig[nal] rockets wer[e] sent up from shore. There is a little town by the name of Castres {Castries}. On each side of the harbor are very high Mountains all most perpendicular. [Margin Note] 300' 350 ft

[2]...high mountains on each side of the harbor in the form of a sugar loaf.

Wednesday May 6 '63

Ran north on the East side of Martinique passed the place where we lay off for the 290 last Sat. at one. Came to St. Pierre & anchored about Four o'clock. The island, a few miles from St. Pierre, is the most beautiful that could be conscienced of. Everything seems to spring up spontaneous. Springs flow down the rocky ravines, fall off the rocks to the sea. Field after field of sugar cane are seen stretching away in the distance. (Thermomiter 95–98 Shade.) Cocoa, Bannanas & Mangolia trees cluster here & there in the ravines, or in groves left standing, or from the shades for long beautiful lawns in front of the stately Mantion {Mansion} of some rich old Planter. Lovely indeed must Eden have been to exceed this island in beauty.

[2]...spontaneiously from the earth and each seems to try to excel the other. Streems of crystal waters flow down their rocky ravines...into the sea with a deep roaring sound...trees mingle in rich profusion in the ravines...Nature, indeed, seems to have done her best to beautify the Island of Martinique.

Thursday May 7th '63

Fired a salute of 13 Guns at 2 1/2 o'clock for the Lord Mayor of St. Pierre. The Amer. consol was of[f] with him. Get up anchor & left at 4 o'clock. Ran north West passed the island of Dominica. This island is in plane sight of St. Pierre. [There seems to be a confusion about whether it is St. Pierre or Pt. Pierre.] The Phaeton arrived as we left. She just wanted to see what the Vanderbilt was up to.

Friday May 8 '63

Continue our course to the Nor[th] West. Saw land early this morning & about four P.M. This was the island of Santa Cruz. Came to the town of Fredrickstad & came to anchor at 9 o'clock.

Saturday May 9th '63

Fired a salute of Twenty one guns with the Danish flag at the fore which they returned from shore. Afterwards the Cap. & Admiral went ashore & they gave him 15 guns which we ans. They went to see the Gov. General of the Island 16 Miles out in the country to Christianstad.[31] Was escorted with a band of music in a 4 horse chaise.

Sunday May 10th '63

The Gov. General came aboard at 2 o'clock. Gave him 17 Guns shortly after the American Consol came, & we saluted him with 9 guns. Both wer[e] returned from shore. In the afternoon all the visitors came from the island & the ship was crowded all the afternoon.

Monday got up anchor at 6 o'clock in the morn & ran over to St Thomas. Arrived at Ten.

Tuesday Wrote a letter home. Commenced coaling off of the Bark, Lucy Frances of Brookville, & Brig, Chas H. Foster of Philada{lphia?}. A Breman Merchant[man] came in and fired a salute of 5 Guns. Was returned from shore.

Wednesday May 13

The Captain of the Squadron overhauled & condem[n]ed the James Bock {Gemsbok}. Sent our letters home by the Eliza M. Strong, St. George. Several Mail Steamers arrived among which are the Clyde, & Trent of the Wilks-Trent affair. She is a Bark rig side Wheeler with one Funnel. Geo W. Kelsy went off with Sergt. Pope after the Wachusetts M.D. Doctor.[32]

[2]...held a survey of the Gems Bock today, & condemned her as unfit for sea service and consequently she is to be used as a store ship...among which wer[e] the Clyde of London...G.W.K. went ashore with Sergt Pope to get the Wachusetts M.D. who was on a bender.

Thursday May 14 '63

Shepard Knapp was towed out by the Oneida & started to sea.

There was Eleven Marines from the Wachusetts came aboard today, Friday[15] with some Sailors. Little else occured.

Saturday May 16 '63

[The following is scribbled over and is noted as a mistake by the author] Six Corporals from the Wachusetts—two corporals [end of marked-over section] Thirty sailors from the James Bock {Gemsbok}. The Thermometer stands 95 shade, eve cools down to 75.

Sunday[17] wer[e] all out to inspection of arms.

Monday[18] the Admiral went aboard the Wachusetts to get the bal. of his things & when he left they gave him 15 guns.[33]

19 Tuesday got the Brig, Fair West, of West New York, along with more coal. Joined the Orderly Mess May 18th 1863.

Friday May 22d 1863

Ship is now coaled, painted & ready for sea agen. Expected to go to sea today but was delayed because the cabin was not finished.

[2]...delayed on account of some slight alterations in the cabin stairs which was not quite completed.

Saturday [23] wrote a letter & sent home by the Wachusetts which left this Sunday [24] morning at daylight. As she left the harbor, cheer after cheer was given them by us which they returned in a hearty manner. Afternoon some of the marines went aboard the Alaba[ma], visiting.

[2]...She is going to NY to get new boilers. Potts went on her by order of our M.D.

Monday May 25th 1863

Got up anchor in the afternoon. Went to sea about four o'clock. Passed Santa Cruz on our way. Before dark ran south.

Wednesday May 28 '63

Still running south. Ran up & stopped by the side of the little island of Santa Marie, & sent the boat off to Two Amer. Whaling schooners which lay at anchor a short distance from the land. The island is barren & sandy without trees or any apparent vegetation. Although could see herds of cattle in the distance, could not see any sign of inhabitants.

[2]...The island is a barren waste to all appearances with here & there a green patch with a little hut in the middle...cattle & horses can be seen very planely roaming without any thing to keep [them] under control except the ocean.

Thursday May 29 '63

We lay off this island yestardy after taking the Capt. of schooner back two or three hours. Then started off in a south westerly direction. About daylight this morning saw land on our Port bow. Was the main land of Venezuela. The Mountains rise abruptly from the watter to the height of several thousands of fect & continue the same h[e]iylil as far as we went. About Ten arrived at the Town of La Guirie {La Guaira}.[34] There is very little chance for building here except on the hillside. The Mountain is higher here than any other place I have seen. Fired a salute of Twenty One Guns at 12 M., & 7 for the American Consol when he left at Ten o'clock. (Heared the Shepard Knapp was wrecked while at La Guaira).[35]

[2]...mountains which appear higher here than in other places, frowning down on the little villa at their base, which would take but a few rocks sent them diving from their dreadful summits to destroy it...

Friday May 29th '63[36]

The Captain & Admiral started for Caracas about 5 this morn. Together with several Officers accompanied by Sergt. Pope for Bodyguard. There is no harbor or protection to vessels here. They must anchor off the land. The swells are very big and the sea is roughf all the time. The weather is cool enoughf to make a watchcoat comfortable at night. The Thermometer stands their at 65 to 70. In daytime 95–100 in Shade. Bands of Gurillies {Guerrillas} are in the Mountains. Can hear their firing & see their camp fires at night.

[2] Friday May 30th...bodyguard for the Ad. They are going to transact some business relative to finances or loans by the U.S.A. to Venezuela. La Guyra {La Guaira} harbor or anchorage would not be called a harbor for there is not shelter from the sea. There is a trementious ground swell here. The weather is very hot...Gurillies {Guerrillas} are in the mountains back of the town and they expect an attack every night.

Spanish Man of War came in today, Monday June 1st, to protect the Town. Down on the level with the sea on the beach, the trees are very green and fields of sugar cane can be seen. Above this as you begin to ascend the hills, they are barren or only covered with stunted bushes. While near the top are cultivated fields, beautiful trees and shrubry.

[2]...protect the town from the guerillies bands. Expected the Admiral & Capt. back. They did not come, however.

Tuesday June 2

The Capt. & Admiral wer[e] expected back yestarday but have not returned yet.

Thurday June 4 '63

At 8 o'clock we hoisted the Spanish & Venezuilean flags at the fore, side by side. At Twelve M. fired a salute of Twenty One guns with them still flying. The Spanish Man of War lying here hoisted the Amer. and Spanish flags at the fore and fired a Salute of Twenty One Guns at Twelve. Also the fort fired a salute at the same time, which was to celebrate the day called Corpus Christe, a religious day with the Spanish Catholics.

Friday Jan {June} 5 '63 A D

3 P.M. The Officers that went the second since Caracas returned today & the gig has just gone after the Admiral. The Thermometor at Twelve o'clock in the shade was 85° with a good breeze. The Admiral returned about 5 o'clock. We got up anchor & left at 8 in the Evening running North by West.

Saturday June 6

Saw the island of Buen Ayre {Bonaire} at Eleven, & at Twelve was at Curacao[37] City of [Willemstad] But they would not allow us to enter as we had expected, on account of our just coming from La Guayra {La Guaira} where the Small Pox was raging. Unless we should lay 15 D[ay]s at quarantine which we concluded not to do. So we went on towards St. Thomas.

[2]...As we did not want to see the place bad enoughf to wait that time, we started on toward St. Thomas.

Sunday June 7th '63

Weather very roughf. Decks keep washed down well by the watter coming in at the ports. Was read off as Corporal at muster.

Monday June 8 '63

Boarded a schooner from St. Thomas one day out. At Eleven in the evening ran into Fredrickstaid, Santa Cruz, & anchored.

Tuesday June 9

Got up anchor at 8 and started for St. Thomases where we arrived about two. We ran up to sail rock & fired 42 Rounds with the Guns at it nearly all of which struck it. Some of them fell short and rochisked {ricocheted} & hit afterwards. The Alabama is the only Amer. Gunboat here.

Wednesday June 10 '63

Commenced taking coal off the Gems Bock today.

[2]...Fired a salute of 17 guns as he passed from the sloop to shore. They gave him 15 on shore.

Saturday June 13th 1863

Admiral Wilkes transfered his blue penant to the U.S.S.S. Alabama at Two o'clock today to the satisfaction of all on board, & Especially the Marines. We gave him a present and 13 Guns when he left. I believe he was called home.[38] Yestarday we fir'd a salute of 17 guns for the Danish Gov. General as he passed on his way from the sloop of War to the shore. He was rec'd with a company of soldiers and 15 Guns by the Danes. Afterwards they ret'd our Salute. Are now preparing to get up anchor. 2 1/2 o'clock. Expect to go down to Brazil. Got up anchor & under way about four o'clock.

Sunday 14 June

Passed the islands of St. Kitts, Mountsurat {Montserrat} & others. Saw the list of killed & wounded in the 154 Reg. N.Y.S.V. {N.Y. State Volunteers} among whome wer[e] some particular friends. Oh, when will this Unhallowed Rebelion cease. This was at Chancellorsville, Va.[39]

Monday June 15th 1863

Lay off Gaudelup {Guadeloupe} all night and ran into Point-to-Petrie {Pointe-a-Pitre} & anchored at 12 M. Preparing to take on coal agen. The Oneida is coaling here now.

[MARGIN NOTES, LISTS & ACCOUNTS] Rio d' Janeiro Aug 2d 1863...M.M. Oviatt...Olean, N York...Mississippi....

French Words & Meanings[40]

Affaire d'amour—A love affair
Al'Francaise—After the French Mode
Al'Mode—According to custom
A Main Armee—With force of Arms
Au revoir—Adieu until we meet agen
Aux Armes—To Arms
A voitre sante—To Your Health
Beau ideal—A perfect Model of Beauty
Beau Mond—Fashionable World
Bon Vivant—A jovial companion
Cap-a Jue, Frombread to fort—all over in Paris
Champs Elysees, Elysian fields—a park
Douceur—Sweetness, A Bribe
Ducit amor Patriae (Latin)—Love of country, me guiles{?}
Dum vivi mus Viva mus (Latin)—Let us live, While we live
Enmasse—In a body
En Route—on the way
Femme Couvert—Married Woman
Femme sole—Unmarried Woman
Garde de corpse—A body guard
Le beau monde—The fashionable World
Protege—One protected
Bona Fide (Latin)—In Good Faith
De Facto—From the fact
Dum Spiro spero—While I live, I hope
Ex officio—By virtue of office
Facsimile—A close imitation
File Non Armees—By Faith not arms
Fortes fortuna juvat—Fortune assists the Brave
Paretur pax bello—Peace is produced by War
Prima Donna—Principle actress
Post Mortem—After Death
Pro Temp—For the Time
Sine Die—Without date
Verbatim et literation—word for word, letter for letter
Vivi Vula—Far[e]well & be happy
Vox populi—Voice of the People

Some think the Bark Rig Steamer which passed when we wer[e] getting up anchor at St. Pierre, May 5, was the 290.

Towed the Johana Elisabeth into Table Bay Aug 31. [SEE BOOK 2 FOR DETAILS]

U.S.S. Vanderbilt

Dec 28 Rec'd of the Pay Master	5.00
Jan 1 Clothing & Stores	21.70
Feb 15 Cash	5.00
	31.70

Germain, Chief Eng.

Chas. Baldwin, Cap.

Daniels, 1st Lieut.

Kiser, Lewis, McGloin, Masters

Rec'd 4.25 Grog Mony Apl 6	31.69	31.69
		33.00
		64.69

At Fayal {Faial} Oranges sold @	.75 cts	100	
" Havanna " "	2.00 cts	100	
" Kingston " "	1.00	100	
" St. Thomas " "	1.40	100	
" Martineake " "	2.50	100	

The U.S.S. Vanderbilt took 1600 Tons coal before leaving the Brooklyn Navy Yard, Oct 5, 1862, to go cruising after the 290 or Alabama.

[This has been scratched out by author] We have got 39 Com[missioned] Officers besides the Capt. on board this Vessel.

Signed account Aprl 23 for Bal till Aprl 1st

May 2	31.69
Drew 1 Pr Shoes	1.81
" 2 Bar Soap	.50
" 2 B. Peper 16c	.32
Shd{?} 6 Sks Silk	.18
" 1 Tobaco	.12
	3.56

Direct to the U.S. Steamer Vanderbilt

   Directions

M.M. Oviatt

U.S.S. Vanderbilt

Care Naval Lyceum

Navy Yard

Brooklyn, NY

M.M. Oviatt Dr To Ed McKee Mony	3.00
Towles Mony	1.20
Will Inglesol	3 cts
Geo Bandfield	6 cts
Towles Mony	1.00

Morgan Liberty	1.00	
Wm Smith Dr For Mony Lent	1.06	
G.W. Kelsy Dr For Mony	.25	
For Show Ticket at Miltons		
{Miblins?} Garden	.20	
Wm Smith Dr For Ticket at Miltons		
{Miblins?} Garden	.20	
Wm Smith Dr For Mony of	1.00	13.70
[Above entry scratched out and marked Paid]		<u>22</u>
Geo Kelsy Dr For Figs	.20	35.70

Angus	Towle
Brothers	Bandfield
Deslin	Smith
Darling	Serg Morgan, Or.
Carbery	Serg Pope "
Gregg	Corp McCandless
Harris	Corp Kane
Ingersol	Music Harper
Johnson	Music Hraps{?}
Kelsy	
Kinmerly	
Gunning	
Murdock	
McKee	
Oviatt	
Potts	

Dec 29 Paid P.S. Towle	2.00
" " " Ed McKee	1.50
" " Rec'd of Wm Smith	1.00
" " " of Tolfree Paymt	5.00
Jan {Jun} 3 " " "	3.00

24 May 1861 Ellsworth Assasinated.[41]
Recp for Jan 6, 3 cts 1863

Port Watch	Starboard
Kelsy	Bandfield
Johnson	Gregg
McKee	Harris
Towle	Ingersol
Carbery	

CHRONOLOGY OF U.S.S. VANDERBILT
[AS WRITTEN BY MILES M. OVIATT]

Nov 10th, 1862 — Left New York first time
Nov 20th, 1862 — Arrived at Bermuda
Nov 21, 1862 — Left Bermuda

Nov 30, 1862 — Arrived at New York
Dec 10, 1862 — Left New York
Dec 24, 1862 — Arrived at Fayal
Dec 31, 1862 — Left Fayal
Jan 17, 1863 — Arrived in Hampton Roads
Jan 29, 1863 — Left Hampton Roads
Feb 3, 1863 — Arrived at Havana
Feb 4, 1863 — Left Havana
Feb 8, 1863 — Arrived at Kingston
Feb 9 — Left Kingston, Ja.
Feb 13 — Arrived at St. Thomas
Feb 23 — Left St. Thomas
Feb 25 — Arrived at St. Thomas
Feb 26 — Left St. Thomas
Feb 28 — Arrived at Agguidella
Feb 28 — Left Agguidella
Mar 2 — Arrived at Point a Petrie
Mar 3 — " " " "
Mar 4 — Left Point a Petrie
Mar 6 — Arrived at Barbadoes
Mar 7 — Left Barbadoes
Mar 8 — Point a Petrie
Mar 13 — Left Point a Petrie
Mar 14 — Arrived at St. Thomas
Mar 15 — Left St. Thomas
Mar 17 — Arrived at St. Niclos
Mar 17 — Left St. Nicols
Mar 20 — Arrived at Havanna
Mar 22 — Left Havanna
Mar 22 — Arrived Key West
Apr 1 — Left Key West
Apr 2 — Arrived Havanna
Apr 11 — Left Havanna
Apr 15 — Arrived New Providence, Nassau
Apr 16 — Left Nassau
Apr 18 — Arrived & left St. Salvador
Apr 20 — Arrived Cuba
Apr 25 — Left Cuba
Apr 28 — Arrived St. Juan, P.R.
Apr 29 — Left St. Juan
Apr 30 — Arrived & left St. Thomas
May 2 — Arrived Fort Royal
May 4 — Left Fort Royal
May 4 — Arrived St. Pierre
May 7 — Left St. Pierre
May 8 — Arrived Santa Cruz

May 11 — Left Santa Cruz
May 11 — Arrived St. Thomas
May 25 — Left St. Thomas
May 29 — Arrived La Guaira, Venezuela
Jun 5 — Left La Guaira
Jun 8 — Arrived Frederickstaid, St. Croix
Jun 9 — Left Frederickstaid
Jun 9 — Arrived St. Thomas
Jun 13 — Left St. Thomas
Jun 15 — Arrived Point-a-Pitre

Crew list on the Vanderbilt; Oviatt's cash ledger

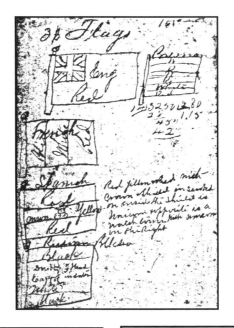

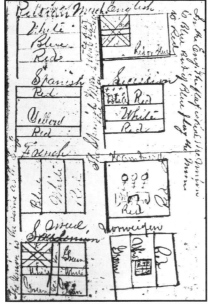

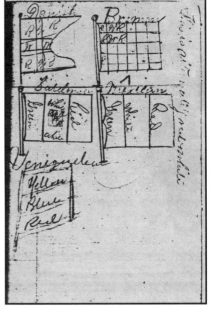

Flag identification charts

Route and ports in the Caribbean southward to Venezuela

THE CONTINUING VOYAGES OF THE U.S.S. *VANDERBILT*

U.S.S. Vanderbilt written by M.M. Oviatt while on board, continued from old Log

Log of the U.S.S. Vanderbilt

[MARGIN NOTES ON DIARY FLYLEAF]—Gen Guiseppe—M M Oviatt—John M Oviatt, Olean, NY—John B Calvin—G H Bandfield—Homer—Kenney—United States of America—Good Hope—M.M. Oviatts Log Book written on board the U.S. Steamer Vanderbilt—Marg. th Gent.{?}

To OSM	Dr	
Mony 1/2 Sov. 1/2 Milrea		2.42
1 Pr Gloves 25 cts		.27
1 Ps Rd Cloth		.25
		2.94
		.50
	Total	3.44

To OSM	Dr	
Candles 1 Pr Week since May 1st		
" 1 Pr Sissors		33 cts

Point-a-Petrie June 20 '63

Left Point-a-Petrie at 6 1/2 this morning. Wrote a letter home which expect to send at Barbadoes. Pass'd two or three small islands before noon, one of which said to be Amerigo Island. While lying in Point-a-Petrie, a slaver came in flying the Braman {Breman} flag with a cargo of slaves, five or six Ne[...], I believe.

Sunday June 21 '63

Saw a sail this morning on our port quarter. She came in sight & showed the French flag. Made Barbadoes about 4 o'clock. Amer. Consol came off, but did not bring any news of the 290.[1] But quite a number of rumors are circulated about her coaling on the other side of the island, as usual. Sent our mail off to an American Brig & then left without dropping anchor. Running south East by East 1/2 East.

Monday 22d '63

Continue the same course as yesterday. Sent the Top Masts down this morning as we sent the Yds down last evening. Weather very heavy. Watter coming in at the ports keeps Gun deck well washed.

Wednesday June 24 '63

At 4 Boarded a Spanish Brig Thirty days out of Montevedo Bound to Havanna. Says the 290 boarded an Eng Bark since she left off the island of Ferdinandes. Also says American vessels are lying in port all along the South American coast.

Thursday June 25 '63

At 4 o'clock boarded a Pourtegese Brig from Pernambuco. Says the 290 & Georgia left Bay of All Saints on the 23 of May & the Mohegan {Mohican} arrived three days after. Also the Octorora at Pernambuco on the 25 getting repaired. At 12 M was in Lat 8° 52" 15.

Friday June 26 '63

Had bag inspection this afternoon. At quarters this evening loaded our muskets. Had night quarters at Three bells which was not very pleasantly received. Lat 6° at 12 M.

Sunday June 28 '63

Running south East by East 1/4 East. Had inspection of arms. Loaded at the usual time. The sea has calmed down & weather very pleasant. Lat 5° 22" 59" at 12M.

Monday 29 '63

Fired at target at quarters with gun, 42 Rounds. We making best shot that was fired the first time. I was made second Capt. while we wer[e] excercising. Rec'd Grog Money, Five Dollars in Am[erican] G[reen] B[acks].

Tuesday June 30th '63

Filling in forward to protect the Boilers which shuts up the forward gangway South South East by S[outh]. Lat 4° 7" 27". Afternoon we got into the South East Trade winds. In this lattitude a little north of here, they are the North East Trade Winds.

Wednesday July 1st

Ch'd our course to south East this morning at Ten. This sail reported right ahead came near enoughf to fire at 11 1/2. When we fired a blank from the

Howitzer and another a few minutes afterwards, but she did not stop. We the[n] fired the fore Pivot & when she hove to, was an Eng. Bark. Said the Mohegan {Mohican} was Blockaded by the two Rebels vessels, Alabama and Georgia. This news was 4 Ds from Pernambuco. Lat 2° 25" 12M.

Thursday July 2d '63

Neptune[2] made his appearance this morning at one o'clock. First hailed the ship then came over the bow to inquire if we had any of his children that he had not seen. On being informed we had, he said he would call on the morrow and then disappeared in the form of a tarbarrel over the stern in a flame. At twelve o'clock M was twenty-five miles from the line and at One the shaving (as it is termed) commenced. The lances men wer[e] all shaved, the[n] the Darks afterwards. They thought to shave the Marines, but as they had not taken any part in the proceedings, they strongly ob-jected. About half past three, they made a rush after them, who had antici-pated an attack & have staid below on the gun deck for the purpose of resistence, if necessary. Accordingly, when they came down, they wer[e] rec'd with Muskets and bayonets which rather discouraged some from at-tempting anything farther Till Marines put up their arms. Then came the tug with hand, spikes & fists—Marines ahead. In the mean time they brought the hose down to drive them on deck but we succeeded in turning it on them. Some few knocks wer[e] rec'd by the blue jackets. About this time, Mr. Daniels & Mr. Parker made their appearance and quieted the row. Mr. D. then went to the Captain to know if he could, by main force, take us up an[d] put us through the process, which he did not think adviseable to undertake. So they left us alone.

Friday July 3rd 1863

At 7 this morning boarded two brigs, one American and the other Norwe-gian. One from Montivedo & the other from Rio Jenairo {Rio DeJaneiro} with coffee. Say the 290 was cruising down off the coast of Brazil. Went to quarters at Nine as usual. While there, saw a long Brig Rig Side Wheel Steamer, a little on our port bow. Stopped excercising and got ready for an engagement. Overhauled about 11 & boarded her. Was a French Mail boat from Pernambuco to Bordeaux, France. No news of importance that I heared. Saw a brig ahead before quarters at 6 in the evening & fired a shot to have her heave too. She ran down abreast of us. Partly came round after we stopped & then put off before the wind agen. So we did not board her. So we went on. On our way, fired three shots to bring the steamer too.

Saturday July 4th 1863

Got up at 4 this morning. We wer[e] laying by, wating for daylight to see a vessel which went out of sight. Started at 2 Bells having seen & made her out to be a Brig. At 7 saw land ahead. Was then running South West. It was the island of Fernando [de] Noronha, a Brazilian Convict island. A little after Nine, came along side, stopped & sent the Gig with sailing Master off for news. While we wer[e] wating for them to return, we amused our selves by sending up Masts & Yards which took till noon. At 12 Started on agen running South by West. The island is composed of several rocky portions on which are situated fortifications. They are but little ways apart. We had Bread Poultice & coffy for Breakfast, Been Soup for Dinner with Pork, & Hard Tack for supper with coffee. As we had ch'd our course, we made sail and ran with sail all the afternoon.

Sunday July 5th 1863

Muster & Articles of War on the Half deck by Mr.Daniels. At Ten, saw land on the starboard bow. At eleven, stopped & took soundings off Cape St Rogue about 3 miles from shore. Was 25 fathoms. Where the watter is greenish-looking or white rather near a shore, it is called soundings. Made Pernambuco[3] & came to anchor at dark, of the town, about a mile. 45 fathoms of chain out. Weather cool.

Monday July 6th 1863

An American Whale Boat came off this morning with the Capt. of the Bark. Afterwards they left for the States with one Thousand barrels of oil. Got up anchor and left at 2 o'clock. At 3.30 Boarded the Sail Ship "City of Bath" from Calleo {Callao, Peru} home. Said the Privateer, Georgia, had captured our ship, Constitution, from Philla[delphia] to Shanghai, and was coaling off from her at the island of Trinidade. The Captain, wife & mate with 15 of the crew wer[e] on board. They also said the 290 was hourly expected there to coal. The "City of Bath" was boarded and let go for she had an English cargo to U.S.[4]

Tuesday July 7th 1863

Sent down Masts & yards this morning. We saw some cattamarans on Sunday as we came into Pe[r]nambuco. They are used as boats by the natives, made out of logs on which they put sails (For further information see Bandfield's log treating on the subject) to propell them. They are often seen out sight of land. Are made with slanting bottoms. Heavy head winds with roughf sea prevails. Lat 11"2 22.

Wednesday July 8th 1863

One of the forward boilers gave out this morning. But was pluged up so that it did not delay us any, as the steam was up in the after boilers. At 12 M. was in Lat 13"54.

Thursday July 9th 1863

Have been making great preparations for a fight tomorrow. & also have been righting up ship with water barrels & ashes as we are getting very light.

Friday July 10, '63

Called all hands at 4 o'clock this morning. Had coffee prepared over night, and had coffee as soon as we wer[e] up. Afterwards, went to quarters just as we passed Martin Vas {Vaz} Is[lands] and remained till we had went around the Trinidade. Had our guns all trained around ready for action but wer[e] disappointed. Neither the Georgia, Constitution, or any other vessel was to be found. Run outside and lay off to send up Masts & Yards. Also sent a boat to shore & sent up the recalls & fired a gun before she returned. At 2 P.M. left. Saw pleanty of burnt pieces of timbers, apparently ship timber, ps. of plank, coals of chared wood & etc.[5]

Saturday July 11th 1863

Nothing unusual occured today till about 8 o'clock when we wer[e] about to turn in. When we saw a light right aft and on the Starboard side. The whole ship was an uproar in an instant. We ran past it as every one thought & was going to let it pass off so. But the Cap. did not think so, for we ran past far enoughf to furl sail. Then ch'd our course & made for the vessel which we made out to be a ful rig ship. & beat to quarters. Overtook her about 10. Hailed her & board[ed]. She was the British Ship, Wayfarer, 38 Ds from Liverpool to Singapore, loaded with Iron.

Sunday July 12th 1863

Saw three sails a little after daylight. Overtook one, a Bark, at 8 o'clock. Was French.

Tuesday July 14th 1863

Nothing occured since last I wrote worthy of note. This morning saw land or lighthouse off Cape Fria. Saw land at daylight ahead. Ran into Rio [de] Janeiro and came to anchor at 10 o'clock. At 12 fired a salute at 12 of 21 guns with the Brazilian flag at the fore. When we came in & cross[ed] what is called the Rolling Way, I began to think Old Vand. it was gone for. It, in one of the rolls, the bottom of the Port Wheel cleared the watter about six feet. At the mouth of the harbor there is what is called the Rolling Way. A Brazilian Frigate rolled her masts out not long since. The City of Rio [de] Janeiro stands on the Port side of the harbor & Rio Grand on the Starboard as we enter. There is a sugar loaf on the port side 2200 feet hight.[6] The only man ever at the top was an American Comodore. M.M. Oviatt

Wednesday July 15th 1863

The American Minister, Jas. Watson Webb of the courier and Reporter formerly of New York, & the Rusian Ch'g De Affaires wer[e] aboard about noon. The wife of the former was also with them. When they left, we fired a salute of 17 guns each for them. Some of the Blue Jackets went on liberty today. Commenced coaling this morning. The Cliper Ship, George Griswold, is discharging a cargo of coal at the wharf. The Captain of her gave $700,000 Dollars Friday. One of the Eng. Men of War left today, the Leander.

Saturday July 18 1863

This is a general holoday ashore. At 8 o'clock this morning we hoisted the Brazilian flag at the Main mast. At a quarter to one, fired a salute of

Twenty One guns. The same was fired at the fort and also on the Eng. Man of War.

Sunday July 19 1863

This is the first Sunday since the ship has been in commission that we have not had inspection or muster. This day Eleven Months ago enlisted in the Marine Corps of the U.S. States & many times have I rued the day that I did so.

Monday July 20th 1863

At Eleven this morning, word was passed for the Marines that had not been on liberty to draw their mony & get ready to go. I was one of the number & was on hand for my mony, $5.00 of American Gold. We wer[e] hurried into a boat, and as there was some Niggars going, we had their company. Our being hurried off with out any notice, & then having to be put off with niggars, had rather got the best of my better nature. & consequently was in no humor to enjoy liberty. However, we arrived on shore in the course of time which was about half past Twelve. Went to a Brokers & got my $ changed for 9 Milreas or four Dollars & fifty cents American mony. Then was in for a stroll through the city which we did for about an hour. When the callings from the inner man had to be attended to. Five of us then went to "Hotel de France" & called for dinner, but they could "No comprehende". But we fell in with an Eng. Gentleman who could talk the lingo & went back & had our dinner of dishes with wine for the sum of 11 Millreas. We then started off for a cruise around the city till 6 o'clock when we had supper at "Hotel des quarte Nations" for 1 1/2 Milreas each. Where we engaged lodgings for 1 1/2 Milreas each but when we went to turn in, found we must pay before we saw our beds. Think this will not go down with us & we finally persuaded them to let us take a look at them. When we found that there was only beds enoughf for three of us. Accordingly, we paid our dinner bill & left. After wandering about till near Midnight, I procurred a shore boat for 2 Millreas to bring me off to the ship.

Wednesday 22

Several rumors are circulating about the ship that the "City of Bath" had been taken, and that there was a privateer crew on her when we boarded her togather with guns & ammunition. The U.S. Man of War, Mohegan, came in at evening. She is a 7 Gun Propellor Bark rig, Two Eleven in 32" Rifle fire. She left three days before we came in. Has been south as far as Montivedio or in the direction.

Thursday July 23d 1863[7]

Dressed ship this morning with the Brazilian flag at the maine, and the American Stars & Stripes at the fore & signal staff withe the Blue Jack at the bow. Fired a salute of Twenty One guns at 1 P.M. The Mohegan came up to coal where we coaled. We having finished coaling this morning &

commenced painting ship all over. The Emperor has issued a proclamation that the Rebel, Florida, shall not enter any Brazilian port, and the others shall remain but 24 hours.

Saturday July 25

Finished painting & coaling and after dinner ran down to the town. Fired a salute of 13 guns on the way for the French Ad. Comodore which they immediately returned. One of the Brazilian Frigates has been firing at the target all the forenoon, as has the forts.

Sunday July 26th 1863

Made preparations for receiving visitors. After noon one of the ferry boats loaded with visitors came along & then went back agen & brought another load off & carried the first back agen. Then came & got the ballance. The French Admiralship fired a salute of twenty-one guns Three times at 8 A.M., 12 M. & 6 P.M. to celebrate the birthday of Louis Napolean.[8]

Monday July 27

Very stormy most all day. Scrubbed Hammocks this morning. Asked permission to scrub last night but the officer of the deck, Hawkins, would not let me do so. So had to get up this morning after standing the mid watch to do it. The French Admiral off of the Frigate, Astra, went aboard the Mohecan after noon. When he left we fired a salute of 13 guns. He came aboard here. When he left, we gave 13 guns more. Each wer[e] returned by the Astra.

Tuesday July 28th 1863

Our Minister, J.W. Webb, came aboard with his wife. At 4 o'clock we rec'd him in uniform. The Cap't gave them a grand supper at 8 o'clock this evening togather with Executive Mr Daniels & Captain Gleason of the Mohican. They wer[e] invited guests.

Wednesday July 29 '63

At daylight this morning, we fired a salute of Twenty One guns and hoisted our flags. The American at the fore, Brazilian at the Main and American at the ensign staff. I noticed that all the Men of War in the harbor also fired a[t] the same as we. And the Brazilian, 3 in No., dressed their ships in a rainbow as did a Pourtigues, also. Afterwards learned that it was to commemorate the birth of the (Empress Imperial), daughter of the Emperor of Brazil. At One fired another 21 guns. But did not at night, neither did the Eng. or French Frigate have been expecting for two or three days.

Thursday July 30 '63

Nothing very important. Mr. Parker went ashore & came back about one P.M., regular Hog: Oh, tyght.

Friday July 31

Hoysted the Pourtigese & Brazilian flag at the Main, Stars & Stripes fore & aft at 8 this morning. At one, fired a salute of twenty one guns in memory of

Sketches of entrance to the bay at Rio de Janeiro
Probably drawn by George H. Bandfield.

Oviatt's personal cash ledger
and sketch of entrance to
Rio de Janeiro

the day Don Pedro was made Emperor or the day Brazil declared herself independent of Pourtigal. At 2 P.M. the Mohican got underway. As she passed the Eng. and French frigates, they played Hail Columbia and the French Man Maned the riging & gave three cheers which they returned. We also did the same. Spalding, Rodgers & Durvy's Circus just left on a Man of W. Brig at 3.

Saturday August 1st 1863

Had a letter wrote to send this morning but the mail left before I got it ready. Saw the Emperor pass in his Yaucht (steamer) at 1 o'clock. Several distinquished persons came aboard between one & two, among which was the French Admiral & Captain. The Captain of the "Egmond" & Lady, Russian minister, Eng. Consol, American Consol, the Pope of Rome's Enuncio & suit, Dr. Reins & Lady who owns the ferry line here from Rio [de] Janeiro to Rio Grand. We gave them all a present & three rolls. Gen. Webb went ashore about 4 in full Dress with Capt. Baldwin. We fired a salute of 7 guns when all wer[e] on board. A South Hampton Mail steamer arrived at 4 P.M. Bringing news[9] of 40 vessels destroyed in the bay of Funda [Sunda?] by the Privateers, of Dupont being superseded by Dahlgarun {Dahlgren}, Hookers Resignation. Burnside defeated at Port Hudson, Reb. Gen Lee in P.A. and that the merchants of New York had sent out two Privateers, the Atlantic & Baltic.

Sunday Aug 2d 1863

Inspection at quarters at ten o'clock. At one began to make preparations to go to sea such as making up swing booms, hoisting boats, bringing the chain too, fastening awnings, etc. At half past four got under way & steaming South East by South. Did not roll as bad as when we went in. There is a hill on the right side of the harbor over 2200 feet high on the top of which is a convent.[10] One side of the hill is a perpendicular rock almost from the base. The other is a very steep slope.

Sunday Aug——1863

Very pleasant & beautiful. The sky is clear & transparent. Sea smooth and shows i[t]s dark transparent blue to the best advantage. Everything seems quiet as if keeping the Sabath.

Sunday Aug 9 1863

This day dawned upon us with renewed splendor. I can almost hear the birds sing their praises & ringing of the distant church bells one after another as they used to do summoning their congregations togather to worship God on some beautiful October Sabath day back in old Cattaraugus. A sort of reverence for the day pervades the ship and all is so quiet that one is led to thank God for the sabath. The past week, have been quite unwell with chills & fever; have lost 3 turns of post. From Rio d'J. cruised around North East & touched at the isle of Trinidad on H——{?}——Then after running around it, started off in a South E by E course. Last night overhauled a French Bark from Bordeaux. Fired 4 shots to fetch her up. Chased her near half-days run out of our course. 47 Days from Bordeaux to Bourbon—Eleurie.

St. Helena Sunday Aug 16

I had calculated to copy this till now. We left Rio De Janeiro the 2d and arrived here the 14 making 13 days. We had strong head winds and heavy sea all the way. We fired two salutes last night. One of 21 guns Nation salute and the other 7 for the consol. The island of St. Helena is very rocky and barren and very high. There being but few places where a boat can land. The place where we anchored is well fortified. There is several forts on top of the hills. One on the right side of the town. To which a lader of 683 steps, nearly perpendicular leads to this, is cut in the rocks. Heared that the 290 & Georgia wer[e] down at Cape Goodhope and expect to [go] there next.

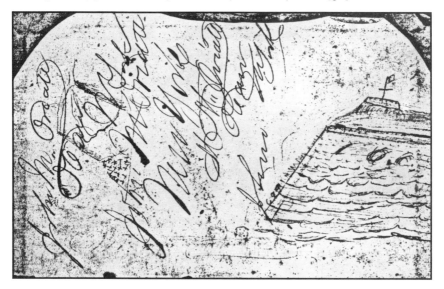

Fort at Island of St. Helena

Sketch of fort at Island of St. Helena reached by 683 steps cut in the rock face; also reference to John M. Oviatt.

St. Helena Monday Aug 17th

Got up anchor and left about one o'clock. Ran to the south. Sent down masts and yards. The wind blowing directly from south and could not run very fast. Very heavy sea.

Tuesday Aug 18th

Ch'd our course at 5 this morning to due North and will not go to (Cape Town) according to that as we expected, till we coal agen. Sent up masts and yards and made sail agen. Saw a sail at 10 A.M., starboard beam. Came to St. Helena & came to anchor agen at 5 o'clock.

Wednesday Aug 19

Commenced coaling this morning from an Eng. Bark. $34 pr ton. 12 mos enlisted today.

Thursday Aug 20th

Coaled all night for can not stay here but 48 hours according to queen's proclamation. Finished coaling and Weighed anchor and got under way about dark. Started south E. qr. E. Are good for Cape Goodhope this time. Took on 400 Tons coal.[11]

Saturday Aug 22

Cloudy and unpleasant with heavy sea. Wind nearly ahead. Masts and yards wer[e] sent down yesterday. Running South E. by E. Several sails reported to day.

Thursday Aug 26

Fired at target at quarters with large guns with shell and shrapnel. We fired the first shot and was the 2d best shot made. The effect of the shrapnel was surf rising for half a mile. They burst raming a perfect shower of shot which would sweep the decks of a ship. Friday sent up yards and made sail. We have had heavy South E. trade winds & heavy weather till today when they ch'd. & now it is quite pleasant.

Sunday Aug 30

Saw land at daybreak. Passed the Cape of GoodHope about ten. At Eleven boarded an American Merchant ship* 38 ds from Mauritius but did not get any news of the privateers. At Two, run into Table Bay or to the mouth of the harbor. And met a pilot who declared upon his oath that he piloted the Georgia, Confederate St'r, out last evening at 7 o'clock. After a delay of an hour or so, ran out to sea agen & started due South. Shortly after, saw a black smoke ahead. We immediately got up fires under both boilers & made all possible speed to overtake her as we supposed. But when she got in sight she proved to be coming toward us. Went to quarters and boarded her but got no news. She was the "City of Cape Town." The pilot said the Alabama left 15 ds before. *(The American vessel was the John Watt of Bath.)

Monday Aug 31

At ten oclock boarded a Danish ship 13 weeks from Shanghai bound to London but got no news from the Rebel vessels. About noon, boarded [a] Dutch ship in distress from Batavia to Antwerpt with a cargo of Tobacco. She was disabled the 27 of July in a gale. Her top masts & yards & gib boom wer[e] carried away. & she had been within one hundred miles of Table Bay since, but could not run in. We took her in tow & started for Cape Town about one o'clock. Her name is Johanna Elisabeth.[12] Her Cap'n says he saw an Eng. Gunboat two weeks ago but she took no notice of him. He saw a low bark rig st'r standing to the southard & Eastward Sat. night with yards down. Saw a steamer about 4 o'clock. Thought at first she was a line of Battleship. She turned & ran towards us. We went to quarters & sent a boat off when she came along. She was an Eng. Mail boat ship rig from London bound to Calcutta with quite a number of passengers. Got some NYork papers from her. At dark boarded the bark, Napoleon, from Shanghai 3 Mos. bound to London. Got no news of the privateers.

Tuesday Sept 1st '63

Ran to the mouth of Table Bay with the Johanna Elisabeth and then let her go to run in herself. And we started out to sea agen. We had to have her cut the Hausers before we got loose & took one belonging to him aboard. When he was gone, he sent his best thanks to Capt'n Baldwin for his servises, by means of signals. Capt'n Baldwin answered that he was entirely welcome. At one, signalled a bark for about half an hour. Then went away and left her. Did not hear who or where she belonged. At 4 P.M. hailed the barque, Natal of St. John's, N.B., from Boston to 65 ds bound to Delagoa Bay. Got several N.Y. papers from her. She was an American Bark sailing under Eng. colors.

Wednesday Sept 2

At 7 this morning boarded an American Barque from Manilla to Boston. She was short of provisions. Sent her some Beef & Pork. About ten, signaled an Eng. Ship from Liverpool to Calcutta. Got no news, however, of the privateers. The Amer. barque was loaded with Segars {cigars} & Tobacco. Nabob was her name. At half past eleven, signaled two Eastern-bound vessels at the same time. But got no news. One was Eng. Did not see the others Colors. In the afternoon signaled an Eng. barque homeward bound and at 4 P.M., a full rig ship under close-rafed top sails. Had had her rudder post carried away in a storm. She was built of iron, was Eng. Clipper built. Saw the account of the loss of the Nabob in a Boston paper today. She was said to be lost off the Cape some place with 7 men and a woman. Had quite a squall towards night. Wind blowing from the North-West.

Thursday Sept 3d

Ran into Simons Bay about ten this forenoon and came to anchor in 8 fathoms of water. Ran out 75 fath[oms] of chain and droped the other anchor. The Johanna Elisabeth is lying here instead of Table Bay which I supposed. The Eng. Frigate, Narcissus, is flagship here. The Admiral lives ashore.[13] Fired two salutes, one of 21 guns, the other 17 for the Admiral.

Sunday Sept 6th

Have engaged a thousand tons of coal & have taken on three hundred tons of it. The Admiral gave us permission to remain here 15 ds.[14] Was much longer as it was necessary to coal, as the 290 lay here and in Table Bay 15 ds in all. "The South African" says The Confederate Str., Alabama,[15] left Table Bay Sept 9th with the best wishes of the majority of the people of the Capital of the Colonies. It also speeks of her gentlemanly officers & gives their names; and the Cape Town artist proposes to furnish photographs of them for any one who desires them. She was repairing and did not get quite through, so she ran into this port Monday and finished. The Tuscaloosa, formerly the Sea Bride,[16] a sailing vessel taken off this place by the Alabama and carries two guns, was in with her. They lay here ten days and when she, Alabama, left, the Narcissus maned the riging and gave her three cheers. The Georgia lay here 15 dys & coaled and gave liberty. One of the officers of the Alabama was killed while ashore gunning and they raised a monument to his memory.[17] Simons Bay or harbor is a large surface of unprotected watter extending several miles in width. The South W. winds blow in, making it unsafe for vessels sometimes, and they are liable to drag their anchors. The town is of the same name as the bay. It is, however, but a Military Station like a great many other Eng. ports. There is but few inhabitants. In fact, there is not room as the mountains extend to the waters edge nearly. They are covered with white sand which fills the air when the wind blows a good breeze.

Sunday Sept 13

Left Simons Bay Friday night at 12 o'clock. Ran south-east. Saw land Sat. morning still on our Port side. Saturday boarded a barque bound to London with 130 passengers. Had been 70 Ds from her starting place wich I did not learn, although one of the East Indies. She was becalmed when we boarded her in sight of land, and a party wer[e] out sporting in a small boat. Never saw the sea more calm or the weather more beautiful than yesterday & today have been.

Monday Sept 14th

Sent up T gallant yards yestarday as a good breeze sprang up & made sail. About four this morning took in sail as the wind was blowing a gale. Sea had become very roughf. Continued roughf all day.

Thursday Sept 17

The weather has cleared up agen and is quite pleasant so that we scrubed Hammocks. The weather Monday & Tuesday was very roughf and was not very pleasant yestarday. But got calm enoughf to Drill and we had squad drill. Serg't Pope first guard, Corp Kane No. 2, & myself the last, each of us having a squad to practice on of a[n] hour each day. This was the first of my attempts at drilling, myself acting instructor. The Paymaster got a little dog in Simons Town this forenoon. One of the Blue Jackets broke its leg and was confined on bread and water. The pup, after having a Medical inspection, was confined to the deep with about 100# iron tied to his neck. Running south E of E.

Saturday Sept 19

Was running East qr North Friday till this morning at 4 then ch'd to half north. About noon saw something floating on the watter. Ch'd and ran to it and found it to be the carcass of a whale with the bluber cut off. A flock of Allabatrosses had taken possession of it.

Sunday Sept 20

Inspection at ten. Mr. P. gave each Non Com. charge of the arms of his squad. Weather very fine. Sea calm. Making 10 Nots.

Monday Sep 21

Four sails reported within half an hour after Eight. At 9 over hauled the ship, Fuchu, from Bomba[y] bound to London with a general cargo. She flew the Eng. flag and after she made us out, twisted the American at the mizen. She belonged in the U.S. S[t]ates. Half an hour after, boarded an Eng. barque. No news, however, was obtained of either of the privateers. Got news from the bark to the effect that our gunboat Sloop of War, Wyoming, was coming home from the China Station.

Tuesday

Weather a little roughfer than for a couple of days. Have been making 16 Nots a part of the day. At 12 M. was in Lat 2"20.

Wednesday Sept 23

Ch'd to nearly north. Have expected to sea land early this morning. Did not, however, sight it till 2 P.M. on the port bow. At drill yesterday, had inspection which made some fun for the boys. Did not drill today. Had quarters at 3 bells last night just to sea what we could do. Some of the guns wer[e] ready in 3 minutes, the longest was 5. Ran along the island of Mauritius. At dark, saw a vessel and went to quarters at 8 bells. Was only a barque. Boarded her but got no news. However, said the Privateers wer[e] last heard of off the Cape.

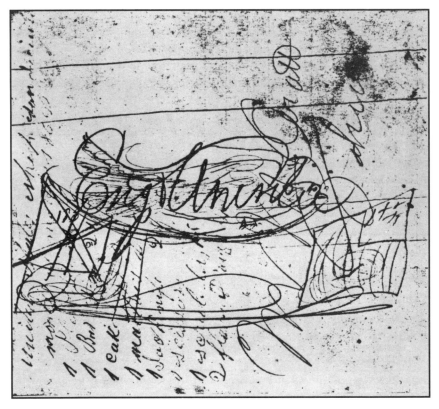

Fuchu from Bombay flew two flags, American and English

Thursday Sept 24

Ran in Port Louis this morning about 8 A.M. Moored our ship and fired a salute of twenty one guns at ten with the Eng. flag at the fore which they ret'd from the shore.[18] At half past ten fired five more for the Amer. consol. The difference between the time here and N.York is 8 h[rs] 16 m[in]. Considerable excitement was created by the barque rig Str. heaving in sight around the point from the southard. But she came directly in and droped anchor by the side of us, and it passed over. She was Engl. from the east, I believe. A large Amer. Merchantman of NYork came in. Said to have a cargo of ice. Port Lewis {Louis} on Maritius {Mauritius} is situated on a beautiful harbor of considerable extent. At the entrance on the left side stands Port Lewis {Louis}. On the right is another fort which is not quite so extensive. The land is low and level for half a mile back from the bay then rises to high mountains. The city resembles Kingston Ja[maica] in scenery. It is all built among trees which hide the buildings. On the right side of the harbor is the Cemetry. A long lane of palm trees extend to it. It is surrounded by a wall, inside of which are trees of all kinds. There is a dry dock here 300 Ft. by 40.

On the left is a coal yard and a road from it to the city made of stone which forms a wall about a mile & connects with it and the fort. This is the most business place I have been in for some time.

Friday Sept 25

Four full rigs ships came in today besides a St'r from Bombay. Commenced to coal. She coaled up & left at night. Tolfree, Parker & Beldon came off at night, tight. The latter, after undressing, lay down on the port guard aft till morning from 12 M.

Saturday Sep 26

The ship (Hampden of Liverpool) built in Maine went out to day. Nearly all the American ships are sailing under Eng. colors now. Heared that the St. Jago had run the Florida down in port at Bermuda. Also that the crew of the Tecona {Tacony} which took the Caleb Cushing[19] wer[e] being 14 in No. The celebrated Paul & Virginia are buried a little way off near a high bluff of rocks.

Sunday Sep 27

Had church service on board by a Rev'd of the Episcopal order at 3 1/2. Quite a number of visitors wer[e] on board today. Also Mr. Parker & Tolfree came aboard tight at 12 Mid N[ight].

Monday Sep 28

Served out Grog mony this afternoon. I rec'd $4.84. At 6 all hands wer[e] called and the Capt. told us that the speed of the ship was or would be lessoned for reasons which he did not state. And, therefore, when in conversation with strangers, be careful not to mention it for fear it would come to the ears of some piratical agent which might tend to make them bolder. He also said it would, perhaps, shorten our cruise but did not endanger the safety of the vessel. I, afterwards, learned that the shaft was cracked on the Starboard side inside the boxing.[20]

Tuesday Sept 29 [No entry for this date]

Thursday Oct 1st '63

Have been taking on provisions for a couple of days & have nearly finished coaling. A ship came in yesterday which says the Georgia boarded her between this and Seychelles Island. News today that she was near this island. The carpenders are putting braces under the shaft to prevent it falling down if it breaks off.

Sunday Oct 4

Inspection and articles of war for the better Gov. of the Navy at ten o'clock. Some of the boys went over to the battleship to church. The American ship, "Wild Hunter" of Boston, came in yesterday. One Eng. ship, two Eng. Bark, one Breman Bark & a French Bark went out between 4 & six last eve.

Tuesday Oct 5th

The American ship, "Western Chief," went out this afternoon bound to London from China. She has 4+ 24" Howitzers. Her Captain says he will fight till his ship sinks before he will let her fall into Semmes[21] hands and his wife says Simmes {Semmes} never shall have her Cronometor[22] to doat over.

Wednesday Oct 7th

The Eng. Mail left for Bombay via Suez at 6 P.M.

Thursday Oct 8 '63

The French frigate, Hermona, came in, anchored, and fired a salute of 21 guns with the Eng. flag at the Maine. She is taking off her guns & preparing to go into dry dock. News that the Alabama [text ends here.]

Thursday Oct 8th

A 22 gun French frigate came in this morning and fired a salute with the Eng. Ensign at the maine. She brought news that the Rebel Alabama burned a vessel[23] off the Cape the day after we left and ran into Table Bay. Several ships are discharging guano here.

Sat Oct 10th

Unmoored ship this morning & went out to sea. Ran East then E. by south then ch'd about 7. Ran West by qr South.

Sunday Oct 11th '63

Running West qr South. Saw the island of Borbon at Half past nine this morning. Came to the harbor of St. Denis and waited till the pilot came off. Saw a large crowd at the town attending a horse race. There is a tunnel around the hill at this place.

Raphael Semmes
Captain of C.S.S. *Alabama.*
U.S. Naval Historical Center

Thursday Oct 16th '63

At 12 in Lat. 28.36.59. Stoped at Noon and took soundings as we have been running on soundings all day. This can be seen by the greenish color of the water & heavy ground swells. Run out 100 fathoms but found no bottom. This was off Cape St. Mary {Marie}.[24]

Monday Oct 19

Saw land this morning off or near Algoa Bay about 400 miles from the Cape.

Tuesday Oct 20

Rainy this forenoon but cleared up in the afternoon. Had target practice at qrs this morning & fired 4 shots or shells. The 3d exploded at the muzzle of the gun flying in every direction. It was not decided who did the best for could not tell very definite on account of the fog. At 5 P.M. boarded the American ship, Hamlet of Boston, from Manila bound to New York. Got no news from her, however, that I heared. At dark, could just see a sail ahead. Overtook & boarded her about ten o'clock. All hands to quarters. She was a dutch ship. No news from her. Monday forenoon at ten, ran into Algoa Bay. The Vice Consul came off. Got papers from Eng. to the 6 of Sept. The 290 or Georgia has not been in here.

Wednesday Oct 21

Saw land early this morning on the str[board] side, the Cape of Agulhas. This is the most southern point of Africa. After passing this, we kept more to the Northard in sight of land all the while. About noon, boarded an Eng. Brig & got a bundle of papers. News of the 290 between Madagascar and Mauritius.

[There is a three-page insertion in the daily log at this point. The following notations are included on these pages:] United States ship San Jacinto.

Month of March 1862

1 Plug tobacco
1 Bar Soap
1 cake
1 mattrass
1 jac knife
1 scrub brsh
2 flacon Draught
Jamestown, Virginia 1600, This is a specimen of my hand writing Nov 16, 1863, while on the U.S.G.R. Vanderbilt from St Helena to Bahia; Jamestown in Virginia 1670 1607; John M. Miles[25] (vs) M.M. Oviatt, Corporal of Marines at the time....Revenge, tis sweet and I will Love it....The Union Forever....E.M. Davis...M.M. Oviatt....Olean, NY

Wednesday Oct 21 [continued from above date]

At night ran into Simons Bay & took the pilot on board after taking a look around. Run out and continued on our course.

Thursday Oct 22

At daylight this morning saw this land agen & we stopped on account of the fog. But after this cleared up, we ran into Table Bay & came to anchor. Saw by the papers of Cape Town[26] that the Alabama came in to Simons Bay on the 17 having lain off in sight of land 4 ds.[27]

Friday Oct 23rd

Wind blows almost a gale. The fog totally envelops Table Rock. Flags are flying half mast on account of the death of Capt. of a Merchantman death. It appears that at night he was uneasy & could not sleep & took a dose of Laudlum [Laudanum] and went to sleep & never woke.

Saturday Oct 24

Cleared up this morning. Wind died away & the cloud cleared off of Table Rock. Made preperations for coaling & got one lighter alongside and was discharging the coal when an order from the Gov. came telling us to stop. So we had to stop without taking on but 20 tons. I believe the Capt. had been to the Gov. requesting permission to coal but was refused and took the responsibility of coaling. But as soon as the Gov. found it out, he made us stop.[28]

Sunday Oct 25 '63

Very warm & pleasant. Had a great many visitors on board in the afternoon but disappointed as many more, as we did not allow any on board after 7 bells. There was in all two to three thousand.

Monday Oct 26

Had quite a number of visitors agen today. Fired a salute of 13 Guns for the Gov. today when he left.

Tuesday Oct 27th

Got up anchor this afternoon and went to sea at 4 P.M. As we went out, saw a large Secesh flag flying on the Port side hoisted near a large house. Had

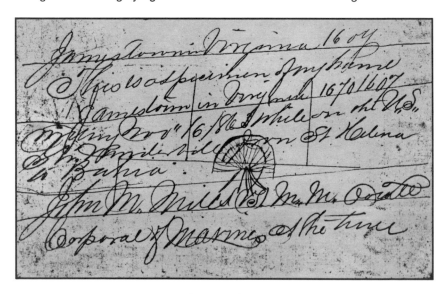

Specimen of Oviatt's handwriting

a fair view of the Lion as it is called. There is three peaks besides Table rock.[29] One is the Lions head, the Lions rump, & the devils peak. There has been large rewards offered for any person that would climb the Lions head and hoist an Eng. flag.

Thursday Oct 29

Boarded a schooner this forenoon from Walwich {Walvis} Bay to Cape Town. She says the Sultanna is taking on the wool from Ichaboe which was discharged there by the Tuscaloosa (vs) Bark Conrad.[30] She, the Sultanna[31] discharged coal & is now taking on wool.

Friday Oct 30th

At two this afternoon ran into Angua Paquana {Angra Pequena} Bay & came to anchor and sent a boat off to the barque, Saxon of Cape Town, which was lying at anchor here. She had taken on a cargo of wool that is supposed to have been left here by the Tuscaloosa.[32] They brought back her papers saying that she had no owner for the wool. Sent Mr. Keith aboard to take possession of her. Mr. Kiser went off to look for coal which was said to be here. He found what he estimates to be 300 tons. About six, a bark made its appearance coming around the point from the southard but as soon as she saw us, she changed about. We fired two shots to heave her too, but they did not reach her and she put off. We then got up anchor and gave chase. Overtook her about Nine & hove her too. Her Capt. made the excuse that he came to steal the coal that was here.[33]

Saturday Nov 1st [Oct 31]

Lay too till four this morning. After overhauling the bark last eve. Then ran back to the bay of Angua Paquanna {Angra Pequina} and run in. The Saxon's flag was flying at half mast. Found afterwards the boat came off that Mr. Denenhon, our Masters Mate, had shot her 1st mate. Mr. D. had ordered him to go forward. When he replied that No G.D. white-livered yankee S.b.-h. could make him go, at the same time attempted to colar Mr. D., when he drew his revolver & shot him through the head. We sent a coffin & buried him at night on the island on the west side of the bay. Also sent a crew on board of her to take her to New York under E.S. Kiser, Act. Master. Also Masters Mates Wyman & Cornell, the latter Capt. Baldwin appointed.[34]

Sunday Nov 2d [1]

Got up anchor at 6 and ran around to the East side of the island,[35] on the E. side of the bay & commenced taking on coal in our boats and one we found here. Sent our boat to the barque & took her crew ashore[36] and brought their Captain on board. About half past ten she left and with longing eyes, I followed her till lost in the distant from the heightest rock on the island where I was on the lookout. This island is a barran rock to all appearance. The sea has overflown it. Sometime there is no inhabitants on it. But there has been some one on it and dug the "Guano" up in heeps. There is two graves side by side. One is to the memory of W. Searles of the Prince

Edward, who died Feb 29th 1839. The other is merely marked grave on a board which stands at the head.

Monday Nov 2

Coaled ship all night. This morning sent a party of Marines to coal ship. A Schooner came in and anchored afternoon.

Tuesday Nov 3d

Went on lookout this forenoon. A party went this morning on an expedition in a boat and brought back a bale of wool, ten #s. About sundown got up anchor & ran out into the open bay.

Wednesday Nov 4

Got up anchor at 2 o'clock this morning & went to sea. Ran North West. Weather quite unpleasant with dense fogs.

Thursday Nov 5

Thirty-nine men reported their times out today. Sent up T. Gallant Yards & made sail as we got good southwesterly trade winds. I believe we took on between three & four 100 tons of coal at Angua Paquena {Angra Pequina}.[37]

Friday Nov 6th

The weather is considerable warmer today than what it has been previous for a few days. We have expected to touch at St. Paul de Loanda till now, but have given that idea up because we keep in this NorthWest course...

Saturday Nov 7

Running North West with light Southwest breezes. Weather warm & pleasant. Sails clewed up, making nine or ten Nots.

Sunday Nov 8th

Saw a full rig ship about Nine o'clock this morning standing to the N.E. Passed her on our port side. She flew the French flag. Continuing N.W.

Monday Nov 9th

Continuing North West with very light breeze. Making 6 or 7 Nots.

Tuesday Nov 10th

Came to St. Helena at ten A.M. Passed the Johanna Elisabeth before going in. Also the Western Chief. She ran in while we wer[e] there. We did not come to anchor but lay too, & sent a boat off. The consul came off but brought no news from the privateers. Left about one P.M. running North West by W 3/4 W.

Wednesday Nov 11th

Continuing the same course as yesterday. Very warm & pleasant weather.

Sunday Nov 15

Nothing has transpired for the past few days. Have been running West Norwest qr West. Have seen no sails since we left St. Helena till this morning when we overtook & boarded the Clipership (Minna Ha Ha) of Boston. 2800 tons was from Caleo {Callao} bound home. Have night qrs at 2 bells last night. Thermometor stands 79 in shade.

Monday Nov 16th 1863

Saw a sail about noon. Ran out of our course for 4 hours & boarded her. She was the French ship T.B. from Callao bound to Haver.

Tuesday Nov 17

Came near running into a ship at one this morning before seeing her. At 10, a sail was reported. We overtook her a little after dark. She was an Eng. ship 57 ds from London bound to New Zealand with passengers. At 11 1/2 had a narrow escape from running into another ship.

Wednesday Nov 18th

Saw a sail this forenoon. Ran for and overhauled her about two P.M. First thought her to be a wreck but found her to be all right. She only had her fore top mast down. She gave us a lot of papers but no news of the privateers was rec'd.

Thursday Nov 19

About noon six sails wer[e] reported a little on the Starboard bow. At one saw land ahead. Ran into Bahia[38] and came to anchor at half past three. Fired a salute of twenty one guns. The contrast is very striking between this place and Angua Paquana {Angra Pequina}. There the eye beheld nothing but barren rocky wastes, dismal looking sand hills on one side & a broad expanse of water on the other, rendered still more dreary by the circumstances which attend it. While here everything is luxuriant. On the right as we enter, the harbor is a high elevated table land on which stands the principle part of the city. Numerous telegraph stations are built at a little distance apart to signal vessels as they enter. About midway or opposite to where we lay, is a splendid park in which a band plays every night.

Friday Nov 20

Commenced coaling this forenoon & took on 196 tons.

21 - Coaling all day. Thermometor 80° shade.

22 - Coaled all day.

Sunday Nov 29

Finished coaling on Thursday last. Marines had three days on the ship. Sat[urday] Painted all over the outside, and today are receiving visitors in our uniform. Several mail strs. have came & went during the week. Afternoon had service on the half deck by a Rev of the Episcopal order. Ten–11 Matthew 28 & 29 vs.

Wednesday Dec 2d 1863

Hoisted our flags at daylight when the Brazilians hoysted theirs. & saluted them with twenty one guns & had their ships dressed. At 12 M. we fired a salute of 21 with the Brazilian at the maine, where we flew it all day.

Thursday Dec 3d

Got up anchor at half past one and went to sea. Ran East qr north. Weather warm & pleasant. Sea a little roughf.

Friday Dec 4

Rained very hard last night & wind blew strong from the Nor. East. I caught a severe cold and feel quite unwell.

Saturday Dec 5th '63

Continuing the same as yesterday with strong head winds. Weather warm & pleasant.

Sunday Dec 6th '63

Lay still all night till four this morning. Started up then & ran into Pernambuca & came to anchor at 9 A.M. An American Barque 70 ds from Baltimore came in soon after. She brings news of the destruction of the Vanderbilt off Cape Good Hope by the Georgia and only 30 out of 500 saved.[39]

Monday Dec 7th '63

Fired a salute of 13 guns this forenoon for the Admiral of the Brazilian Frigate which came in last night. This afternoon another American Barque 47 ds from Baltimore arrived.

Tuesday Dec 8th '63

Got [up] anchor at 10 1/2 this morning & went to sea running North by East qr East. The sun is very hot but there is a good cool breeze blowing nearly ahead. The thermometor stands 84° in the shade.

Wednesday Dec 9th

Fired at target. At qrs. this morning we fired 4 shots or shells & did the best of any. At 6 said to be 36 Miles from Fernando Narhonag {de Noronha} and was running a[t] one Not so as not to get there before morning.

Thursday Dec 10

Arrived at Fernando[40] at 9 this morning. Sent a boat off with Mr. Beldin. Sent T Gallant Yds & made sail as we left at 11 A.M. stearing more N. East. Thermometor 82° shade.

Friday Dec 11th[41]

Went to quarters at 3 this morning for a barque. At a little after 8 sighted a side wheel steamer. Ran after her till could make her out then changed to our old course.

Saturday Dec 12th

Changed to due North this morning. Crossed the line at half past 8 last night. Weather very warm with showers. At 12 was 2°—North.

Sunday Dec 13

Rained nearly all of the afternoon. It was pleasing to see how eager all wer[e] for a little fresh water. Ch'd our course to North West by North.

Monday Dec 14

Cloudy nearly all day with showers. We have the North West trade winds which we struck when we left Fernando. Making 10 or 11 Nots.

Tuesday Dec 15th 1863[42]

Hot & cloudy with showers. At 12 M. was in Lat 8° 30" 43" North running Nor W. North. Long. 42" 32".

Wednesday Dec 16th

Cooler today. The wind has shifted to south East runing West NorWest. At 12 M. Lat 9" 37" 58 Long. 46° 59. Wind is not strong enoughf to fill the sails well and they sway back and forth against the Masts. There is a tremendious swell on the sea & the ship rolls heavy.

Thursday Dec 17th

Cloudy with frequent showers. Running West NorWest at 12 M Lat 10° 21" 11", Long. 50. Sea very roughf with strong winds.

Friday Dec 18th

Pleasant with fine breezes. Continue the same course as yesterday. Lat. 11" 45". Long. 54" 50".

Saturday Dec 19

Arrived at Barbadoes at 10 1/2 A.M. Did not come to anchor but sent a boat off for news. To {two} Eng. Frigates wer[e] at anchor here, the Imortalite and Iriadley. Left about 2 P.M. running North West qr. North.

Sunday Dec 20

Arrived at St. Pierre, Martinique, this morning at a little after daylight. Lay too and sent a boat off. Left at half past nine.

Monday Dec 21

Ran into St. Thomas this [morn—scratched out] today at 4 P.M. & came to anchor near the town so as to be handy to coal. Two Mail Strs., Eng., wer[e] repairing here, the Thames, & Conway of London. Expected to get some Mail here but as the rendesvou of the West Indies fleet has been ch'd to Nicholo[s] Mole, Hayti, it was reported to have been sent there.

Tuesday Dec 22d

Commenced coaling this morning with Gov. coal. There is 200,000 tons of it here belonging to the West India fleet. We wer[e] serenaded by a party on shoar last evening.

Wednesday Dec 23

A mail Str. from Halifax came in yesterday & lay a while & went on agen. Are taking on coal still. Weather very warm & pleasant. Thermometer stands in shade 85°.

Christmas Dec 25

The day passed off very pleasantly. We got a dinner of chicken, rost beef, eggs, pies & etc. which cost us the sum of two dollars. Had rec'd three dollars the day before & consequently had enough by using it equmonical {economical}.

Friday Jan 1st 1864

Everything being in readiness this morning at 7 o'clock. Got up anchor and left St. Thomas agen and ran West qr North. Nothing very interesting or exciting did transpire while we wer[e] lying in St. Thomas. We rec'd papers from N.York as late as the tenth of Dec. Not a day has past but two or three Strs. have come & gone. Among them was the noted "Trent". We finished painting ship on the inside on Tuesday last. And on Wed. sent our boats ashore to bring off visitors. & agen we wer[e] made a public exibition off for the gratification of the spectators & off[icials]. Passed San Juan, Porto Rico, about 4 P.M.

Saturday Jan 2d 1864

Saw land this forenoon. Supposed to be Cape Vieux. After, steared North West.

Sunday Jan 3d 1864

Ch'd to North West qr West then afterwards to North E qr East.

Tuesday Jan 5th

Ran North East between the isle of Caicos, then N.W. to Abaco, then south E. till came to Nassau, instaling what Orpheus C. Kerr would call a stra[te]gic moove.

Wednesday Jan 6th

Lay still off Nassau all night. At daylight or half past five, saw a steamer laying too, wating for daylight to run the Keys into Nassau. She, however, made us out before we did her, & was off nearly one hour & a half ahead of us. We made chase but had no pilot for the shoal water and so did not catch her. She was loaded with cotton, & to lighten her, they threw about 120 bales over board. We fired 15 shots from the forward pivot. Chased her till she was about running into the harbor & then turned back & picked up 50 bales of cotton.[43]

Friday Jan 8th

Saw a steamer this morning while cruising around & chased her. She turned & ran from us for the purpose of having a chase but we could not gain on her. When we fired a gun & she hove too, she was four days from NY, The Eng. St. Corsican, to Nassau. Afterwards we started NorEast and all thought we would go home. But we changed about & finally made up our minds we could not go home yet. On Sunday at three bells in the morning, saw a str. running North East. We made chase, but one of the flews gave out & had to slacken. & did not get fairly under way till after dinner. We then made from 17 to 20 Nots till 12 Midnight. At dark, we wer[e] in sight of her from the deck & kept so till she ran into a dark cloud. About 12 o'clock Capt. Baldwin told Mr. Germain, Chief Engineer, if he caught this one he would go directly home. So we went twenty today while only thirteen after the other when, with this amount of speed, we could have overhauled the other.[44]

Monday Jan 11th

Kept a bright lookout of the Str. this morning but could see no sign of her. Saw Elbow Key a little after daylight.

Wednesday Jan 13th

Signed accts today for $126.03. One hundred & twenty-six dollars & three cents. Weather warm. Thermometor stood at 72°. Thursday, ditto at 74. Runing North West. Friday at 12 M., 63.

Sat. Jan 16th, 36°

Ran into NYork and came to anchor off the battery at 12 M. Passed the Ariel about 20 miles out.

Sunday Jan 24 1864

The first cruise of the Vanderbilt is now completed without accomplishing the object which was intended for her too. Namely, to rid the seas of the privateers, Alabama, Georgia, & Florida, all or any which we might fall in with. But the fault does not rest on the ship's officers or men. For we traveled the seas for over 60 Thousand miles in every direction where they wer[e] heared of or ever supposed to have gone, but still did not get even a sight of them. The nearest we have been to them was at Cape Town where we arrived on Sunday morning, the last of August, 12 hours after

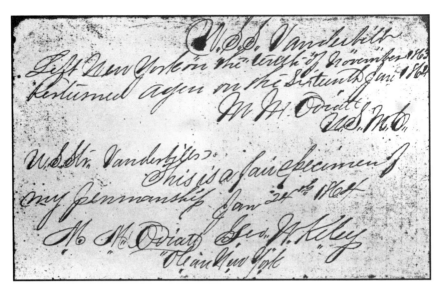

Specimen of Oviatt's handwriting stating length of voyage

the Georgia had left. Had we known that she was there, we might have caught her in the harbor by going directly from St. Helena when we first left, instead of going back to coal, as we did. Thereby loosing 5 ds of time. But if we had kept on and found her there at anchor, we should have been out of coal and could not be prepared to wait for her outside. & while we wer[e] after coal, she would have bid goodbye to this place. And when we came back, she would have been the same as she was when we arrived— gone.

[THE FOLLOWING ARE LISTS AND NOTES WRITTEN ON THE LAST PAGES OF THIS DIARY—SOME ARE SO ILLEGIBLE THAT THEY MAY NOT MAKE SENSE]

Missellaneous — Napoleans' estate at St. Helena is called "Longwood." The Steamer Heymala lay in Simons Bay. He who brought us hither will preserve us. St Helena is 15° 55 South. The Eng. Mail Str, Trent, is side wheeler barque rig with two funnels and has fitted boats on her paddleboxes.

[Chronology of Voyage]

Left Point a Petrie June 20
Arrived at Barbadoes June 21
Left Barbadoes June 21
Crossed the line July 2 at 12 1/2 M.
Arrived at Fernando July 4
Arrived at Pernambuco July 5
Left Pernambuco July 6

Sketch of the English mail steamer Trent

Arrived at Trinidade July 10
Arrived at Rio de Janeiro July 14
Left Rio de Janeiro Aug 2
Arrived at St. Helena Aug 18
Left St. Helena Aug 20
Arrived at Simons Bay Sep 3
Left Simons Bay Sept 13
Arrived at Mauritius Sep 24
Left Mauritius Oct 10
Arrived at Algoa Bay Oct 20
Arrived at Table Bay Oct 22
Left Table Bay Oct 27
Arrived at Angua Paquena {Angra Pequina} Oct 30
Left Angua Paquenna Nov 4
Arrived at St. Helena Nov 10
Left St. Helena Nov 10
Arrived at Bahia Nov 19
Left Bahia Dec 3d
Arrived at Pernambuco Dec 6
Left Pernambuco Dec 8
At Fernando Dec 10
Barbadoes Dec 19
Crossed the line 8 1/2 P.M. Dec 11
Left Barbadoes Dec 19

Arrived at St. Pierre, Martinique Dec 20
Left   "   "   "   "
Arrived at St. Thomas Dec 21
Left on Jan 1st 1864
Captured 50 Bales of Cotton Jan 6
Arrived at New York Jan 16

[Personal Items on Voyage]

White shirts	2	Wa[t]ch Coat	1
Blue shirts	2	Uniform Cap	1
White Pants	2	Uniform Coat	1
Stockings	2 Pares	Feteigh {fatique} Cap	2
Blue Pants	1	Feteigh Coat	1
Boots	2 Pares	Hospatal Chapeau	1

Second Year

Blue Pants	4	Blue Shirts	4
White Pants	5	White Shirts	2
Fetueigh Coats	2	Socks	5 Pares
Fetueigh Caps	4	Bouces{?}	2
Uniform Coat	1	Broughans	4
Uniform Hat	1		

M.M. Oviatt, Olean N York — written on the 4 day of July, 1863,

4° South of 0

Small Stores for the qr End July 1st '63

June 1# Tobacco	.63
" 1# Soap	.25
" 6 Sks Silks 3ea.	.18
" 1 botle Pepper	.16
May 1st l Pr. Shoes	1.81
Tax on Grog Mony	.50
Hospital Fund	.60
	4.13

Small Stores for the Month of June 1863

1 Bar of soap	.25
1 Scrubrush	.19
1 bottle peper	.16
Hospatal	.20

Small Stores July

1 # Soap	.25
1 Spool Cotton	.06
1 Bottle Pepper	.16
1 Fork	.06
2 Ds Mony	5.00

Signed July 1 for $57.69 with out the Extra $2 which Tolfree....

Aug 1 1 Bar Soap	.25		
" Bar Soap	.25		
Sept 27 Rec'd $4.84 G. M. [Grog Money]		$4.84	32.40
Sept Bar soap 2pc	.50	.50	57.69
2 Box Blking 12cts	.25	2\5.34	90.09
Due Oct 1st '63 $95.89		2.67	

39.69	97.38
57.69	-1.49
97.38	95.89

Anthony Kenney on board U.S. Ship Vanderbilt

John M. Oviatt, Olean, NY

M.M. Oviatt, Olean, NYork

Stars Though Henree{?} Thought, Murphy

H.B. Pope, Serg.

Kiss him for her, Mother

T.G. Hopkins

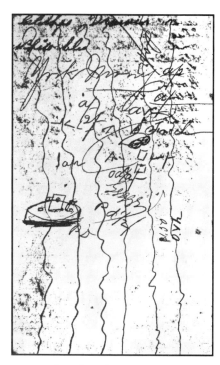

Sketch of a monitor

MESSELANEOUS
AS WRITTEN BY MILES M. OVIATT

Captured the Eng. Blockader, PETERHOFF, on Feb 25th, 1863. She was a brig rig propellor.

Captured the Engl. blockader, GER-TRUDE, on Aprl 16th, 1863. She was a schooner rig.

Captured the Barque, SAXON, loaded with wooll in Angua Paquena [Angra Pequina] Bay, Africa, on 30 day Oct. 1863.

94

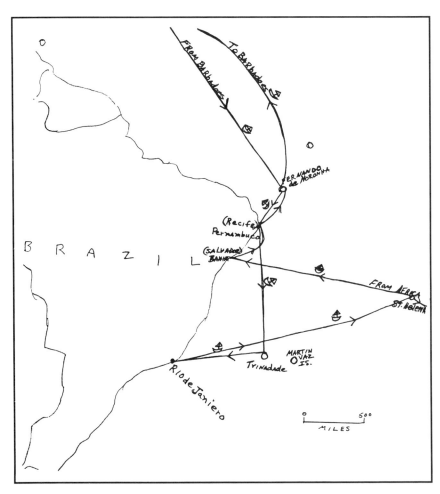

Route of the Vanderbilt on its way to Africa

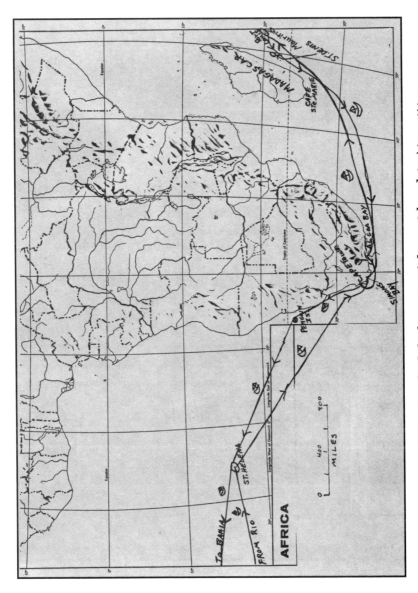

Route of the Vanderbilt from St. Helena Island to Mauritius

Return route via South America to New York

William H. Parker
National Archives: 127-N-517102

George Porter Houston
Courtesy of Massachusetts Commandery
Military Order of the Loyal Legion and the U.S.
Army Military History Institute, Carlisle, Pa.

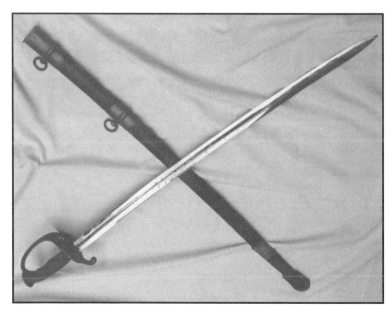

Miles Oviatt's dress sword
Courtesy of Mary P. Livingston

Union and Confederate currency, 1862 and 1863

Diary Book Three

THE VOYAGES OF THE U.S.S. BROOKLYN

EDITOR'S NOTE—A second diary covering the same span of time has been integrated within the following writings. A [2] will indicate that insertion. Only new information will be included.

M.M. Oviatt, U.S.M.C. Brooklyn, N.Y.

This is to certify that I, Miles M. Oviatt, a U.S. Marine, do solemnly swear that I will serve 4 years in the afore said Corpes from the 19th day of August, 1862, unless some{?}——{?}——[2]...took oath in Brooklyn as Pvt. Truth crushed to earth shall rise agen. Olean.

[MARGIN NOTES IN FRONT OF DIARY]—Private Accounts, please keep your hands off. Miles & Little—Bets ——{?}—— Mis Inadaus{?}, Youthful Miss—Susie—Susi Q
1864-5-22-14 1/2
1864-5-10-10
     12- 4 1/2
Mr G. Jones and Co, Nasau N.Y.
Watchword (Frand de boise)
     "   David Dcy
Mauve De Donq.

[2] Guillaume De Lawrence, Fifer, Rue de St.Honor, Paris   We too are citizens of America "Smith & Oviatt" M.M. Oviatt, U.S.M. Sartly{?}, Enlisted August 19, 1862 consequently have 19 mos to serve on this the 18 of Jan, 65.

Miss Hattie Visconsita

Armstrong County

M.M. Oviatt Bought July 8th 1864 At Rio D' Janiero, Brazil,
Price—75 cts. [Could be referring to this diary?]

M.M. Oviatt's Book Feb 26 Canteen Cr[edit]

Mony 1st		5.00
2 Pies @	10c	.20
Mony 2		2.00
Beer		.06
Cheese	2	.20
2 Cigars	5	.10
1 Pie	10	.10
		$7.66
		1.75
Total Due		$9.31

John Steward—Yours with due regard for your high position & etc. Miles M. Oviatt of the USM Corpse, Written on this the 2d Day of July 1864 on board the U.S. Brooklyn off Mobile

The Niagra River recedes 3 ft a year or has receded 130 ft in the last 51 years.

Small Stores	Soap	Mustard	Peper
May	1	1	1
June	1	1	

Carte de visite
Copy of the original carte de visite of the U.S.S. *Brooklyn* sent home by Miles Oviatt to his family.

U.S.S. Brooklyn
Department of the Navy, U.S. Naval Academy Library

Captain James Alden, U.S.N.
U.S. Naval Historical Center

New York Herald says General Mead on a recent visit to Phil. said the army of the Potomac had lost one hundred thousand men since the commencement of hostilities. And wants to know if Mr. Lincoln can't form a joke out of that.[1] Feb 15th, 1864

Puzzle -   Stand   take   to   takings
            I   that u   throw   my

[2] What shall we do when the war breaks the country up and scatters these niggars all around. T.W. Adams, Olean, N.Y. Sergt. Hudson. Casick Skinflint Backbiter. John Wright the Mill Wright cant write his name right. Hallelujah Stialyards. Write me down rightly what right has a wheel. Wright to the rites of the church. Stilyards. Debuk Debuque. San Juan. Spanish Realyo. Pointarenas, Del. S....Accapulco, La Pass, Rio DeJenerio.

[2] Buffalo Sept, Jan Feb...Miss Jane A., Nunda, Livingston Co, NY...Sergt. Owen of the U.S.M.C. Capt H. Miles Mortimer Oviatt, U.S.M.C., Brooklyn, N.Y.

[2] Maurice P. Flynn of the U.S. Marine Corpse now on board the U.S.S. Brooklyn Whome we shall ever have cause to remember on account of association formed in No. 24 Room in the Brooklyn Marine Barracks. M.M. Oviatt. The U.S. Sloop of War Brooklyn carries 20-9" Guns, 2-100# Rifles & 2-60# Rifles, Maned by the Marines Oct 7th 1864

Chem. Chemung, Steuben Courier, Susquehannah

1864 U.[S.]Str. Brooklyn Aprl 14 [repeated several times]
Marine Barracks Brooklyn, Apl 14 [repeated once]
McLane Tilton Captain Com[an]d[in]g
1234567890 Sett Oviatt
Know all men by these presents that I, Miles M. Oviatt of the town....

[2] Written by Miles M. Oviatt on board of the U.S. Sloop of War, Brooklyn, commencing at April 14th, 1864

E.C. Gregg	G.N. Angus
F.R. Harris	W.M. Smith
G.H. Bandfield	Geo. Leland

[2] No. of Posts, Where & Orders
    No. 1 SCUTTLE HOLD
        Order No 1—Allow no person to carry water away except the Yeoman, Dr's. Steward, Fire Men and Cooks for cooking Scouse, Duff, Dryed Apples & Swanky.
        No. 2—Allow no smoking except at proper hours.
        No. 3—No spitting around the post.—Cap Orders—
        No. 4—No quariling around the post nor gambling.
    No. 2 BRIG
        Order No 1—Take charge of Prisoners.
        No. 2—Allow no person to hold any conversation with them.
        No. 3—Allow no person to go into the sick bay except Officers unless passed by Serg. or Corp. or Guard.

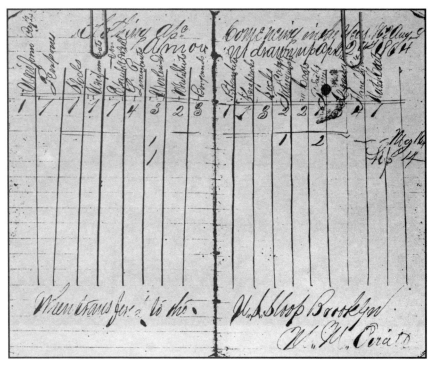

Oviatt's clothing account on the U.S.S. Brooklyn

Post No. 3 COCKPIT
Order No 1—No loafing on this post by any one.

[2] 1864 The Public Debt May 21	Principal	Annual Interest
Debt bearing interest in coin	$817,089,112.55	= 49,973,505.24
Debt bearing interest in Lawful Mony	405,565,023.31	= 21,744,486.24
Debt bearing no interest	508,216,790.97	
Total Principal	$1,730,870,926.83	= 71,717,991.48
Amount in Treasury	15,620,278.93	
Total Debt	$1,715,250,647.90	

1864 U.[S.] Str. Brooklyn Aprl 14, Thursday

N.Y. Harbor Warm and pleasant. At ten this morning was ordered for the U.S. Str. Brooklyn and at one went aboard. At two P.M. the colors and penant wer[e] hoysted as she was declared to be in commision. It is neadless to say that the guard gave a present. The Brooklyn is a twenty-four gun ship—twenty of them, 9 In; two, one hundred pd. Parrot Rifles; and two, sixty pd. Parrot Rifles. Her crew amounts to four-Hundred all told, Three hundred and fifty Sailors and Sandsmen, and forty Marines. She is a ship rig propellor capable of making 15 Nots with sail and steam. It is said, Quarters are not the best, 14 in. only is allowed to sleep in.

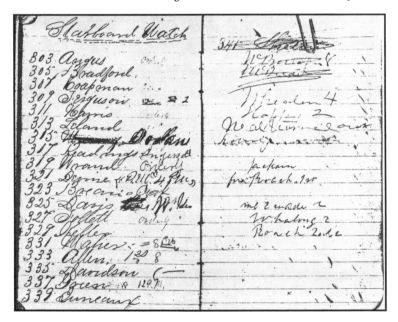

Port watch list and general roll on the Brooklyn

Starboard watch list on the Brooklyn

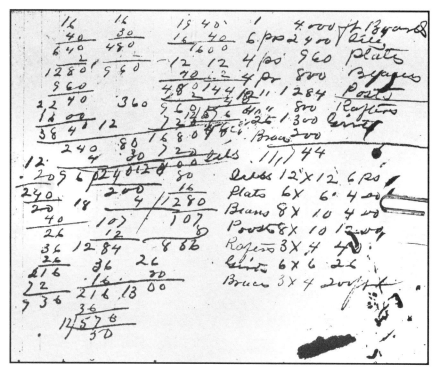

List of timbers that made up the Brooklyn

[2] May 1864 Clothing—Drew 1 Fatiegue Cap
       "   2 Flannel Sacks
       "   1 Blue Pants
Sep 1864 -   " 1 Blue Pants

[2] McBench 24 Hours
   McQuaid 24 Hours
   Neal   24 Hours
To be done at night hours from 6–10, from 12–4

Tuesday May 10th 1864

Got up anchor at 10 A.M. and went to sea. The Marines got their stations at the Guns. We are to man the four guns aft, two of them 9 in. and two 60# Parrot rifles. I was stationed as 2d Capt. of the rifles. We are only making 4 or 5 Nots. The machinery heating very bad so as to keep water running on the journals all the while.

Thursday May 12th

Not much sea sickness yet on board. Excercised a little at making sail. Saw a Steamer about ten runing north. Sent up royals yds and am making about 9 nots with sail set.

Saturday May 14th '64

Weather cleared up this forenoon. We have had considerable sea sickness in the guard for the past few days on account of the storm. At 10 chg'd our course from South-East to East. At 12 M. was in Lat 35°-34. Machinery still heating and still keep the pumps at work on the journal of the shaft. The riging is not in good order and we cannot carry all sails. Heard that the Boatswain was going to call a survey on the riging in the first port.

Sunday 15th '64

At 12 M. three Miles south of Hatrass {Hatteras} making 2 1/2 Nots by steam. Not wind enough to make the sails draw. At 4 P.M. passed a brigantine.

Monday May 16th '64

Weather getting warmer without any breeze. At 12 M. in Lat 32°- 58 South. Saw three vessels on our Starboard beem, apparently close togather. Probably wer[e] on the blockaders. Steaming without any sail and made as high as 4 1/2 nots.

Tuesday May 17th

Rained in the forenoon but cleared up afterwards. Excercised sail in the afternoon P.M. Protem.

Commander Edward P. Lull,
U.S.N.
U.S. Naval Historical Center

Thursday May 19th

Fair winds and pleasant today. Nothing of importance transpired till evening or after sundown when all hands wer[e] called to bury dead. The Capt's Cook was the disceased. He died at 4 P.M. this morning with consumption. Mr. Lull read a few appropriate passages from the Bible and then we consigned his remains to the rolling deep to be given up when the "sea shall give up her dead." The hour seemed a fit one just after the sun had sunk to rest and all nature wore a melancholly aspect. And all present seemed thoughtful as they stood with uncovered heads, not knowing when the same cerimonies might be performed for them. They wraped him up in a sheet of canvas with a hundred pd. shot attached to his feet and threw him over feet first. M.M. Oviatt.

Saturday May 21

For the past few days out the weather has been very hot with scarcely any breeze. We are steeming lazily along at the rate of 3 1/2 Nots. Although for the past few hours, have increased it to 8. At 12 yesterday, passed the hole in the wall on Abaco. 2 this morning, Nassau light [sighted.]. 10, saw 4 sails in sight and several keys on the port beem. Spoke the bark, Pilot Fish of Brunswick, loaded with Molasses.

Sunday May 22d

Pased Sand Key light at 10 A.M. with Key West on our Str. Bow. Ran into Key West at 2 P.M. Mercury...in the shade. All hands wer[e] mustered at ten in the forenoon and at eleven, Mr. Lull. Executive Officer, read service on the Qr. deck. All hands joining in the exercises.

Saturday May 28th

Coaled and watered at Key West and left at 10 this forenoon. Ran West at 4 P.M. Saw the light house of Dry Tortogus[2] on the Str. side in the distance.

Sunday May 29

Saw several sails today. Had inspection at the usual hour and services after by Mr. Lull. Ex. Officer. The yellow feaver was very bad at Key West. Mr. P.S. Towle, Ex Marine & Asst. Paym. of U.S. Navy, was aboard several times. We did not even get an hour on shore but had the pleasure of plenty salt water bathes.

Monday May 30th

It has been a warm beautiful day with a good breeze from the N.E. Making 9 Nots for the after, part of the day before, averaged 7 & 8 Nots. Had quite an excitement last night at 2 o'clock, on account of a schooner ahead which they took to be a Str. and chased her for two or three hours. She was from Philadelphia bound to New Orleans loaded with coal. Saw two or three vessels today but spoke none of them. At to {two} ch'd from West by N. to North by West.

Tuesday May 31st

About noon ran into Pensacola, but did not come to anchor but proceeded on to join the West Gulf Squadron. When we arrived about 5 P.M. fired a salute of 18 guns for the Admiral[3] and came to anchor in sight of Forts Morgan & Gaines. Forts Mc Craig [McRae] stands on the left on a little island. Pickens on the right on Santa Rosa Island and Bar[r]ancas on the mainland opposite Pickens. The Navy Yard is still in——{?}—— "Pensacola."

Wednesday June 1st

Got up anchor this morning by order from a signal on the Hartford as did all the vessels, 15 in No. Sent down yards and made ready for an action. Ran around by order from signals till One P.M. Then came to anchor in the old place. Saw quite a No. of Rebel vesels running between the forts all day. Wrote a letter home.

Thursday June 2d

Nothing unusual occured today. Saw the same rebel Strs. running between the forts and up the bay. One of the Richmond's boats went out sounding[4] and they fired on her from the forts & drove her back but did not hit her. Sent a mail by the Tenesee & Sent down T. Gallant Masts afternoon and Stays. As yet we have not enough of one thing as to cause the monotony that we had on the Vanderbilt.

Saturday June 5 '64

At ten last evening, a vessel ran into the harbor without any resistance. Sent the extra spurs and Masts out this morning to Pensacola. Heared that the vessel we chased coming to Pensacola, was taken the next day by a side Wheel gunboat worth 40 thousand dollars. Sent Sam the rebel. Saw Battie lying over at Fort Morgan today. Admiral Farragut was aboard this afternoon & dined with the Capt.... Miles M. Oviatt.

Wednesday June 8th '64

Warm and pleasant. Fired at a target this morning. We also fired three shots at the lighthouse at Fort Gaines. Two of them struck on the beach. These wer[e] from the 60# Rifle just to try the range. The Mettacomett caught a blockader runner Sunday night trying to run in. She was loaded with Arms & Ammunition.

Sunday June 12

Nothing very important has transpired for the past few days. Last night between 12 & 2, a vessel ran out between us and the Laccawanna and we not over 200 yds apart.

[2] Tuesday June 14th '64

Cool & cloudy with a good fresh breeze from the N.E. One of our gun boats D.B. Ender [double-ender] went out with the Admiral to recanoiter the channel. A ram came out to meat

Rear Admiral David G. Farragut, U.S.N.
U.S. Naval Historical Center

her when she came back again. There is two or three rebel vessels anchored in sight.

[2] Wednesday June 15

All quiet with the fleet. Our boats went on pickit at night for the 2d. time as there is but one boat sent at once. Our turn does not come very often. The rebel rams are still anchored in sight.

Wednesday June 22

Warm and pleasant. Red a letter from Geo. & Frank, date[d] 24 May. M——{?}——Conc ce vous, cit vos freare. [The preceding is fairly illegible in fancy script.] M.M. Oviatt

Monday June 27th '64

The weather is very hot, but through the middle of the day, a fresh breeze is always blowing. The Richmond returned from Pensacola,[5] brings word that the Yellow Feaver is raging there very bad. A schooner loaded with all sorts of things for sale to the fleet has arived from Philla. One of the gun boats went up and anchored near the island opposite Fort Morgan. Two or three rams in sight commenced making a very black smoke as if getting up steam.

June 30, 1864

The Admiral and all the fleet Captains went up to Sand Island to recanoder on the....

Friday July 1st 1864

About 4 this morning a blockade runner tryed to run in when one of our gunboats gave chase to her and fired at and ran her aground under the guns of Fort Morgan and near the beach. Six or seven other boats immediately got up anchor to try and destroy her. They lay off at a long range and fired without much apparent effect except cutting away her main mast. They continued the firing at short intervals for the most of the day on the vessel, and the sand bateries along the beach. The most of the firing being directed to the latter till they silenced some of them. At dark they came back only for a flint{?} for there was others sent back immediately where they kept watch till morning.

[2] July 1st 1864 Signed acct for $32.36

```
          $32.36
          28.40
          $60.76
```

Acct 13 pr month in full, 20 cts pr Month out

4 Mos of $12.80	$57.20 [multiplied wrong]
Out for Clothing etc	29.65
Balance Due	$27.55
Total Due	$59.91

From 1st of May, extra pay of $5.00 pr Month,

4 Mos	$20.00	
$7.00 pr Month		
2 Mos	14.00	
	$34.00	
Total	$93.91	
9 Yds Flannel @ .85		$7.65
2 Undershirts		4.00
1 Pr Shoes		2.50
1 Plug Tobaco		1.00
1 Socks Pr.		1.00
4 Brs Soap 50c.		2.00
4 Peper		1.50
Cr.		19.65
Grog Money 4 Mos 1.50 $6.00		10.00
		$29.65

Saturday, the firing was kept up at long intervals as the bateries replied till they wer[e] silenced entirely. Then they would send a few shots at the vessel. There wer[e] two men wounded on the Mettacomett. One had the fuse of a shell go through the abdomen and is feared will prove mortal. It was supposed the rebel rams would come out and assist in getting her off but they kept shy.

Names of the Vessels off Mobile Bay on the Blockade

Hartford, Flagship	Port Royal
Richmond	Genesee
Brooklyn	Itasca
Lackawanna	Pembina
Monongahale	Pinola
Oneida	Kenebeck
Osapee	Mattabesett
Seminole	Tenesee
Galena	Boneville
Mettacomett	Octorora

Monday July 4th '64

At one P.M. the Galena, Oneida, Seminole, Manongahale, & Genesee got under way and went out and engaged the sand batteries. They kept up a sharp fire for 2 hours. Then drew off out of range. The Manongahale fired occasionally, however, at the fort with her 200# at a long range, making some excilent shots. At 5 P.M. all came back to their stations. At 12 M. the whole fleet fired a salute of 21 guns each with the stars and stripes floating gaily from all of the peaks. At Fort Morgan they fired a salute also of 21 guns, with the Confederate flag flying.

[2]...Genesee and a little tow boat...Fort Morgan fired ocasionally and the Manongahale responded with her 200# Rifle Parrot...Her guns are no doubt longer ranged than those on the fort...did not learn the result of the firings....

Tuesday July 5th

At 5 this morning saw rapid heavy firing in the direction of Morgan which lasted 2 hours. The fleet did not engage the batteries today. But we expected to go up and give the Anglo Saxon a few broadsides as the Capt. volunteered to, but was prevented by the Admiral.

[2]...but we expected to go up and see the depth of the water and give the Anglo Saxon a few broadsides....

Wednesday July 6th

This morning at 2 o'clock, our boats set fire to the Anglo-Saxon[6] which burned the inside of her out, but the hul[l] being iron, still stands to mark the spot. The rebs had taken all of her cargo, rigging, etc, out before; consequently they did not loose anything of consequence, as the vessel was a reck.

Sat July 9th '64

An expedition from the Hartford went up last night to blow up the remains of the blockader, but just as they wer[e] going to board her, the rebs on the——{?}——opened on them with a battery they had just built with grape and canister and forced them to retire again. They nearly destroyed the boat & wounded several men, one of them having since died. Heared today that the Monitor, Manhatten, was at Pensacola. The Bermuda had 11 in. shell on board for her.

[2]...The boats left without accomplishing their object. I since learned that three others wer[e] wounded badly and the boat nearly destroyed. There is a monitor at Pensacola wating the arrival of others before she comes here....

Sunday July 10th

Morning dawned upon us with another blockader on the beech close under the guns of Fort Morgan. The Manongahale, Lacawanna & Seminole went over & fired at her awhile. But without any apparent effect as the range was so long, although several shell burst over her. At 4 P.M. a tug came out and tried to get her off but our boats went and made her skedadle back. After a few shots, we could see a large number on the beech, apparently discharging her.

Monday July 11th '64

The rebs came out and took off the blockader last night. Admiral Farragut transfered his penant to the Tenesee as the Hartford is going to Pensacola for coal & etc. She went during the night.

[2]...get the blockader off but wer[e] driven back twice. They succeeded in getting her about twice her length ahead...his blue penant....

[2] Tuesday July 12

The rebs got the last blockader off last night and ran her in.

Friday July 15

Papers from NY arrived today bringing news of the sinking of the Alabama[7] by the U.S.S. Kersage. Called all hands to muster and read the same, then gave three cheers for the "Kersage." [Kearsarge]

Wednesday July 20

Got up anchor and ran over to Pensacola & commenced coaling. Passed the Monitor, Manhatten, on her way to join the fleet. Manned the rigging & gave three cheers.

Wednesday July 27

Finished taking on coal and provisions. Got out our sheet cable & put on the str. side to protect the boilers. Put iron plate around the top for sharp shooters and men at the Howitzers and made a devil[8] to rake up torpedoes.

[2]...protect the boilers for 50 or 60 ft. Took on provisions and some sand...

Thursday July 28th

Ran back to our station off Mobile and came to anchor about 10 A.M. The Manhatten lays at anchor inside of Sand Island in smoothe watter.

Tuesday Aug 2d

Preparations are still going on to prepare the fleet for the coming engagement. Nearly all have been to Pensacola & got supplies and coal. There [are] three iron clad Monitors inside of Sand Island, 2 of them are Doub[le] Terreted from N.O. [New Orleans] Are daily expecting the Tecumseh from N.York. P.S. She arrived on the 4th, 4 P.M.

[2]...5 iron clads inside of Sand Island,[9] 4 of them are from N.O.

[2] [List of ships engaged in the Mobile Bay Battle]—Hartford, Brooklyn, Richmond, Lacawana, Ossipee, Monongahale, Seminole, Oneida, Galena, Mettacomett, Port Royal, Genesee, Itasca, Pembina, Pinola, Kennebec, Mattabesett.

[2] [Watch list] -

Angus-Post	Baker-Sick
Bradford-Post	Harris 1st-Sick
Ferguson-Post	Harris 2nd-Sick
Bray-Post	Davis-Sick
Hill-Post	Ryan-Sick
	Sullivan

Gilligan 4
McBench 4
King 8
Wheaton 2 without
6x10-10x2
Dorrington

Starboard and port watch lists on the Brooklyn

Starboard and port watch lists on the Brooklyn

Rifle gun crew lists on the Brooklyn

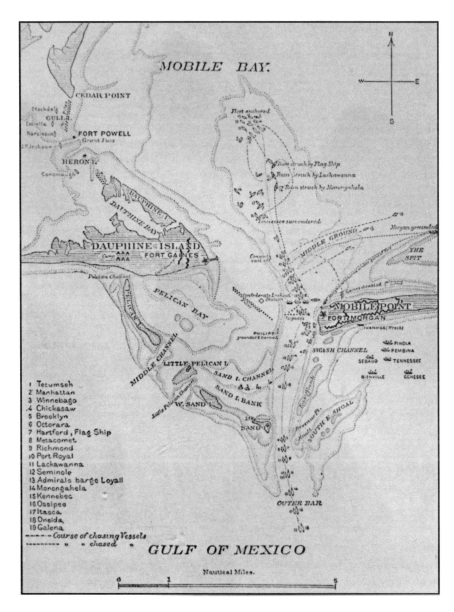

Battle positions of Union and Confederate forces,
August 5, 1864, Mobile Bay

Battles and Leaders

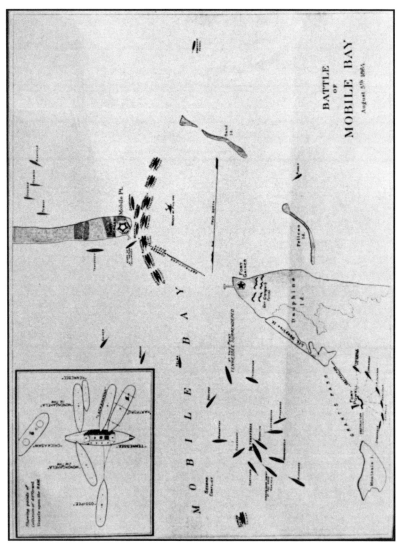

Battle of Mobile Bay

1864 Friday Aug 5th

At three this morning all hands wer[e] called and got breakfast. Took the Octarara along Portside and lashed her fast. At 5, got up anchor and formed in line of battle, we taking the lead of the wooden fleet. The Monitors which wer[e] at anchor inside of Sand Island started about the same time and engaged Fort Morgan, but they did not reply till we had got within range. The first shot from the fort, at 6:50 A.M., was directed to us but fell a little short, striking the water on the starboard bow and richochead over the bow. We immediately replied with our 100# Rifles on the bow, which at first fell short, they being the only guns that could be brought to bear at the time. The firing soon became very rapid and was responded to with equal vigor. When abreast the fort, the Monitor, Chickesaw, stoped and we wer[e] compelled to stop and back about the length of the ship. While doing so, the Hartford, next ship to us, ran past.[10] The Richmond came next and tried to follow the example of the Hartford and get past to a place of safety, but did not suceed.

[2]...Monitors...started about this time and wer[e] ahead of us below the fort, but stopped so as to stop us abreast of the fort. & trying to avoid them, [we] ran into shallow watter and had to back off[11]...While backing, the Hartford came up on the port side and went past. The Richmond tryed to follow, calculating to pass the fort in safety, while we drew the fire & succeeded in getting past, way past, & got through without loosing a man.

About 7:30, the Monitor, Tecumseh,[12] struck a torpedo and went down allmost instantly while going after the rebel, Tenesee. At 9 A.M. had passed the forts and came to anchor inside the bay out of range of the forts. Her Ram came out as we passed and tried to run into our Str. qr., but by superior speed, we avoided her, and she swung round and ran for the Lacawanna, but she avoided being run into. The Ram went across her bow, then came too and gave her a broadside. We had just came to anchor when the Ram came on again, stearing for us. As she approached, the small vessels between us and her got up anchor & left. But still she kept on intending to run us down. But when within a qr. of a mile, we got under way, came around & gave her a broadside. But they might as well been left in the guns for the effect they did. The Manongahale came around head onto the ram & ran against her with all force but without any apparent dammage to the Ram, but smashed her fore-fort in & gave her a few shots with her 200# Rifle. The Laccawanna & Hartford struck her next but with no better effect. We was underway to strike her, when the Hartford ran in ahead of us, and not having the Ram's broadside to her, she struck her near the bow & slid off. Finally, the Monitors came around & set to work but a good ways off. & gave her the contonsc of their heavy guns which, togather with the wooden vessels, began soon to tell on her. And it was seen that her firing was less frequent than at first. Our 100# Rifle on the forecassel carried away her smoke stack, & the 60# Rifle cut the rudder chain which left them in rather a helpless condition. And the Monitors got round & sent some telling shots into her stearn.

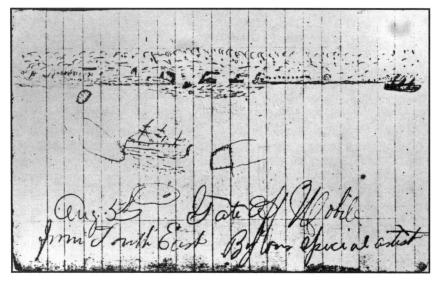

Sketch of the Battle of Mobile Bay, probably by George Bandfield

Comical sketches by George Bandfield

[2]...but with no effect but each gave her a broadside for a parting salute...It was soon seen that she was getting the worst of the battle...rudder chain and she was fearless as a ram & began to steam off towards Fort Gaines. Her flag was shot away & she did not fire for some time. It was supposed she had given up but such was not the case, for directly she came in range of us & gave shot or too but soon we saw the white flag displayed in place of the red battle flag...[13]

When the Reb[el] rag came down, a white one was sent up in its place. Our loss was 14 killed & 30 to 40 wounded.[14] The Brooklyn was struck 59 times, 39 in her hull, 4 in the M. Mast, rest in her rigging.[15] Came to anchor the 2d time at 10:10. The stations wer[e] as follows: The Monitors, Tecumseh, Chicasaw, Winebago, wer[e] to go first. Brooklyn & Octarora, Hartford & Mettacommett, Richmond & Port Royal, Laccawanna & Seminole, Manongahale, Ossipee, Oneida. The Mettacommetts tooke the Reb Str. Selma. Her Armament was 6 Rifles.

In the afternoon, the Monitors went up to Fort Powell. At 11 o'clock, the rebs left the fort & blew it up.[16] In the afternoon, sent down a flag of truce asking leave to send our wounded to Pensacola which they granted provided the vessel would return as we wer[e] all considered as prisoners.[17]

Fort Gaines Monument, Mobile Bay, Alabama
Courtesy of Mary P. Livingston

Fort Gaines, Mobile Bay, Alabama
Courtesy of Mary P. Livingston

Silent guns, Fort Gaines, Mobile Bay
Courtesy of Mary P. Livingston

Looking from Fort Gaines across the bay toward Fort Morgan
Courtesy of Mary P. Livingston

[2]...& fired for 2 or three hours. The Gunboat ran aground trying to run past Fort Morgan & was burned because they failed to get her off...Selma with 8 Rifle guns 7 in. The Tenesee had 6 Rifles 4-6 in., 2-7 in.

Aug 6th 1864

Sent men to take possession of Fort Powell and sent a flag of truce to demand the surrender of Gaines, but they refused to surrender & in the afternoon, sent the Monitors down to bombard the fort. Their firing was very brisk on our side, but was not answered by the rebs very briskly.

[2] Our Gunboats sent men and took possession. We maned the riging and gave three cheers. Afternoon, sent and demanded the surrender of Gaines but our propositions not being accepted, sent the Monitors down in the afternoon to shell them out....

Sunday Aug 7th 1864

The Admiral sent down a flag of truce to demand the surrender of Gaines today, but was refused again. At 3 P.M. they sent off a flag of truce requesting Farragutt to accept the surrender instead of giving it to the Army as he requested. But he refused & gave them till next morning at 8 A.M.

Monday Aug 8th 1864

At 8 this morning, the fort hoisted the American flag. We took possession at 12 M. & fired a salute of 21 Guns and the Hartford's Marines in Fort

Powell. We took 850 Prisoners, 50 or 60 guns & ammunition, & 6 Mos. provisions for the Garrison.

[2] Gave them till next morning at 8 A.M. to decide. When the fort was given up to the Army and Navy and the Good Old Stars and Stripes wer[e] hoisted to the breeze over another strong hold of "Cesesh"...

[2] Saturday, Aug 13
Our boats have raked several torpedoes out of the channel between Fort Morgan & Gaines of very large size, some containing from 50 to 60# of powder. We have also been landing troops over in rear of Fort Morgan so that the present force must be at 15 or 16 thousand men.

Monday Aug 22d

Gen. Granger having his 10 thousand troops in rear of Fort Morgan and guns in position ready for a bombardment. Accordingly at 5 A.M., we got up anchor and ran down & commenced the bombardment, till 11 when we wer[e] ordered to hold off. The Monitors kept up the fire till dark, then left it to the land batteries to continue the fire through the night. Which they did with a spirit which was anything but agreeable to the rebs, "judging by myself." At 8 o'clock the fort took fire which gave our men a better chance to see where to fire, which was still burning in the morning.

Tuesday Aug 23

At daylight a flag of truce was seen flying from the fort. Two Monitors and a gunboat wer[e] sent down to see what was wanted. They found out that Page was willing to come to terms. He was informed that nothing but Unconditional Surrender would do, so he accepted. At 2 P.M. we took a formal possession. They had destroyed the Carriges, spiked the guns, broke up & burned their small arms & swords & Provisions and wet all of the powder. Even Old Page, himself, had no sword to give up. All the vessells fired a salute of 21 guns. We took from five to six hundred prisoners. Page has since been court martialed for destroying everything & acquited honerably.[18]

[2]...to see what was the cause. Since our troops landed in rear of Morgan, they have been building batteries and diging trenches & rifle pits untill they have arrived within a hundred Yds of the fort. We sent two of our 9 in. Guns over to the land. The batteries have fired at the fort as they got into position for the last 3 or 4 days. At dark last night, there was but one gun visible on the fort mounted. The fire of the Monitors was very destructive, throwing the sand into the air 30 or forty ft. The Comander of Morgan surrendered the fort Unconditional at 2 P.M...no sword to give up, consequently we gain nothing but the fort...

Wednesday Aug 24

The Monitors, Chickasaw & Sebago, went up within a few miles of Mobile and engaged the batteries. They report Mobile on fire.

Thursday Aug 25

Went down to the fort to take one or two guns on that had been ashore previous to the bombardment. Two boats crews from the Galena went to bouy the Monitor Tecumseh, then commenced to drag the channel for torpedoes. They hooked onto 5 which wer[e] attached to each other & in getting them out on the beech, one exploded killing 3 men & wounded 18 more, which they brought aboard us to take to Pensacola.[19] Gen. Granger commenced taking the troops off again today, & carried through Grants Pass.

[2]...went to dragging the channel for torpedoes. They grappled onto 5 but wer[e] two heavy for them to draw, & cut two adrift. When they got them ashore & wer[e] rolling them up onto the beech, when one exploded killing 3 men & wounding...12 of them have since died. Commenced transporting the troops back to a point of land west of Fort Powell. The Monitors wer[e] taking in ammunition.

Friday Aug 26th '64

Got under weigh & left for Pensacola. At 11 A.M. called all hands to bury the 4 men that died last night from injuries rec'd by the explosion of the torpedo. Arrived at Pensacola at 4 P.M. & made preparations for some slight repairs before leaving for home.

Rifle gun crew aboard the Brooklyn

Gideon Welles,
Secretary of the Navy
U.S. Naval Historical Center

[2]...Came to anchor off the Navy Yard...

[2] Sept 4, 1864
Miles M. Oviatt was read off as Sergt. of Marines on board the U.S.S. Brooklyn, Sunday morning, in Pensacola harbor while laying at anchor.[20]

[2]Robert Cushley, Washington, D.C.
   Drummer boy on board the U.S.S. Brooklyn

   William Applebea
   Fifer boy on board the U.S.S. Brooklyn

   William Topley
   Orderly Sergt. on board the U.S.S. Brooklyn

   Geo. W. Davis
   Pvt. Marine on board the U.S. Sloop Brooklyn

To Hon Gideon Wells, Secty
Sergt. M. M. Oviatt
John B. M. Oviatt
Winfield Lougrence, Winterport, ME, Seaman
President James Buchanan, Lancaster, PA

Friday Sept 9th 1864

We left Pensacola for home this morning with head winds & heavy swells.[21]

[2] [CHRONOLOGY OF BATTLE OF MOBILE BAY AS MILES OVIATT TELLS IT] Passed the forts & captured the Tenesee and Selma Aug 5th 1864 from 6:50 to 10:10

Rebs evacuated Fort Powell 6th Aug.

Surrendered Fort Gaines 8th Aug.

Bombarded Fort Morgan 22 Aug. from 6 to 11 A.M.

Rebs hoisted a white flag at daylight morning 23 Aug.

Left Mobile Bay and went to Pensacola Aug 25 to coal and repair before going home.

Left Pensacola for home Sep 9th, 4 1/2 P.M.

[2] Sept 14, 4 P.M. before going to quarters. Yes, we are going at a rate of 4 Nots which is considered good time for the Brooklyn.

[2]...light head winds & heavy swells.

[2] Sept 15th, 1864 At 12 M. Lat 31° 45 North

[2] Sept 17th 1864 At 12 M. Lat 36° 1 North

[2] Sept 18th 1864 At 12 M. Lat 38° 37 North

Sept 20th 1864

Arrived at Boston this morning after a stormy and pleasant passage of 11 days.

Sept 23d 1864

Transfered to Barracks for 15 ds or till the ship should be repaired.

[2]...Charlestown Barracks...Navy Yard, Mass...from the U.S.S. Brooklyn till she was fitted up for sea again. Got liberty at night and on the 24, Mounted Guard at the Navy Yard Gate. Sunday, the 25, came off. Monday morning the 26th, Mounted Guard at the Barracks.

October 1st 1864

Was transfered from the Cha'stown Marine Barracks to the U.S.S. Brook-lyn to make a 6 weeks cruise to Wilmington with Capt. Houston, in Com'd of Guard Sergt Hudson, Ordly Sergt.

[2]	Signed acct Oct 1st 1864 For $60.78, for #13 pr Month.	
	From May 1st to Sept 1st, 4 Mos 5 Extra	20.00
	Sept 1 Mo 7 Extra	7.00
	Not Signed for yet, due Oct 1st	27.00
[2]	Rec'd from paymstr, Oct. mony	10.00
	" Pd for Sailors Home	2.00
	1 Br Soap	
	2 Pr. Socks	
	Oct 1st Signed Miles M. Oviatt, Dr. $60.78	

October 6th '64

Left Boston to join Admiral Porter's squadron[22] at Hampton Roads, where we arrived on the 10 inst. We lay at Hampton Roads waiting for troops to opperate against Wilmington with us untill Dec 13th 1864, then left for that place with 12 thousand troops under Gen. Butler. We arrived off that place on the 13 inst. and came to anchor about 40 miles from land to wait for the fleet to get togather.[23]

[2]...and encountered heavy weather most of the way...

[2] Oct 18th, 1864

For the past few days have been firing at target every day for practice. Capt. Aldin was up to City Point[24] and returned today. Have been putting on Sheet cable on Ship's side to protect her boilers. Expect soon to be off for Wilmington, North Carolina. Rec'd a letter from home and answered it immediately.

[2] [THE FOLLOWING IS NOT ADDRESSED, BUT SEEMS TO BE AN UNMAILED LETTER WRITTEN BY MILES OVIATT TO A CLOSE RELATION]

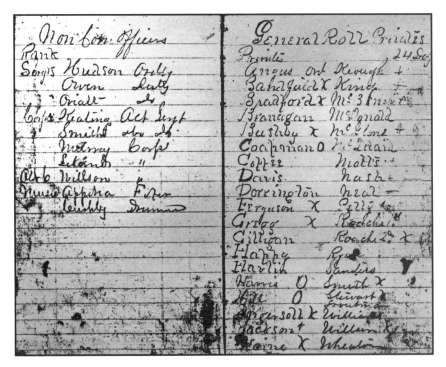

Oviatt's notes and duty roster aboard the Brooklyn

Noncommissioned officers and general roll
aboard the Brooklyn

I do not know that I can employ my time better for an hour than writing to you. We are lying in Hampton Roads, coaling ship at present, which is quite agreeable. Ever since we left Boston the water and sand has been knee deep on deck and everything painted over to get the dirt & coal dust off and now commence again. Oh, I tell you, life in a man of war is very agreeable, pleasant, enchanting. We are the flag ship now. Ad. Porter came aboard yesterday & we hoisted his blue penant & fired a salute to let the people around here know how much we honor Uncle Sam's favorite. I expect in course of a week or so, we shall be on our way to Wilmington. But wheather Porter goes with us or not, I don't know. I hope he does though, for they say he has a great regard for personal safety and if so I guess The Old B. won't get cut up as bad as at Mobile. I hardly know what to think or do nowdays. Sometimes the hopes of getting a discharge and the prospect of coming home (cross me up) (And all the enjoyments). But when I look on the other hand and see a long 22 Mos. yet to serve and still worse, prospect of Wilmington, for I don't like that job at all. & casts a shade over all of my air castles. But I cannot grumble for it is all my own fault.

[2] 1864 U.S. Str. Brooklyn, Hampton Roads vs. Roads vs. Fortress Munroe, Oct 19th. Twenty Six Mos. ago today joined the U.S. Marine Corpse by enlisting under false pretenses. Capt. Haywood, recruiting officer. Expect to go to Wilmington, or get a dischg. every day.

[2] [THE FOLLOWING LETTER WAS ALSO UNSENT AND IS PART OF THE SECOND ACCOUNT OF THIS DIARY] Dated U.S.S. Brooklyn, Hampton Roads, Oct 29th, 1864....Dr. Father, Last night at Qrtrs, Capt. Houston read a copy of an order by the President to the Secy. of the Navy revoking the order to discharge the 62 men and give the bounty of 100 Dollars to all that enlisted from the 8th of May, 62, to July, 63. As I come under that act, it will be of no use to make farther aplications for my discharge. I have had a faint hope of getting out till now. But can patiently wait now that I know there is no possibility of getting out. For I knew that an aplication from some citizen would not be over looked by the Sec'y and I suppose that reason the order was sent here was to stop them so that he could quietly lay back in his chair and sleep on, as Jas. G. Bennett expreses it. G. Bandfield tells me that he is going to get the town bounty of 400 dollars in addition to the 300 county and 75 from the state, if possible, which will count up to $775. Besides 100 Gov. at the experation of term of service.

[2] This is a fair specimen of my handwriting, Oct 31st, 1864, M.M. Oviatt, Bennington, Buffalo, NY.

[2] Left Hampton Roads, Dec. 13th 186[4]. Arrived off Wilmington, Dec. 15 and came to anchor out sight of land in 15 fathoms water.

Dec 17th 1864

Got under weigt and ran in towards land till we sighted it from the Masthead. Then came to anchor again to wait for the troops to come down from

Beaufort, N.C. And a powder boat to go up and explore which was calculated would explode the magazines in the fort or dismount the guns. [2] Ran in 12 Miles nearer. [Dec] 20 went in nearer.

On the 23d, the powder boat went in behind a blockade runner and anchored near the fort & blew it up, but without any apparent effect except broke some light of glass in the Cap's skylight.[25]

On the morning of the 24, got up anchor, formed in line of battle and started for Fort Fisher.

> The Stations of the Vessels wer[e] as follows:
> New Ironsides 1st.
> Three Monitors
> Mohican
> Colerado
> Wabash
> Minnesota
> Powhatan
> Brooklyn
> Susquehanna

[2] Vessels engaged in the bombardment of Fort Fisher
December 24th, 25th, 1864

Frigates—	Wabash	1 Class Sloops—	Brooklyn
	Minesota		Susquhanna
	Colorado		Powhatan
	New Ironsides		

Miles M. Oviatt, Olean, NY

Togather with 50 or 60 vessels of less draft & gunboats. Before we came in range of the fort, the Capt. called all hands up on the quarter deck and Mr. Swan, the Ex. Officer, read a short prayer then gave 3 cheers for the U.S. of America & three for Capt. Aldin. Commenced firing on the fort at 12:45. In 2 hours, had the fort silenced but the batteries kept up an easy fire till we hauled off. Owing to the other vessels not taking their position in as far as was expected, we ran past them & went up opposite the mound battery & came to anchor. But the tide running out swung us off so that we could not bring our guns to bear. We then weighed our anchor and kept in

Rear Admiral David D. Porter, U.S.N.
U.S. Naval Historical Center

motion till 5:15. & then hauled off & came to anchor out of range. The most of the firing was good except some of the small vessels which fell short to some extent. We have about 180 guns bearing on the fort at once. The fleet did not receive much injury from reb. shell — only two or three vessels wer[e] struck. We rec'd one shot only — nobody hurt.

[2] U.S. Brooklyn Dec 24th 1864—At 8 this morning got up anchor and formed in line of battle. The Iron Clads, three Monitors and the new Iron Clads took the lead. Next came the Mohican, Colorado, Wabash, Minnesota, Susquehanna, Brooklyn, Powhatan, Juneauetta {Juniata}, Shamrock, & Vanderbilt. Before opening [fire], called all hands togather & Lieut. Swan read a short prayer & called for the blessings of Providence & asked His protection which rec'd a hearty Amen, if not aloud, every [one] thought it. Then gave 3 Cheers for the United States of America & 3 for Capt. Aldin. At 12:45 opened fire on Fort Fisher. Soon after, silenced the fort but the water batteries kept up a continual fire throughout the afternoon. We came to anchor abreast the mound battery but owing to the current, had to get it up again & keep in motion. The fire from the whole fleet was good & very terrific as we had about 180 guns bearing on the enemies' works at once. The reb's firing was very poor on account of the smoke so that they either fell short or went over. Only a few vessels wer[e] hit at all. The Colorado received 8 shots, the Junetta, two, & Wabash, 1. At 5:15 we hauled off & the firing ceased. The fort was on fire several times but was put out.[26]

Sunday Dec 25

Formed in line this morning at 7 o'clock. Started for the fort but the Admiral signalized us to leave the line & help shell the woods before the troops landed. Commenced shelling the woods & batteries at 11 A.M. And at 3 P.M. the 1st boats reached the shore which was the color guard. When they landed, we maned the rigging & gave three cheers which might have reached the ears of the rebs in the fort if they had not been deafened by the 15 in. shell bursting around them. Our pickets found some rebel troops in the woods & quite a sharp skirmish took place. They took some prisoners & the rest left. Fort Fisher was shelled today by all of the Ironclads, frigates and most of the gunboats. The bombardment was terrific & was returned with considerable spirit part of the time. The Colorado was struck 8 times & some of the other vessels wer[e] hit several times. There was 6 100# Parrott Rifles bursted killing or wounding their crews. We fired the first day nearly 8100 shell & over 400 the second. After taking a view of the shore from his ship, the Ben D Ford, Gen. Butler ordered the troops to reembark & requested us to shell the woods to protect them from a large rebel force which he said was coming down under Gen. Bragg. We immediately set to work & shell as far as our guns would reach in the supposed direction of the rebs, till they either left or hid themselves.

[2]...break the line & cover the landing of troops on the mainland in rear of the fort...at 3 had them silenced & commenced landing the troops....Our troops captured about 100 Prisoners in one of the batteries from whome it was supposed Gen. Butler got some information in regard to the rebs. For soon after, he commenced to reembark the troops. His pickets wer[e] driven in two or three times & we covered them & shelled the woods. The Advance Guard went up in rear of the fort where they captured 4 or 5 hundred more prisoners. It is said they remained in camp all night. The firing from our fleet this day on the fort was terific & grand. The huge monitor shells tearing the earth in all directions. The batteries & Fort wer[e] silenced for several hours. Gen. Butler intended to reembark the remaining force today, but was prevented from doing so.[27]

Monday Dec 26

We expected to cover the reem'ing of the troops today, but the heavy serf prevent them from coming off, so the Admiral sent us to recanoiter around the fort. When we got up close, the rebs opened on us & we gave them a couple of broadsides & left. Next day, covered the reembarking of the troops & prisoners of whome they had about 600. Then hauled off into the stream.

[2]...found the rebs still there. They opened on us with spirit which we returned by the broadside force, short time & then left. Their shots all fell short as they could not get the range of us on account of the heavy forays.

Tuesday 27 1864

[2] Covered the reembarking of the troops & then hauled off from land. The Ironclads went round to Caswell[28] & made a demonstration there.

[2] [Synopsis of above battle] Com'c'd the bombardment of Fort Fisher Dec 24, 1864. Commenced firing at 11:50, ceased at 5 P.M. Sunday, shelled the woods & batteries from 11 till 4 & helped land troops. Fired again in the eve. Monday, 26, reconoitered fort & fired a few rounds alone at the fort. Troops reembarked again on Tues. Those that did not get off on Monday & left. Most of the fleet left today. We covered the Embarking of the troops. Capt[ured] 600 Pris[oners].

Wednesday Dec 28

Took the cable off of the side and at 11 o'clock at night got up anchor and started for Beaufort, N.C. Where we arrived next day to take in coal, ammunition, provisions etc, with the rest of the fleet. Butler & troops went to Hampton Roads.

[2] [THE SECOND ACCOUNT OF THIS VOYAGE INCLUDES THE FOLLOWING LETTER TO AN UNKNOWN PERSON, THAT WAS NEVER SENT—IT CONTAINS HISTORICAL INFORMATION NOT CONTAINED IN THE DAILY WRITINGS] U.S.S. Beaufort, N.C. Jan '65. I rec'd your

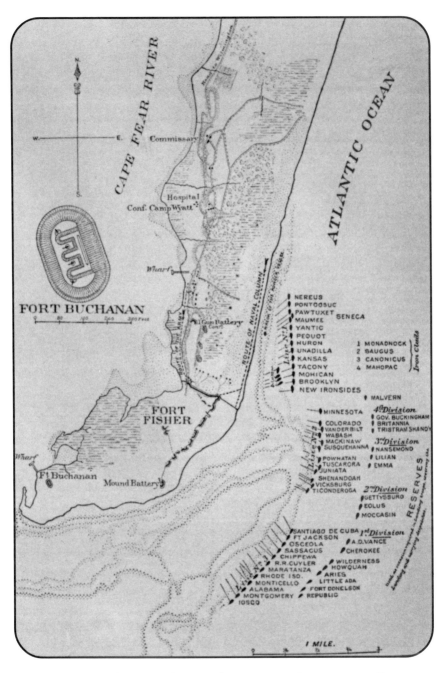

*Attack of Fort Fisher and position of Union vessels,
January 15, 1865*

letter of Sept 6 yesterdy. Was very much pleased to hear from you & was very much surprised because I thought perhaps you had forgotten that I was on the U.S. Brooklyn. Your letter went first to Mobile then to Boston & back to Wilmington, then up here. Since we took the forts at Mobile, I have been to Boston. Was sent to Barracks while the ship was being rep[aire]d, then came down to Hampton Roads, joined Porter's fleet, went down to Wilmington, fought 2 days & began the third & gave it up. Came back here & are coaling up to go there again....[unfinished].

Thursday Jan 12 1865

Got under weigh in the P.M. and started for Wilmington where we arrived about dark the A.M. of the 13, about 6. The Admiral signalized us to go & shell the woods & protect the troops. We commenced about 7 A.M. & shelled the beech for two or three miles. And about 9, the troops commenced to land the second time. They wer[e] all landed by 3 P.M. And at 4, got up anchor & led the way up to fort fisher & commenced firing till dark, when wer[e] ordered off by the Admiral.

Saturday Jan 14th 1865

Afternoon the Ad[miral] sent us up to support the fire of the Ironclads & gunboats on the fort. Got into position about 3 P.M. Continued firing till after dark, & then fired at intervals through the night without changing our position.

At daylight, Sunday 15 inst., prepared for action again but the Admiral signalized us to haul off for ammunition & sent the rest of the fleet in to commence the bombardment. We took on 800 shells by 12 M.[29] Took our station & fired at intervals after 3 P.M. untill we only had 30 left. In the P.M. the Marines & sailors went ashore to storm the fort in front while the Volunteers attacked it in rear.[30] They made the charge about 3, but wer[e] driven back in great confusion with heavy loss & refused to rally. The infantry charged in rear at the same time & fought desperately hand to hand with the rebs for 6 or 7 hours, when the rebs surrendered. All the guns from the fort wer[e] used against them that could be brought to bear on them, as well as those from the Mound battery.

Monday Jan 16th

Our men took the rebel prisoners out of the fort down on the beech about 3 miles to embark them in the transports that brought them down. About 7 o'clock the magazine in the main fort exploded killing 4 or 5 hundred of our men. It is supposed besides, a large number of rebs. It is not known how it happened, but is thought to carlessness of some of the men.[31]

In the P.M. of the 17th, went ashore to look at the fort. It covers an area of 40 acres with the line of defence on two sides forming a letter "L". The land side is much the weekest point. There is only 14 guns facing towards the

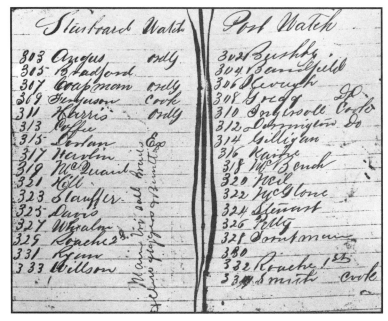

General roll aboard the Brooklyn

Starboard and port watch lists of the Brooklyn

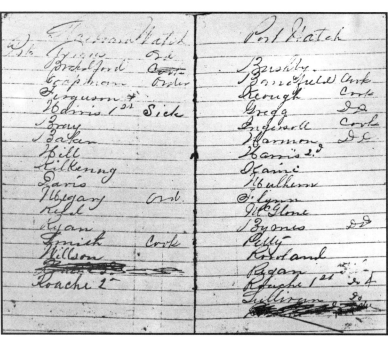

Starboard and port watch lists of the Brooklyn

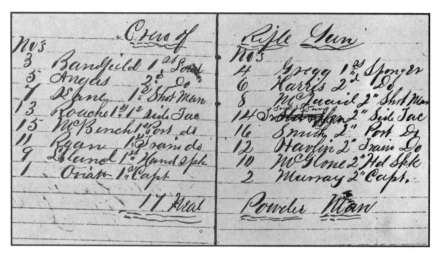

Rifle gun crew aboard the Brooklyn

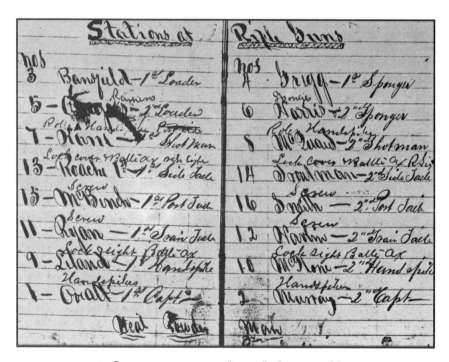

Rifle gun stations aboard the Brooklyn

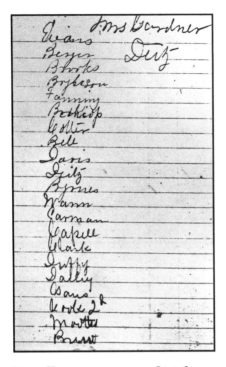

Miscellaneous names list from
Diary 3

land while twice that No. of better & heavier calliber face the channel. I noticed a 150# Rifle of the Armstrong make which was presented to reb Col. Lamb[32] by Queen Victoria. It[s] weight is 16000# pounds. The celebrated mound battery which commands the channel for 7 miles which they said was Ironcladed, was not, but mounts two heavy guns. One is an old fashioned Eleven inch. The other, 100# Rifle.

In rear of all the works & commanding the channel inside is Fort Buchanan which mounts 4 heavy rifles which was not injured. But when our troops got possession of Fisher, they spiked the guns and left. Our men wer[e] at work drilling them out and wer[e] going to turn them on Fort Caswell to see if the rebs had left. As they blew up some the night before which they supposed to be that fort. We saw a fire in that direction which was said to be 3 blockaders on fire. A blockader ran in past the fleet last night & came to anchor inside with our gunboats, supposing that they had got with vessels of her class. When our men very quietly went aboard & took possession of her.[33] The quarters for the troops in the fort wer[e] in the bom[b] proofs under the mounds.

Tuesday night at 10 o'clock, got up anchor & started for Hampton Roads to wait for orders.[34] Where we arrived on the 19th at 12 M. The Capt. went immediately to Washington.

[2] Rec'd Jan 24 pay't of 25 dollars on acc[ount].

[2] [THE FOLLOWING NOTE WAS HANDWRITTEN IN PENCIL ON THE BACK PAGE OF THE SECOND ACCOUNT OF THIS DIARY] I can't find anything of your clothes. No one in your N6 knows anything about them. I shall try & get aboard tomorrow, if I get liberty. Mews{?}, Johnson, Murdock, Stockel are ordered to the Nereus immediately. I am left...[page torn off at this point]...Ed McKee.

[MARGIN NOTES AT END OF DIARY—The later dated and unrelated information probably indicates the flyleaf was used as a scratch pad some time in the future.]

[2]   ORDER BOOK   EXTRA DUTY
      McBench 24   P. McBench 12 h.
      McQuaid 24   Pvt. McQuaid 5 h - Knapsack
      Neal 24 hours each Davis & Coffe

With knapsack, with either cape or watchcoat rolled. Neal to [be] turned out every 2 hours to...unless he turns in at 4 o'clock. Relief in daytime to fall in on deck to be inspected before going on Post.

Non Commes Musick & Orderlies to be turned out when all hands are except those having the 1st & midwatch. 2 Pris[oners] in Iron, full Ration. Centris to be posted with loaded muskets. Orders to fire after haling twice.

Brean and Byrnes on deck after 8 Bells without being properly dressed.

Green 24 hours extra [duty] with knapsack—Davis 1st 4 hours, Dixon, Edwards, Johnson, Williams, Allen 2nd, Murray, Myers 2, Edwards 2, Reading 4, Ephram.

[THERE ARE SEVERAL MORE PAGES OF SIMILAR DATA CONCERNING THE SHIP PERSONNEL AND THEIR INFRACTIONS BUT TOO MUCH LIKE THE ABOVE TO BE INCLUDED HERE]

Potatoes are cut brl. scouce in the morning.

Col. B.B.B.B. to C.C.C.C. Washington
Yours Affe'tly,
Olean, N.Y. Dec 24th, 1893—N.J. Barber to M.M. Oviatt

Dr. 9 1/4 Dys hauling ice @ $4.00	$37.00	
Cr. By{?} Stroys{?} Bile	-33.45	
Bal Due	3.55	
Rec'd Pay't		

Feb 20 By Cash $2.00
Nov 1875

Packing 3 gallon crock	lbs.	or
	5	12
	5	4
	4	14
	4	6
	20 —	6

Miles M. Oviatt's Book, Mobile Bay, June 5th '64
U.S.M.C. on board U.S.S. Brooklyn From Rio De Jenerio Brazil
July 16th 1863 Hotel Des Quartre
This was he of whome I spoke—M.M. Oviatt

Do not ask a girl to be a wife
If you would have a happy life
Rather remain in single bliss
?..................... this.

Mrs. V. Le Hughs

Frankie Oviatt [Miles' daughter born Nov. 26, 1876]
Rio De Jenerio July 7th, 1863
N.Y. Snows til Day 19 Aprl 1874
[There are many columns of figures and grocery items listed, too numerous to mention.]

CHRONOLOGY OF THE VOYAGE OF THE U.S.S. *BROOKLYN*

1864

May 10—Left New York Harbor
May 22—Arrived Key West
May 28—Left Key West
May 31—Arrived & left Pensacola, Fla. continuing to Mobile Bay
Jul 20—Left Mobile Bay
Jul 20—Arrived Pensacola
Jul 28—Left Pensacola
Jul 28—Arrived Mobile Bay
Aug 25—Left Mobile Bay
Aug 25—Arrived Pensacola
Sep 9—Left Pensacola
Sep 20—Arrived Boston
Oct 6—Left Boston
Oct 10—Arrived Hampton Roads
Dec 13—Left Hampton Roads
Dec 15—Arrived Wilmington, N.C.
Dec 24—Left Wilmington
Dec 24—Arrived Fort Fisher
Dec 28—Left Fort Fisher
Dec 29—Arrived Beaufort, N.C.

1865

Jan 12—Left Beaufort
Jan 13—Arrived Wilmington
Jan 13—Left Wilmington
Jan 13—Arrived Fort Fisher
Jan 17—Left Fort Fisher
Jan 19—Arrived Hampton Roads

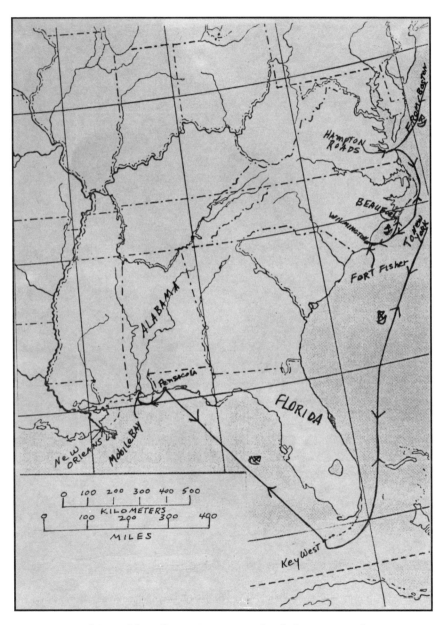

Route of Brooklyn from Boston to Mobile Bay and return

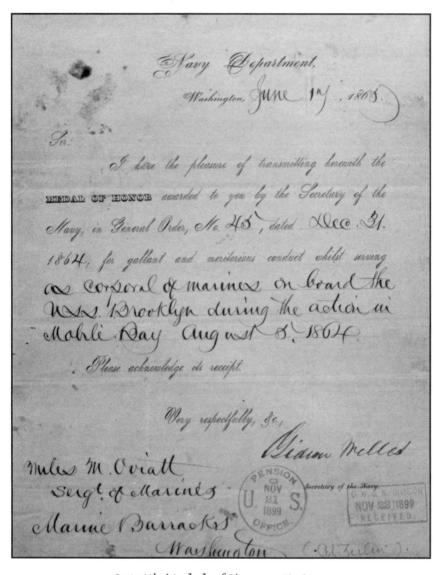

Oviatt's Medal of Honor citation

Courtesy of Mary P. Livingston

Oviatt's Medal of Honor

Courtesy of Mary P. Livingston

142

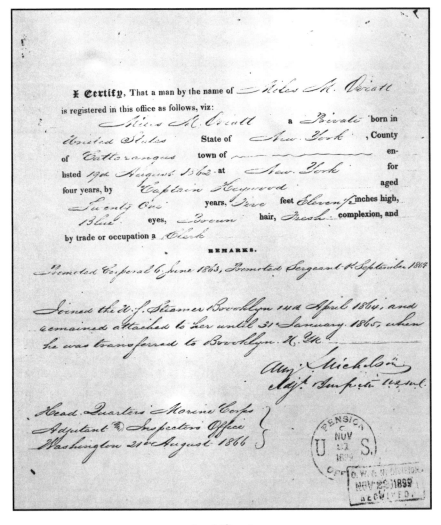

Certificate

143

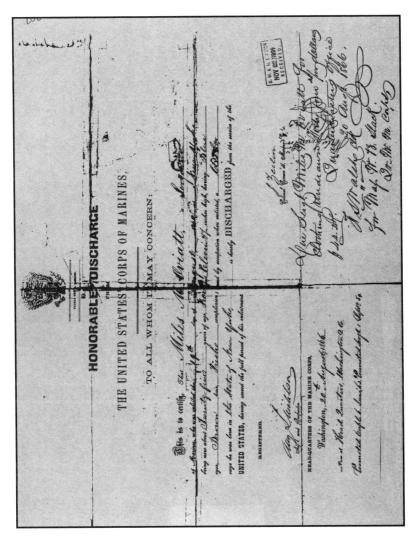

Discharge from the U.S. Marine Corps, August 20, 1866.
Notice dates of promotions.

Receipt for payment

Receipt for payment in full of all owed to Miles Oviatt during his enlistment in the Marine Corps, August 21, 1866.

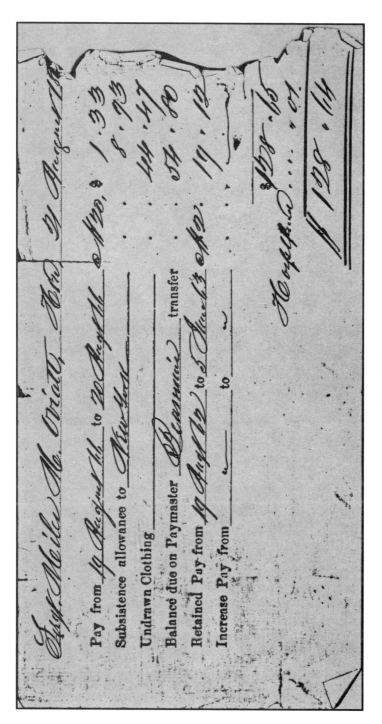

Pay from ___ to ___ @ Mo. $ 1 . 33

Subsistence allowance to ___ 8 . 93

Undrawn Clothing ___ 44 . 47

Balance due on Paymaster ___ transfer 54 . 80

Retained Pay from ___ to ___ 17 . 12

Increase Pay from ___ to ___

$ 128 . 14

August 20, 1866, pay record

CHIPMAN, HOSMER, & CO.,
Attorneys, Claim Agents,
AND
Solicitors of Patents,
No. 446 FOURTEENTH ST.

Washington, D. C., Jany 21 1867

Miles M. Oviatt Esq
Olean N. Y.

Dear Sir;
In answer to yours of the
15th inst. which is just at hand, we
will state that the "Petahoff" is
not yet adjudicated for the reason
that its condemnation has been
long contested, and a large sum of
money spent in litigation by the
Owners to save it. The "Tennessee"
has been adjudicated, with many
prizes Captured in Mobile Bay, and
if you will send us a full statement
of your claims we will prepare &
forward you all necessary papers.
Our Fees are $10 pr ct in these claims
Yours, truly
Chipman Hosmer & Co.
pr S.

Prize money for ships captured during the Civil War was difficult to get from the U.S. Government. Miles' requests ranged over a two-year period after his discharge, as evidenced by these three letters.

(No 11.) 11

Treasury Department,

Fourth Auditor's Office,

March 21ᵗʰ, 1867.

The application of *Milos M. Oviatt*

late of the U. S. S. *Brooklyn*, for prize money, is received, and Discharge herewith returned.

The claim will be disposed of as early as possible, and the result communicated to you.

I am, sir, respectfully,
Your obedient servant,

S. J. W. Tabor,
Auditor.

E. C. Brooks
Olean
Cattaraugus Co
N. Y.
&c.

148

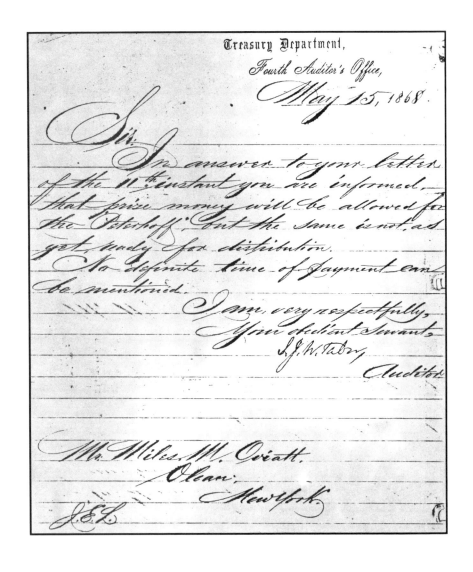

Treasury Department,

Fourth Auditor's Office,

May 15, 1868.

Sir,

In answer to your letter of the 11th instant you are informed, that prize money will be allowed for the Peterhoff, but the same is not, as yet, ready for distribution.

No definite time of payment can be mentioned.

I am, very respectfully,
Your obedient Servant,
S. J. W. Tabor,
Auditor.

Mr. Miles M. Oviatt.
Olean,
New York.

J.E.L.

Top: 629 Main St., Olean, N.Y. Boyhood home of Miles Oviatt.

Left: Receipt for coin silver spoons by Allison Oviatt, brother of Miles Oviatt, given to Miles' widow, Lucetta. The spoons are engraved "LJO," initials of their mother, Lydia Jane Rice Oviatt. They are currently proudly displayed in the home of the editor.

Right: Obituary of Miles M. Oviatt, published in a local Olean, N.Y. newspaper, probably during the week of November 1, 1880.

Lost to Earth.

On Monday last, Miles Oviatt departed this life, and crossed over the river to join those gone before. He was about 35 years of age, and leaves many who will mourn his death. Early in the opening of the campaign he began taking an active part in the work of organization, and when the cavalry company from Pleasant Valley was organized he was chosen captain. He was ever effective and vigilant on the side of right, and his command was among the best drilled in the battalion. When the boys went to Buffalo Mr. Oviatt was with them. He took a severe cold, from the effect of which he passed away, as stated above. The funeral was held at his home in Pleasant Valley, on Wednesday. It was largely attended by the members of the Garfield and Arthur Club, of the city, as well as by hosts of relatives and friends. The services were conducted by Rev. Sooy, of the Methodist church.

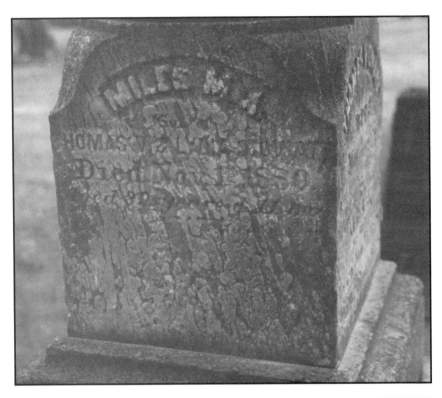

Bronze marker and old marble tombstone
Pleasant Valley Cemetery, Hinsdale, N.Y., north of Olean.

Courtesy of Mary P. Livingston

OLD WAR AND NAVY DIVISION.

3—070.

RG, *Ex'r.*

Ord. Or. No. 18,758.
Lucetta Oviatt (now Turner)
w'd of Miles M. Oviatt,
U. S. M. C.

Department of the Interior,

BUREAU OF PENSIONS,

Washington, D. C., *Sept 14* , *1899*

N. W. & N. DIVISION
OCT 4 1899
RECEIVED.

SIR:

For use in the above-entitled claim for pension, you are requested to furnish this Bureau with a descriptive list and a history of the service, including the names of stations and of vessels upon which he served, and the dates of transfer from each, of *Miles M. Oviatt* who, it is alleged, enlisted at *New York Barracks* *August 19* , *1862*, served on *U. S. S. "Vanderbilt"* *and "Brooklyn"*

and was discharged *August 20* , *1866* at *Washington Barracks.*

Please forward your report through the Bureau of Medicine and Surgery, Navy Department.

Very respectfully, BUR. M. & S.

51736

J. L. Davenport
Acting Commissioner.

The Adjutant and Inspector,
United States Marine Corps.

SEP 29 99

4962b1m11 97

Report

Lucetta A. Oviatt, widow of Miles Oviatt, now Mrs. Turner, began correspondence with government officials in 1916, trying to collect back prize money and pension on her late husband's naval war service. These four letters give the facts.

CHARLES M. HAMILTON
43D DISTRICT NEW YORK

REPUBLICAN WHIP

House of Representatives
Washington, D. C.

Washington, D. C.
January
Fourth
1 9 1 7.

Mrs. Lucetta A. Turner,

   321 Tompkins Street,

      Olean, New York.

Dear Madam:

   Replying to the letter of Mrs. Mary A. Wood, R. F. D. #1, Portville, New York, in which she enclosed certain letters and documents in your behalf with reference to prize money, etc., due Miles M. Oviatt, on account of his service in the Civil War, will say I have communicated with the Auditor of the War Department in regard to this matter and am enclosing herewith his reply together with the papers which were sent to me. It would seem, from the records of the War Department, that Mr. Oviatt received all the prize money to which he was entitled under the law.

      Very sincerely,

      C. M. Hamilton

*Dictated but not read.
Mr. Hamilton was compelled to leave before this letter could be transcribed.*

ACT SEPTEMBER 8, 1916

3—607

DEPARTMENT OF THE INTERIOR
BUREAU OF PENSIONS
WASHINGTON

MAR 1 5 1918

Hon. Charles M. Hamilton,

H. R.

My dear Mr. Hamilton,

I have the honor to inform you that the ___Original___ claim for pension of

___Lucetta A. O. Turner, former widow of Miles M. Uviatt___

late ___Sgt., U. S. Marine Corps___

whose address is ___143 S. Union St., Olean, N. Y.___

has been allowed under certificate No. 840,182 ___ at the rate

of $ 20. ___ per month from Apr. 11, 1917 and

$ 25. " " " Oct. 6, 1917

and that the certificate will be forwarded at an early date to the beneficiary.

As you personally called up this claim while pending, I deem it but courteous to inform you of this action.

Very respectfully,

Group 1

E. C. Tieman

Acting Commissioner.

B

CHARLES M. HAMILTON
43D DISTRICT NEW YORK

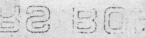

House of Representatives

Washington, D. C.

Washington, D. C.

March

Sixteenth

1 9 1 8.

Mrs. Mary A. Wood,

R. F. D. No.1,

Portville, New York.

My dear Mrs. Wood:

I am enclosing herewith communication from the Commissioner of Pensions stating that the pension claim of Lucetta A. O. Turner, former widow of Miles M. Oviatt, U. S. Marine Corps, certificate No. 840,182, has been allowed at the rate of Twenty Dollars per month from April 11, 1917, and Twenty-five Dollars per month from October 6, 1917. I trust the result is satisfactory to you and the claimant.

Very respectfully,

C. M. Hamilton

Afterword

BY MARY P. LIVINGSTON

Time seems to have a way of taking incidents and memorializing them, making legends out of insignificant occurrences bearing errors that future generations don't want disturbed, no matter how well the errors can be documented. One such legend is the story of Admiral David Farragut's famous line, "Damn the torpedoes, full speed ahead!" During the research for this transcription, I found many official documents, diaries, and letters written by reliable officers stating personal observations at the site of the Battle of Mobile Bay where Admiral Farragut uttered this battle cry. I thought it appropriate to include them here to underline this historic event.

The U.S.S. *Brooklyn*, commanded by Captain James Alden, was the contributing factor preceding this event. Miles Oviatt, a Marine assigned to the Brooklyn wrote, "...abreast of the fort, the Chickasaw stopped & the Brooklyn was compelled to stop and back about the length of the ship...{Hartford ran past}...we tried to avoid them...we ran into shallow water & had to back off..." The Hartford passed on the port side.

Captain Alden, in his ship's log recorded "...Backed the ship clear of two buoys, evidently attached to torpedoes, there being also but 16 or 17 feet of water...the Hartford sheered under our port beam." He also reported to Admiral Farragut, "We were now somewhat inside the fort, when shoal water was reported, and at the same time, as the smoke cleared up a little, a row of suspicious-looking buoys was discovered directly under our bow. While we were in the act of backing to clear them our gallant Admiral passed us and took the lead."

The steam log of Mortimer Kellogg, chief engineer of the *Brooklyn*, states, "The Brooklyn was headed up the channel, followed by the rest of the fleet. Moved the engine first slow, stopped and backed quite frequently in accordance with the bell signals from deck."

The log of the U.S.S. *Richmond*, commanded by Captain Thorton A. Jenkins, gives this interesting report. "...the Hartford was observed steering to the northward and westward and the Brooklyn backing athwart the bow of this ship and very near; order given to back hard by this ship and the Port Royal. As soon as the Brooklyn commenced going ahead with starboard helm, the order was given 'Hard a-port and four bells' and when about in the wake of the Hartford and a little to the starboard of the Brooklyn's wake..."

The U.S.S. *Hartford's* acting signal officer, 1st Lieutenant John Coddington Kinney, 13th Connecticut Infantry, was quite observant in his report: "Brooklyn came opposite the fort and approached the torpedo line, she came nearly alongside the monitor...at this critical moment the Brooklyn halted and began backing and signaling with the Army signals...the sudden stopping of the Brooklyn threatened to bring the whole fleet into collision, while the strong inflowing tide was likely to carry some of the vessels to the shore under the guns of the fort. Brooklyn signaled 'The monitors are right ahead; we cannot go on without passing them.' The Admiral sent the reply, 'Order the monitors ahead and go on.' But still the Brooklyn halted...The whole fleet became a stationary point-blank target for the guns of Fort Morgan and of the rebel vessels. It was during these few perilous moments that the most fatal work of the day was done to the fleet." Lieutenant Kinney was in a position to know just what signals were given as he was in charge of the signal positions.

Admiral Farragut was less colorful in his report to Naval Secretary Gideon Welles. "As we steamed up the Main Ship Channel, there was some difficulty ahead and the Hartford passed on ahead of the Brooklyn."

I must include here the unbiased eyewitness accounts of the Confederate officers as they observed the Union ships proceeding past Fort Morgan. The commander of the Rebel Ram *Tennessee*, James D. Johnston, reported, "This event was the most startling and tragic of the day, causing the almost instantaneous loss of 93 lives."

The commander of Fort Morgan, Brigadier General Richard L. Page, wrote, "The Brooklyn, the leading ship, stopped her engine, apparently in doubt...Farragut's coolness and quick perception saved the fleet from great disaster and probably from destruction." It is interesting to note the respect that military men had for each other's prowess, disregarding the position each took during the war.

To understand the initial cause of this blunder we look at Farragut's Supplementary General Order No. 11 of July 29 where he charts the enemy torpedoes. The admiral was a cautious man and had planned this battle carefully, looking for all possible obstacles and ways to circumvent them. More than a month before the August 5 engagement, Farragut had been patroling the waters outside the bay, sending in small boats to look for and count torpedoes, and to map out the best avenue for his fleet. He found that black buoys were strung across the west side of the channel toward Fort Morgan and that mines lay between these buoys. His instructions to the vessels were that they take care to pass eastward of the easternmost buoy which was free of obstructions. The easternmost buoy was red and figures in all accounts of the battle. On August 5, the Rebel *Tennessee* was lying to the rear of the torpedo obstructions and west of the red buoy. When the Union monitor, *Tecumseh*, drew near the buoy and was influenced by the narrowness of the channel to the east, and eager to get at the *Tennessee*, Commander Tunis Craven disregarded the instruction and pulled his ship to the westward, striking the torpedoes and causing the instant sinking of his ship and the loss of his own life, as well as most of his crew. The column behind him was subsequently crowded to the westward and no choice was left to the *Brooklyn* and the fleet that followed. The *Brooklyn*, seeing the ravaged *Tecumseh* and the menacing torpedoes under its bow, stopped her engines and tried to take another course.

We see from the above quotes a brave, but troubled, *Brooklyn* unable to immediately carry out her orders. How exasperating to be faced with both a line of torpedoes and shallow water when the entire success of the mission depends on your lead. Captain Alden did the only thing that could be done—stop, reverse engines away from the shallow bottom, and go on. Admiral Farragut's plan included the ability of his own ship, the *Hartford*, to take the lead if necessary. His knowledge of the torpedoes in his path did not keep him from ordering the *Hartford* ahead; it was providence that the snapping torpedo-primers under the bottom of the ship as it passed failed to explode them, probably due to corrosion from lying a long time in the water.

One more aspect to this incident is of Farragut being tied to the mast during the battle. Note No. 11, Book 3, details this moment. Farragut, himself, was amused by the reports that followed of his heroic posture. When informed of the many stories, he said to Captain Percival Drayton, Farragut's chief-of-staff, "How curiously some trifling incident catches the popular fancy! My being in the main rigging was a mere accident, owing to the fact that I was driven aloft by the smoke. The lashing was due to your own fears [Drayton's] for my safety." After the war he posed for a portrait in the lashed-to-the-mast position, thus forever immortalizing the moment.

Epilogue

BY MARY P. LIVINGSTON

Nearly 130 years have passed since the War Between the States ended, leaving a ravaged, scarred, and confused country, still torn by loyalties no longer important. Families managed to put themselves back together, many headed by women who had lost their husbands and sons to the bloody battles. Cities have slowly rebuilt. Political machines drew new governmental guidelines. Wars have come and gone. And with each one has come a change in beliefs, and more willingness to surrender the old, letting in new ideas of brotherhood and love of humanity.

The current generations are too young to remember first-hand the Civil War, or a Soldier, Sailor or Marine who fought in it. But there is a fever amongst all of us to know the past and what happened to bring us to where we are today. The past decades have brought forth from attics, basements, trunks, old buildings, the remnants of the war that tell the story of the men who fought it. Old uniforms, swords, diaries, guns, medals have been unearthed and are once again bringing the heartwrenching story to this generation. The diaries herein transcribed, and the Medal of Honor earned so gallantly at the Battle of Mobile Bay by Miles Oviatt, plus a dress sword, a picture of himself, and pictures of his family are all that remain of a man who wanted peace in our land and fought to bring it to his country.

In the summer of 1992, I learned of the great interest in the Medal of Honor recipients of the Civil War. Oviatt's medal had always been stored carefully by his descendants and had found its way to my hands upon the death of my parents. For many years it hung on the wall of my home office along with the Citation where the family could see it. The Marine Corps Museum in Washington, D.C. had never been able to obtain a Marine Corps Medal of Honor from the Civil War, and when they heard that one truly existed in excellent condition in my hands, they contacted me. In my work as a genealogist, I had gathered many original documents, including the medal, that would be better off in libraries and museums. By the summer

159

of 1993, arrangements had been made for me to donate the medal and the citation to the Marine Corps Museum for permanent display and security. Officials from the museum brought me to Washington, D.C. for a presentation ceremony on August 6, 1993, the anniversary of the Battle of Mobile Bay. An illustrious group of people gathered in the Special Exhibits Gallery for the occasion: Brigadier General Edwin H. Simmons, USMC (Ret.), Director of the Marine Corps History and Museums Division; Lieutenant General Robert B. Johnston, USMC, Deputy Chief of Staff for Manpower and Reserve Affairs, representing the Commandant of the Marine Corps; Mr. David M. Sullivan, noted expert and author on the Marines of the Civil War; Richard A. Long, Head, Oral History Unit; Lieutenant Colonel Thomas Richards, Head of the Historical Branch; and other staff members and representatives of the Historical Foundation, photographers and Navy television cameramen.

The memory of Miles M. Oviatt was alive again in that room as the principals recounted in detail his Marine Corps career and gallant actions during the Battle of Mobile Bay. The Medal of Honor and Citation were presented to General Johnston and then placed temporarily in the Civil War case for the photographers. It will be part of a current acquisition display and be available for young Marines to view and learn about valor and pride in country from a century past.

One additional record of Oviatt exists on a permanent monument. The Congressional Medal of Honor Society National Headquarters relocated to Mount Pleasant, South Carolina, in the fall of 1993. The location includes the U.S.S. *Yorktown* as part of the Patriots Point Naval and Maritime Museum, and a 100-foot silver wall bearing the names of the Medal recipients. Among such heroes' names as General Jimmy Doolittle, James Stockdale, and Navy Ace Commander David MacCampbell, is the name of Miles M. Oviatt. He is in good company with others who put personal safety aside for the good of their country. These monuments and museums keep alive the spirit of liberty that Americans pass on from generation to generation, and the spirit of the men who made it possible.

Jottings by Miles M. Oviatt

TAKEN FROM THE PAGES OF HIS CIVIL WAR DIARIES

EDITOR'S NOTE—These writings may or may not be original—every effort has been made to find and verify the author of each. In any case, they reflect the feeling of the times.

"STAR OF THE TWILIGHT"

Star of the twilight, Beautiful Star,
Gladly I Hail thee Shining afar.
Rest from your labor, Children of Toil,
Night closes ore ye, Rest ye awhile.
This is thy greeting signaled afar.
Star of the twilight, Beautiful Star,
Star of the twilight, Beautiful Star.

Eagerly watching & wating for thee
Looks the lone traveler on the dark sea.
Soon as thou shinest soft on the air
Borne by the light [breeze] Floating the Prayer,
Watch on him kindly hence from above
Light thou his pathway, Beautiful Star,
Star of the twilight, Beautiful Star.

U.S.S. Vanderbilt June 29 1863
M.M. Oviatt

When the summer breeze is sighing
Mournfully along When with Angels
I am sleeping down on the road gutter
All I ask of you to bring me is a bottle of porter.
Then you may gently rouse me while I take a snooter,

Then with courage gathered from it I will gently rise
and go down to old Zimmers
and brush the cobwebs from my eyes.

    U.S.S. Brooklyn - M.M. Oviatt

Oh, Dixie, dear Dixie, the land of my birth,
I love far dearer than all others on earth.
I love you, adore you & by you I'll stand
For you will I die defending our red, white & red.
Our banner is simple and by it [I] stand,
It waves from the Potomac to the great Rio Grand.
As Lee, Boreguard, Johnson and others have said
We will all die defending our red, white and red.

    Ex. of S. of C.S.A.

        M.M. Oviatt, U.S.M.

    "The Capt & Etc."

They marched through the town with their banners so gay.
I ran to the window to hear the band play.
I peeped through the blind very cautiously then,
For fear the neighbors would say I was looking at the men.
Oh, I heard the drums beat & the music so sweet be
But my eyes at that time caught a much greater treat.
The troop was the finest I ever did see
And the Capt. with his whiskers took a sliyh glance at me.
But he marched from the town And I see him no more.
But I think of him oft and the whiskers he wore.
When we met at the ball, I, of course, thought twas but right
To pretend that we never had met before that night.
But he knew me at once, I knew by his glance,
And I hung down my head when he asked me to dance.
We sat down togather at the end of the seat
And the sweet words he spoke I never shall forget.
For my heart was enlisted and could not get free
As the Capt. with his whiskers took a sly glance at me.
Oh, I dream all the night and I talk all the day
Of the love of the Capt. who has gone far away.
And still I remember with superbundant delight,
How we met in the st[reet]s and danced all the night.
And keep in my mind how my heart jumped with glee
As the Capt. with his whiskers took a slyh glance at me.

Home Sweet Home. Home, there's no place like home. There
is no place like home. Written by Miles M. Oviatt of the U.S.M.C.

What visions crown our youthful breasts,
What holy asperations high.
[Inspire] the young heart to do its best
And wait the promised by and bye.
We hear it at our Mother's knee
With tender smile and love lit eye.
She grants some boon of childish plea
In these soft accents bye & bye.

"They that seek thee shall find Thee"
"Honor thy Father and thy Mother that thy days May be
long on the land which the lord thy God givith thee"
     Oct 1864

Be kind to thy sister. Not many may know the deapth of
true sisterly love.

Notes

DIARY BOOK ONE – [PART A]

1. COOPER UNION INSTITUTE — A private professional college in New York City, founded in 1859 by Peter Cooper as a free night school for the working class. Free forums and lectures are held in the Great Hall; Abraham Lincoln gave an address there on February 27, 1860.
   LYMAN TREMAIN — 1819–1878-New York lawyer, district attorney N.Y. State Attorney General 1858–60; N.Y. State Assembly 1866–68; U.S. House of Representatives 1873–75.
   GENERAL WADSWORTH — President Lincoln ordered Mass Meetings held in many cities for the purpose of recruitment. Important orators and Army officers were often the speakers who excited the patriotic spirit of those attending; enlistees were signed up on the spot.
2. HOLY STONE — A soft sandstone used to scrub a ship's deck.
3. CASTLE GARDEN — formerly a fort. In 1850, the largest opera house in the nation, holding 7,000 persons. Situated on a small island 200 feet beyond Battery Park at the tip of Manhattan Island. A wooden bridge connected the two. Today, Castle Clinton National Monument marks the site of the fort built in 1807. The U.S. Customs House is situated at the edge of Battery Park today.
4. LAFAYETTE — Marie Joseph Paul Yves Roch Gilbert du Motier de Lafayette, born September 6, 1757, died May 20, 1834. President James Monroe invited Lafayette to come to the United States for a visit in February 1824, which lasted over a year.
5. JENNY LIND — A Swedish singer, famous for her lilting bird-like soprano voice. Born October 6, 1820, died November 2, 1887. She gave her first American concert at Castle Garden on September 11, 1850.
6. *SYMMETRY*, an English Bark — Official Records of the U.S. Navy, hereinafter cited as ORN, Captain Charles H. Baldwin reports to Hon. Gideon Welles, Secretary of the Navy, that on the morning of November 15, 1862, the *Symmetry*, loaded with grain from New York bound for Belfast, collided with the *Vanderbilt*. The *Vanderbilt* had stopped engines, hailing the bark for boarding. However, the *Symmetry* was not able to stop to avoid the collision that carried away its head boom and bowsprit; the fault lay with the master of the bark.
7. BURNSIDE'S EXPEDITION — General Ambrose Burnside was assigned to guard the Atlantic Coastal area and called upon the Navy for use of their vessels. His first battle at Fredericksburg was a disaster with a great loss of lives on the crossing of the Rappahannock River. General Joseph Hooker replaced him. Burnside's beard style became known as "Sideburns."

8. BARRELL OF SLUSH — This may be an award of beer to the crew.
9. CORCORAN'S LEGION — Brevet Major General Robert O. Tyler was assigned to the Army of the Potomac. His brigade was named The Corcoran, or Irish Legion, probably due to the great number of Irishmen attached to the brigade.
10. FLORES — Portugal-owned Azores; also see Faial Island, City of Horta. The C.S.S. *Alabama* was known to have been in the Azores transferring guns and ammunition, and burning whaling vessels.
11. *TUSCARORA* — The U.S.S. *Tuscarora* was at the Harbor of Horta earlier than the U.S.S. *Vanderbilt*. Three naval officers, Captain John A. Winslow, Lieutenant Commander James S. Thornton and Lieutenant John Weidman, were aboard the *Vanderbilt* with orders from the Navy Department to disembark at Faial for other assignments. (Later, Rear Admiral Winslow was captain of the U.S.S. *Kearsarge*, and Captain Thornton was executive officer at the time of the capture of the C.S.S. *Alabama*, June 12, 1864. See *B. & L.*, Vol. IV, Pg. 615.)
12. COAL — December 30, 1862, ORN record $4,994.50 drawn by Acting Assistant Paymaster James E. Tolfree to pay for 350 tons of coal.
13. TOMPION — A tompion is a wooden plug or a metal or canvas cover for the muzzle of a gun.
14. WASHINGTON — Diary of Gideon Welles, Tuesday January 20, 1863, Vol. I, Pg. 224. "...Baldwin of the Vanderbilt came up today from Hampton Roads where he arrived yesterday from an unsuccessful cruise for the Alabama, his vessel having been detained by Wilkes which defeated the department's plans."
15. *MINNESOTA* — The flagship at Hampton Roads in March 1862, during the famous battle of the *Monitor* and *Merrimac*. She played a big part in the defense of Union ships there.
16. *BRANDYWINE* — A forty-four-gun frigate, built 1825. Destroyed by fire at Norfolk, Va., September 3, 1864. Offered to Marquis de Lafayette by the United States for his last trip to the U.S. and his return to France in September 1825.
17. MONITORS — These vessels were running into Hampton Roads to get supplies and prepare for the voyage to Port Royal, S.C. by orders of Admiral Samuel F. DuPont to make ready for the attack on Charleston, S.C. They were given a trial on the Great Ogeechee River at Fort McAllister, Ga. on January 27, 1863.
18. CAPTAIN BALDWIN'S ORDERS — ORN January 27, 1863; Secretary of the Navy, Gideon Welles' orders to Captain Charles H. Baldwin of the U.S.S. *Vanderbilt* instructed him to resume his search for the C.S.S. *Alabama*, visiting Havana, Cuba, for new instructions. He was to proceed to the West Indies, then Brazil, Fernando de Noronha, and Rio de Janeiro; continue to Cape of Good Hope, St. Helena, Cape Verde, the Canaries, Madeira, Lisbon, Western Islands, and New York. If the *Alabama* was found, he was to disregard instructions and pursue the rebel vessel and destroy it.
19. U.S.S. *ATIS* — It is not clear what Oviatt is referring to. It could be President Lincoln due to the Jack flying at the Main. Or it could be president of the steamship company. There is no U.S.S. *Atis* listed in any Civil War documentation researched for this book.
20. ORDERS — ORN January 28, 1863, telegram from Gideon Welles to Captain Baldwin informing him of the destruction of the *Hatteras* off Galveston, Tex. by the C.S.S. *Alabama*; the *Vanderbilt* was to proceed with all dispatch to Havana, as the C.S.S. *Florida* was there on the twentieth.

DIARY BOOK ONE – [PART B]

1. MASON & SLIDELL — October 1861, James Mason and John Slidell, Confederate Commissioners to Britain and France, respectively, aboard the British steamer *Trent*, left Havana, Cuba. Captain Charles Wilkes of the U.S. screw-sloop *San Jacinto* stopped and removed them. The incident was contrary to International Law which dictated that Wilkes should have brought the *Trent* to an American port where a prize court would have reviewed the case. This created a major crisis between Britain and the United States. President Lincoln and Secretary of State William Seward found a way around the problem. Britain, herself, had not always followed the International Law, so Seward good-naturedly

congratulated her on finally agreeing to follow the law along with other nations. The incident helped to clear the way for better relations.

2. *SAN JACINTO*— Not true, as this ship was in service until January 1, 1865, when she hit a reef at No Name Key off Great Abaco Island and sunk.

3. *RINALDO*— This British ship was assigned to take Mason & Slidell and their secretaries from Provincetown, Mass. to Southampton, England, after the unfortunate *Trent* Affair. They departed January 1, 1862, and after a rough voyage, arrived at their destination January 29, 1862.

4. PORT ROYAL — Early capital of Jamaica, destroyed by earthquakes in 1692 and 1907; entrance to Kingston Harbor. Many ports visited by Union and Confederate ships during this period maintained neutrality, but allowed repairing and coaling for a brief time so they could be on their way.

5. BLUE BEARD — Bluebeard's Tower, now a hotel.

6. SANTA ANNA — General Antonio Lopez de Santa Anna (1794–1876) was a fiery revolutionary who became dictator of Mexico. He stormed the Alamo in Texas, but was finally defeated in 1836 in the Battle of San Jacinto.

7. BLACK BEARD — This five-story stone watchtower built in 1679 was probably used by the notorious pirate Edward Teach; also was Fort Skytsborg and now a small hotel.

8. *JACOB BELL* — February 12, the Rebel Privateer *Florida* (aka *Oreto*) destroyed the American ship *Jacob Bell* in latitude 24° 01' N., longitude 65° 58' W. en route to New York from Foo-Chow, China. Captain Frisbee, four passengers and crew were put aboard the Danish bark *Morning Star* on the fourteenth near the Island of Sombrero.

9. COALING — ORN indicate 240 Tons of coal were purchased from Baring Bros., London on 60 days' account. The engine and boilers were also under repair.

10. *PETERHOFF*— ORN corroborate Oviatt's details of the events. Captain Jarman of the *Peterhoff* had a lone manifest for seven [7] boxes of tea, but the cargo also contained kegs, cases, and boxes for which there was no manifest. A crew member confessed they had fieldpieces and arms on board. Captain Jarman also denied having any passengers, yet seven were discovered; some were found to be quite violent when informed of their capture. Later it was discovered that one was a colonel in the Confederate service. As the *Peterhoff* had run the blockade before, Captain Baldwin sent a dispatch to the Navy Department asking that she be declared a lawful prize. He followed International Law by sending the *Peterhoff* to Key West to be adjudicated. Also see March 30, 1863, entry for further word on this crew. See illustrations for details of the prize awards for her capture. A full description of this incident, including correspondence by those involved, can be seen in ORN Series I, Vol. 2, "Operations of the Cruisers," Pgs. 98–104. On December 23, 1863, under Acting Volunteer Lieutenant Pickering, she was stationed at Throgs Neck, in Long Island Sound. She spent the rest of her days in U.S. service and was sunk in a collision on March 6, 1864, off the North Carolina coast. Her value was $80,000.

11. COMMANDER WILKES — Rear Admiral Charles Wilkes, commanding the West Indies Squadron, transferred his pennant from the U.S.S. *Wachusetts* to the U.S.S. *Vanderbilt* on February 26, 1863, thereby contradicting the sailing orders of the *Vanderbilt* given by Secretary of the Navy Gideon Welles.

12. POINTE-A-PITRE — A 4,869-foot volcano, Soufriere, on Guadeloupe, may have been responsible for the upheaval.

13. ST. PIERRE — Completely destroyed by the eruption of Mont Pele in 1902. Its history is preserved in a museum that depicts the city before and after the disaster. Approximately twenty miles south is Fort De France, the new capital of Martinique; also called Fort Royal in Civil War days. Napoleon's Josephine was born at Les Trois-llets in 1763.

14. BARBADOS — Known for its parrot-green sugarcane and lush gardens at Francia, and the many trellised vines at Villa Nova, former home of Anthony Eden, Prime Minister of England, 1955–57.

15. FORTS — Citadel Henri, the Sky Fortress of Haiti, sits on a 3,000-foot cliff at Bishop's Bonnet on the northern coast of Haiti. Henri Christophe, born October 6, 1767, a freed slave and self-appointed king and protector against the French invasion that never came,

1804–1820, built the fortress; the only emperor of a western hemisphere nation. Palatial mansions and plantations dot the hill at the capital of Cap Haitien, overlooking the harbor. In a valley stands Christophe's ruined palace, Sans Souci. The Citadel's thick stone staircases stand unmoved by the earthquake of 1842 that destroyed San Souci. Christophe shot himself in the head October 2, 1820, after the revolt of his people; his officers smuggled his body from the palace and buried it in a pile of quicklime. Over the years, the quicklime melted away, exposing the whole skeleton. 1847 saw a fitting burial with a stone slab marking the grave. Islanders say his restless ghost still wanders among the cannons of the fortress.

16. BAHAMAS — Admiral Charles Wilkes examined the Old Bahama Channel on the way to Havana, Cuba.

17. GRISWOLD — George R. Griswold deserted while in charge of a boat. ORN affirm that Captain Charles H. Baldwin asked the U.S. consul in Havana, Cuba, to offer a reward for the apprehension of Mr. Griswold, and that he be kept in prison until the *Vanderbilt* returned to Havana.

18. *IROQUOIS* — Although this Union ship spent most of her naval career blockading the Mississippi and James Rivers, she also took a tour of duty in the Caribbean Sea, as evidenced by a report of November 23, 1862, when she was eluded by the C.S.S. *Sumter* in the port of St. Pierre, Martinique. See *B. & L.*, Vol. II, Pg. 135.

19. *RETRIBUTION* — Seven prisoners were received from the U.S.S. *Alabama* who were taken from the privateer *Retribution*. ORN Correspondence, Captain Baldwin to Gideon Welles.

20. COALING — ORN Correspondence, Captain Baldwin reports to Gideon Welles, that 1,100 tons have been taken on the *Vanderbilt* on this date, and scaling and repairing the boilers will be finished the next day. The report also includes a detailed description of recommended repairs that were needed to ready the ship for further service. The *Vanderbilt* had been ordered by Admiral Wilkes to leave the Havana, Cuba, harbor and proceed to Key West for coal, and return.

21. RELIGIOUS DAYS — This may have been the Lenten period before Easter.

22. *CUMBERLAND* — Sunk in action with the *Merrimac*, also known as the *Virginia*, March 8, 1862, off Newport News, Va.

23. CASTLE MORRO — El Morro was begun in 1589 and completed in 1630, designed by Italian engineer Antonelli after one in Lisbon. The lighthouse tower was added in 1844; FORT — La Punta, a fort built in 1590 to catch pirate ships entering the harbor. A heavy chain was strung from El Morro to La Punta to close the harbor.

24. CHARLESTON — The Attack on Fort Sumter began on April 7, 1863.

25. *GERTRUDE* — A British blockade runner, James Raison, master, captured by the *Vanderbilt* off the Island of Eleuthera, east of New Providence I. Her cargo included 250 barrels of powder which marked the *Gertrude* as a contraband trader. She ran toward Harbor Island but after 28 miles was caught and boarded by the crew of the *Vanderbilt*. The pilot, George Oliver, a citizen of Charleston and a passenger on the *Gertrude,* was held as a prisoner to be sent to the United States. He confessed to being a trader. ORN Correspondence on this date from Admiral Wilkes to Gideon Welles tells of being 130 men short in the squadron due to prize crews being sent to U.S. ports with prisoners and asks for speedy return of the men to active duty.

26. COLUMBUS — There is still speculation today as to the correct Bahama island that Christopher Columbus named San Salvador. Even though Cat Island does not entirely fit Columbus' description of his landing place, a map from 1642 by the cartographer Jan Jansson places the legend "Guanahani o San Salvador" beside Guanima, the Indian name of today's Cat Island. In the 1800s, this error was so commonplace, that even the natives themselves adopted it. Admiral Samuel Eliot Morison, in 1942, stated evidence showed first landing place to be Watling (Cat Island), already renamed San Salvador; Long Bay on Watling has a white cross marking reputed spot of the landing. National Geographic Society, in 1986, concluded Samana Cay to be San Salvador, based on evidence in Columbus' diary in his words "The people here call this island Guanahani." There have been nine

different landfall theories in the last 200 years. The Taino natives of these islands were profoundly affected by the arrival of the Europeans; smallpox, famine, enslavement nearly wiped them out; West Indies became a back-water till 17th-century trade in sugar.

27. FORT — Morro Castle built in 1640–42, designed by Antonelli; this fortress commands a view of the Oriente coast.

28. CAPTAIN WYMAN — ORN contain Admiral Wilkes' correspondence to Gideon Welles wherein he reports the *Senoma* joined the *Vanderbilt* at Cape St. Nicholas Mole. As the *Senoma* was on its way toward Cuba, Admiral Wilkes transferred Captain R.H. Wyman to that ship with orders to take command of the U.S.S. *Santiago de Cuba* when it was intercepted at Key West.

29. WILKES — Admiral Wilkes reports to Gideon Welles that he and Captain Baldwin had business with the authorities, Mr. Latimer, and the U.S. consul, Mr. Hyde, in which they discussed a slight misunderstanding. This may have to do with neutrality which was a constant problem between the U.S. and foreign-owned ports.

30. GALION BAY — East side of Martinique.

31. CHRISTIANSTED — ORN contain correspondence to Gideon Welles from Admiral Wilkes that he and Captain Baldwin stopped at Santa Cruz to have an interview with the Governor of the Danish Islands concerning the objections by the secessionists of St. Thomas about U.S. vessels lying at that port. A more friendly attitude was attempted so as to convince the Danish officials to deny coaling and repairs to the Confederate ships. Christiansted was the tiny capital of Santa Cruz at that time.

32. DOCTOR — ORN read that Admiral Wilkes reviewed his crew on the *Wachusetts* upon returning to St. Thomas and found Dr. Otis in poor health; therefore, ordered him to return home.

33. ADMIRAL WILKES — Gideon Welles wrote in his diary on Saturday, May 16, 1863, that the admiral's special mission had been the capture of the *Alabama* and, in this, he had totally failed. In his zeal to catch blockade runners and get prize money, the admiral had seized the *Vanderbilt* for his own use and had aborted their orders, thus defeating the Department's plans.

34. LA GUAIRA — Birthplace of Simon Bolivar; the port for Caracas.

35. *SHEPHERD KNAPP* — See May 14, 1863; however, published records state that the *Shepherd Knapp* was wrecked on a coral reef at Cape Haitien in the Caribbean on May 8, 1863, and abandoned.

36. ADMIRAL WILKES — Gideon Welles, in his diary, wrote on Friday, May 29, 1863, that the C.S.S. *Alabama* continues to elude capture, even at Fernanda de Noronha, due to the continued interference by Admiral Wilkes, of the Vanderbilt's orders; the admiral, finding that the comfortable accommodations on the *Vanderbilt* were to his liking, had deliberately attached her to his squadron for too long a time.

37. CURACAO — Aruba, Bonaire, and Curacao are small Dutch islands off the coast of Venezuela; others in the area — Tortuga, Los Testigos, Margarita, Los Roques.

38. ADMIRAL WILKES — ORN indicate that Gideon Welles sent orders to Admiral Wilkes to return to Washington at once, and was to be replaced by Commodore James L. Lardner.

39. CHANCELLORSVILLE — May 1–5,1863; Eleventh Army Corps, Second Division, First Brigade of 154th New York, Colonel Patrick H. Jones, wounded, Lieutenant Colonel Henry C. Loomis, in charge. *B. & L.*, Vol. III, Pg. 236.

40. FRENCH — U.S.S. *Vanderbilt* cruised islands owned by France, so it was necessary for the crew to learn some of the language. As indicated, the focus was only on conversational French.

41. ELLSWORTH, Colonel E. Elmer — 11th New York (1st Fire Zouaves) killed Alexandria, Va., by hotel owner. He lay in state in the East Room of the White House as he was a good friend of President Lincoln. *B. & L.*, Vol. I, Pg. 179.

DIARY BOOK TWO

1. 290 — The C.S.S. *Alabama* was known as "No. 290," that being her number on the list of ships built by Lairds Brothers of Birkenhead, England. However, the American consul

informed Captain Baldwin that on June 20, six men and two officers had come ashore in a small boat and reported that their vessel had been captured by the Florida and forced to sail at an undisclosed latitude and longitude; after thirty days, being out of provisions, they had burned their vessel and came on shore at Barbados. See ORN.

2. NEPTUNE — The mythical God of the Sea; when ships cross the equator, Neptune is said to arise from the sea and instruct sailors to go through an initiation process.

3. PERNAMBUCO — Former name of Recife on the coast of Brazil, north of Natal.

4. *CITY OF BATH*— ORN substantiate this report; she was going to Antwerp with guano (a fertilizer chiefly composed of seafowl excrement); the crew of the American ship *Constitution* was on board having left that ship at Trinidad, 800 miles S.S.E. from Pernambuco, where the Confederate ship *Georgia* was coaling off her. The *City of Bath* had paid a ransom bond of $20,000 as the cargo was foreign property.

5. CHARRED WOOD — ORN state Captain Baldwin believed that this wreckage was the remains of the *Constitution*, judging by the currents and location, 30 miles E. by S. from the Trinidade.

6. SUGAR LOAF — Sugar Loaf Mountain (Pao de Acucar), conical in shape, is 1,300 feet high. However, Corcovado Peak is 2,300 feet. Today, the Statue of Christ, The Redeemer, 124 feet, stands on the top with outstretched arms. "River of January" was the name given Rio de Janeiro by the Portuguese discoverers, January 1, 1502, thinking it was the mouth of a river.

7. *VANDERBILT* CONDITION — ORN: Captain Baldwin reports on this date that his ship's boilers have given up on him several times, requiring patching, and one time scalded a fireman; the tubes are now so thin that scaling is impossible, therefore, increasing the coal consumption. Five or six days are required to ready the ship for sailing; provisions until August 1 have been obtained. In August, 40 of the crew will have passed enlistment time, with others falling due in the next months; 1,200 tons of coal have been loaded; prices are not excessive, $11 to $12 per cardiff, in gold; coaling is not allowed at Santos and Santa Catharina, but Bahia, Pernambuco, and Fernando de Noronha are cooperative.

8. LOUIS NAPOLEON — (1808–1873) Napoleon III, son of Louis Bonaparte, nephew of Emperor Napoleon I.

9. NEWS — July 6, 1863: Admiral DuPont was relieved of his command by Admiral Dahlgren due to DuPont's failure to take the city of Charleston. The Navy Department failed to back up its statement to share the responsibility if the plan failed; General Hooker replaced by General Meade after Hooker's conduct at Chancellorsville; Port Hudson battle July 8, 1863, the Confederates surrendered; Confederate General Robert E. Lee at Gettysburg, Pa.; private businessmen spent their own funds to help with the war effort.

10. CONVENT — There were many convents in Rio de Janeiro. On the right side of the harbor entry is the town of Niteroi, the state capital 1835–90, with many 16th-century churches and forts. Overlooking the bay is Fortaliza de Santa Cruz, built in 1565 and still used by the military; also the 18th-century Santa Teresa Convent.

11. COAL — ORN confirm the loading of 400 tons of coal as allowed by Sir Charles Elliot, governor of St. Helena, if it could be loaded by 5 P.M. on the twentieth.

12. *JOHANNA ELIZABETH*— ORN confirm this ship's plight; a Dutch bark from Batavia to Amsterdam with cargo of sugar and tobacco, both valued at L40,000 and 15 officers on leave with their families; Captain Baldwin's report to Gideon Welles states he could not, in all humanity, refuse to help the stricken vessel and crew, and instead of abandoning their ship, the *Vanderbilt* towed it 100 miles to Simon's Bay, putting the *Vanderbilt* behind in its mission. On September 8, 1863, the U.S. consul at Cape Town, South Africa, received a letter from O.J. Truter, consul general of the Netherlands, praising Baldwin and his crew for the generous rescue of Captain Junius and his ship, the *Johanna Elizabeth*, passengers and crew, without thought of salvage claims or personal good; this incident would be brought to the attention of his Netherlandic Majesty's Government. The Cape Town newspaper carried the story. The act further strengthened United States–Netherland relations.

13. ADMIRAL — Sir Baldwin Walker was the English admiral of the station at Simon's Town. See *B. & L.*, Vol. IV, Pg. 605. He gave the *Vanderbilt* permission, with proclamation of neutrality, to coal and make repairs, according to correspondence in ORN.

14. *VANDERBILT* CONDITION — ORN state that her forward smokestack was almost gone, the lower part of the fronts of all the boilers were in poor condition, constantly giving out, the iron being so thin there was nothing left to rivet to. Two engineers were taking prizes to ports, and others were quite sick; 904 tons of coal had been taken on; 46 of the crew's time had expired, with November 10 making it 100.

15. *ALABAMA* — *Raphael Semmes* by Colver Meriwether reviews the movements of this Confederate vessel, Pges. 235–36: She was nearly caught in Simon's Bay, when, one night the middle of September, the mighty *Vanderbilt* flew past after chasing the *Alabama* across the Atlantic, shuttling back and forth between Simon's Town and Cape Town, just missing the Rebel ship each time. The crew of the *Alabama* admired the *Vanderbilt's* prowess in keeping the trail all the while. As the *Vanderbilt* used 80 tons of coal a day to keep her going, and had the problem of constantly retracing her route to find coal, the *Alabama* avoided a confrontation in the Straits of Sunda, where the *Vanderbilt* might have been stationed. On June 19, 1863, the C.S.S. *Alabama* captured the *Tuscaloosa* that had been trading between Montevideo and New York. She actually had 4 guns when turned into an armed tender.

16. *SEA BRIDE* — This is a different ship, commanded by Captain White, that was also captured by the C.S.S. *Alabama* on August 5, 1863, at the entrance to Table Bay. See U.S. consul, Cape Town, Walter Graham, December 16, 1863, Chronology Log, Pg. 572, and Pg. 428, report by Edward Cooper of the Bark Urania, August 19, 1863. ORN, Series I, Vol. 2. Both *Tuscaloosa* (*Conrad*) and *Sea Bride* are referred to many times as separate ships.

17. MONUMENT — *Civil War Times Illustrated,* June 1991 issue, Pg. 10, letter from Major Warner D. Farr, M.D., U.S. Army: The only Confederate serviceman buried in South Africa is 3d Assistant Engineer Simeon W. Cummings of C.S.S. *Alabama,* born in Connecticut, lived in New Orleans for 12 years prior to the service, served aboard the C.S.S. *Sumter* early in the war. *Alabama's* 1st officer, Lieutenant John M. Kell, performed the grave-side ceremony. Cummings died after a shore-side ostrich hunting trip when he was shot by his own gun while boarding a cutter to return to the *Alabama.* British Royal Navy officers from Cape Town, South Africa, later erected a permanent headstone at Cummings' grave to honor the *Alabama.*

18. ARRIVAL AT MAURITIUS — ORN confirm Captain Baldwin's correspondence with Edward Rush Worth, acting colonial secretary to Major General Johnstone, commander in chief of British Naval Forces, and governor of Mauritius; permission granted the *Vanderbilt* to remain in port for the purpose of repair and coaling with this to be accomplished at all possible haste as the port was under neutrality proclamation. Baldwin found Johnstone to be kind and "hearty in manner" and was invited to dine at the governor's country house.

19. *SANTIAGO DE CUBA* — This U.S. steamer captured the *Victory* after a long chase in June 1863, but never caught up with the *Florida*; *CALEB CUSHING* — Confederate schooner, seized June 27, 1863, and blown up that same day.

20. *VANDERBILT* CONDITION — ORN details correspondence from Captain Baldwin to Gideon Welles that during the overhauling of the ship in Port Louis, a two-foot crack in the shaft, and into the side of the ship, was discovered, a portion of it quite recent which probably occurred during the heavy weather on the way to this port. Low steam at 7 to 9 pounds pressure was used at that time. The *Vanderbilt* had used 20 to 25 pounds on her usual peacetime runs between New York and Le Havre. A platform of heavy timber was constructed to catch the shaft should it break off. 600 Tons of coal on board, boilers very bad, but the crew did the best they could. Speed to be reduced. Hoped that the Department would agree with the decision to return home, but would continue visiting ports on the way in case a rebel might be found.

21. SEMMES — Captain Raphael Semmes of the C.S.S. *Alabama.*

22. CHRONOMETER — An accurate timepiece that contains a compensating balance, useful on a ship.

23. BURNED VESSEL — There is speculation that this may have been the *Sea Bride;* however, U.S. consul, Walter Graham, Cape Town, entered in his report to Captain Oliver S. Glisson, USN, on December 16, 1863, ORN, that on December 15, a vessel corresponding

to the *Sea Bride* arrived in Madagascar, discharged cargo and was up for sale. This report begins with July 27 and ends with December 15 and does not note any vessel-burning by the C.S.S. *Alabama*.

24. CAPE ST. MARIE — The southern-most tip of Madagascar.

25. JOHN M. MILES — There is no explanation for Miles Oviatt's obsession with this name and that of John M. Oviatt. A search of LDS AGI files reveals the following: Oviatt, John Milton born about 1811—Steuben Co., N.Y. The two men lived in adjoining counties; Miles' father, Thomas, was born in 1809, so there is probably some relationship.

26. NEWSPAPER — *Cape Argus*, Cape Town, South Africa, October 20, 1863: Quote from the original, Page 2 under Summary of "Cape News." "The Alabama finally left the Cape on the 25th of September." "The Vanderbilt went from the Cape to Mauritius." This newspaper was brought back to the United States by Oviatt and has been stored in an attic until found recently by this editor.

27. ALABAMA — The biography of Raphael Semmes exposes the intimate thoughts of the man who commanded the infamous rebel vessel *Alabama*. His countenance was one of courage and deliberation, masking the growing weariness and sinking spirits that were taking a toll on the man as he continued to avoid the *Vanderbilt*. The constant hardships and discomforts of the sea, plus the desertion of fourteen men, however, were obstacles to be overcome. His strategic enlistment of volunteers as "passengers," working their passage, from the Cape Town port solved his crew needs.

28. COALING — ORN reveal correspondence to and from Sir Philip Woodehouse, governor of Cape Colony; Rawson W. Rawson, colonial secretary, and Captain Baldwin at Table Bay. To the appeal for coal from Baldwin, the colonial secretary denied the request on the grounds that the *Vanderbilt* had coaled at St. Helena, Simon's Bay, Mauritius and again wanted coal from Cape Town, all within a three-month time frame; this was in opposition to Her Majesty's instructions. Permission to remain in port for repairs was granted, however.

29. TABLE ROCK — Clouds form on top of this flat mountain and spill down over the sides, making a formation like a table cloth. It is 3,500 feet above sea level. Lion's Head and Signal Hill are two nearby mountains now reached by roads. Table Mountain has a cable car to the top as well as more than 300 foot paths.

30. WOOL — This was at the Port of Angra Pequena [Penguin Island].

31. *SULTANNA* — This is not the passenger steamer *Sultana*, loaded with 2,000 liberated Union prisoners, that exploded near Memphis, Tenn. April 7, 1865, killing 1,200 men.

32. *SAXON* — ORN detail correspondence from Captain Baldwin to Gideon Welles, October 30, 1863: 200 tons of coal destined for the *Alabama* was at Angra Pequena and that a cargo of wool and goatskins had been discharged by the *Tuscaloosa* there. The *Vanderbilt* found the British bark *Saxon*, laden with 160 bales of cargo but no proof of ownership. The captain, Stephen Sheppard, revealed a letter without signature directing him to come to this port and load any cargo he could find. Due to her association with the *Alabama*, the *Saxon* was considered a war prize and sent to a court of adjudication in New York.

33. SHIP — The British bark *Good Hope* reported that she was stopping at various ports to load guano. Reports from Cape Town tell of the *Good Hope's* orders to load the coal belonging to the *Alabama* and to warn the *Saxon*, as the two ships were under the same charter.

34. DANENHOWER — ORN detail this incident with reports from Captain Baldwin, Acting Master A.M. Keith, Captain Stephen Sheppard of the *Saxon*, 2d Mate David Aitchison, and Governor of Cape Colony, Sir P.E. Wodehouse: Acting Master Keith in charge of the prize crew, along with Acting Master's Mate Charles Danenhower, were supervising the *Saxon's* crew while Baldwin gave chase of the *Good Hope*. During the time they were ordering the crew below, Mr. Danenhower's cocked pistol went off accidentally, killing 1st Mate James Gray of the *Saxon*. It is noted that there were no arms aboard the *Saxon*. Baldwin had a coffin made and burial was done on the mainland on October 30, 1863, by the men of the *Vanderbilt*. No *Saxon* men were present, except for Captain Sheppard.

35. PENGUIN ISLAND — British territory. The *Vanderbilt* was desperate for coal and risked British anger, even though this area was outside its jurisdiction.

36. *SAXON* CREW — ORN include Captain Sheppard's account of the preceding incident: November 1 the Saxon crew was landed on the mainland with insufficient supplies, plus their personal items. They walked the coast and crossed to Halifax Island in a boat. November 3, the schooner, Isabel, rescued them, taking them to Ichaboe, then Hottentot Bay, where they boarded the ship, Lord of the Isles, and arrived Table Bay, November 21.

37. COAL AND REPAIRS — ORN state that 293 tons of Hartley coal were taken on at Penguin Island, and that coaling at Loanda was not necessary. Hartley was inferior to Cardiff coal for use on the *Vanderbilt.* $13 per ton was a fair value estimate, being the same price charged at Cape Town for the same quality. The crack in the starboard shaft had not increased in size but was under great strain when observed in motion.

38. BAHIA — Also Salvador on the coast of Brazil.

39. DESTRUCTION — This is one of many examples of erroneous reporting that was probably done by enemy forces so as to weaken the morale of the Northern troops.

40. FERNANDO DE NORONHA — A former penal colony, seven square miles, northeast of Natal, Brazil.

41. ADMIRAL WILKES — ORN for this date include correspondence to Gideon Welles from Admiral Charles Wilkes concerning his unjust treatment in regard to his detaining the U.S.S. *Vanderbilt* in the West Indies. Wilkes complains in detail that being squadron leader gave him the full authority to use the ships in that area as he saw fit to track the *Alabama* and other rebel vessels. The *Vanderbilt* was cast in a bad light in this letter; it could not have carried out its assignment due to needed repairs, which Wilkes took credit for ordering at Key West. He blames lack of vessels in numbers and efficiency for the failure to capture either the *Alabama* or the *Florida.*

42. NAVY DEPT. — ORN for this date contain a scathing letter from Gideon Welles to Admiral Wilkes detailing Wilkes' inexcusable conduct in transcending his authority, taking upon himself direct contradiction of orders. The *Vanderbilt* was not allowed to proceed to her destination as per her order from the Department, thereby preventing her from the possible capture of the rebel vessels. Wilkes' replacement, Acting Rear Admiral James L. Lardner, was ordered for the West Indies Squadron. The official report to the president accused Wilkes of dereliction of duty, and that relieving his command was in order.

43. COTTON — ORN report on January 6 the *Vanderbilt* chased a steamer, 900 tons, small sidewheels and two smokestacks at about 13 knots up the Douglas Channel at New Providence, Nassau. About 200 bales of cotton were thrown overboard, most picked up by other ships, leaving the balance of 50 for the *Vanderbilt.* Captain Baldwin questioned what to do with the 50 bales plus the one bale of wool picked up on November 3 at Angra Penquina, part of the cargo of the *Conrad.* He blamed the conditions of his boilers for not being able to catch the privateer.

44. CONDITION OF SHIP — ORN verify the chase of two vessels on January 10 by the *Vanderbilt.* Captain Baldwin details his ship's condition to excuse his inability to catch them: at 14 pounds, a forward boiler gave way filling the fire room with boiling water; a wooden wedge resulted in pressure of 22 pounds; the cracked starboard shaft opened more and several tubes gave way; chief engineer recommended a complete repair could be done in two months at a large shop if the *Vanderbilt* was required for immediate service.

DIARY BOOK THREE

1. GENERAL GEORGE G. MEADE — Meade felt strongly that Gettysburg was not handled correctly and that too many lives were lost. See *B. & L.,* Vol. III, Pges. 406–19: Sickles-Meade correspondence, Gettysburg soldiers' diaries.

2. DRY TORTUGAS — A small group of islands 68 miles due west of Key West. Fort Jefferson National Monument.

3. ADMIRAL — Admiral David G. Farragut, Union Commander, West Gulf Squadron.

4. SOUNDING — The bay was trapped with mines and torpedoes laid down by the Rebels.

5. *RICHMOND* — The Hartford had been Farragut's first choice to lead the attack on the Rebel forces in Mobile Bay. His captains advised against this, and due to the *Richmond's*

delay in returning from coaling and escorting the *Tecumseh* from Pensacola, Farragut selected the *Brooklyn* to take the lead because she had torpedo catchers on her bow.

6. *ANGLO SAXON* — Map sketches of the bay and ships show the wreck of the *Ivanhoe* southeast of Fort Morgan. According to "Warships and Naval Battles of the Civil War," the *Anglo Saxon* was a Confederate ship and captured by the Union forces, no date given.

7. *ALABAMA* — On Sunday, June 12, 1864, the U.S.S. *Kearsarge,* commanded by Captain John A. Winslow, captured and destroyed the Rebel ship, C.S.S. *Alabama* in the bay off Cherbourg, France, thus ending the long reign of Raphael Semmes as the nemesis of the Union forces.

8. DEVIL — Webster's Dictionary defines this as a device or machine. Images in "Civil War Naval Chronology 1861–1865" depict a "devil" as a crude raft of wood having perpendicular posts running through it to snag the torpedoes gently enough to prevent explosion. Many years after the war, abandoned devils could be found along the river banks and in the reeds along the shores.

9. MONITORS — ORN list 4 iron clad monitors inside of Sand Island: single-turreted *Tecumseh* and *Manhattan*, and double-turreted *Winnebago* and *Chickasaw*.

10. HARTFORD — [A] Reports of Admiral Farragut being lashed to the main during this battle have been substantiated in many accounts. 1st Lieutenant John C. Kinney, Acting Signal Officer on the Hartford, reports that due to the low-hanging smoke from the guns, Farragut went up the rigging of the mainmast to just below the maintop. Fleet Captain Percival Drayton ordered Signal Quartermaster Knowles to fasten a rope around Farragut to prevent him from falling if he should be wounded, thereby being killed by falling to the deck. J. Crittenden Watson, USN, also recounted in detail this incident, noting the bravery with which Farragut stayed in that position all during the shelling from the forts. [B] Kinney also recounts that a signal came from the *Brooklyn* and taken from the forecastle of the *Hartford*, indicating torpedoes lay in their path. It took ten minutes for the admiral to decide to pass the *Brooklyn*, and, on doing so, heard another vocal warning from that ship. The popular story has it that the admiral contemptuously answered the warning with "Damn the torpedoes." However, the din from the battle was so great it is doubtful that a voice could have been heard from the other ship. And if the remark was made it was probably made to his men nearby.

11. *BROOKLYN* — There are many opinions on this incident. Some of them are detailed in the Afterword.

12. *TECUMSEH* — Captain James Alden of the *Brooklyn*, in his official report to Admiral Farragut, exclaimed "Sunk by a torpedo! Assassination in its worst form! A glorious though terrible end for our noble friends, intrepid pioneers of that death-strewed path! Immortal fame is theirs; peace to their names." ORN, Series I, Vol. 21; Pg. 445. Captain Tunis A.M. Craven, the officers and crew, with the exception of the pilot and 8 or 10 men, went down with the monitor and drowned.

13. *TENNESSEE* — This description concerns the defeat and capture of the Rebel ram *Tennessee* commanded by Admiral Franklin Buchanan. The prisoners were 20 officers and about 170 men.

14. CASUALTIES — ORN: Admiral Farragut's dispatch No. 338 to Gideon Welles states the *Brooklyn* incurred 11 killed and 43 wounded. Surgeon George Maulsby, of the *Brooklyn*, lists them in his report to Captain Alden — Pges. 408–9 of ORN, Series I, Vol. 21.

15. DAMAGES — ORN, Series I, Vol. 21, Pges. 449–51, contain detailed damage reports of Edward Lull, executive officer; R.G. Thomas, carpenter; John Quevedo, acting gunner; Charles A. Bragdon, boatswain, USN. Gunner Quevedo also lists the amount of ammunition used during the siege in his report. Farragut reported to Gideon Welles on August 16, 1864, dispatch No. 350, that "some vessels would have to go into the dockyard and be thoroughly repaired; the *Brooklyn* could not be safely sent to sea farther than Pensacola or New Orleans unless temporarily repaired. The *Brooklyn* is terribly cut up; half her hanging knees on the starboard side have been cut from under the beams, and this ship's [*Hartford*] starboard side was so crushed in by the collision with the *Lackawanna* that neither she nor the *Brooklyn* would be safe in a gale."

16. FORT POWELL — The *Chickasaw* under the command of Commander Perkins shelled Fort Powell and blew it up after the approximately 10 p.m. evacuation of the fort's officers and men to the mainland. *B. & L.*, Vol. IV, Pges. 398, 400.

17. WOUNDED — Farragut sent a flag of truce to General Richard L. Page, Commandant of Fort Morgan, to say that if he would allow the wounded of the fleet as well as Admiral Buchanan, who had a compound fracture of the leg and faced amputation, to be taken to Pensacola to the hospital, then Farragut would send a vessel out if she would be permitted to return safely. Page assented and the *Metacomet* was dispatched. Among the wounded prisoners from the *Tennessee* sent to Pensacola was one Thomas Thompson, who was said to be a deserter from the U.S.S. *Brooklyn*. Farragut requests of Commodore William Smith, Commandant of Pensacola Navy Yard, that the prisoner be returned for court-martial when he recovered. ORN, Series I, Vol. 21, Pges. 406, 452.

18. FORT MORGAN — Brigadier General Page, C.S.A., Commander of Fort Morgan, wrote a detailed and descriptive report on the battle and surrender. *B. & L.*, Vol. IV, Pges. 408–10.

19. EXPLOSION — This incident is chronicled in V.C. Jones' story of "Farragut at Mobile Bay." The abstract log of the U.S.S. *Seminole*, Commander Edward Donaldson, states that their men were hauling torpedoes ashore when, at 5 p.m., a torpedo exploded, killing and wounding many. The Admiral's steam barge, *Loyall*, took the men to the *Brooklyn*. The next day the body of Charles Milliken was sent ashore and buried. The abstract log of the U.S.S. *Brooklyn*, Fleet Surgeon James C. Palmer reporting, states that four of the wounded died during the night. Seven survivors were then taken to the hospital at Pensacola. The next day at 10:30 a.m. all hands were called, the burial service was read by Lieutenant Thomas L. Swann, and the remains of the four men were consigned to the deep. ORN, Series I, Vol. 21, Pges. 786, 853. The names of all dead and wounded are listed there.

20. MILES M. OVIATT — ORN, Series I, Vol. 21, Pges. 447–49 contain a report to Captain James Alden from Executive Officer Edward P. Lull recommending many of the *Brooklyn's* crew for the Medal of Honor. Oviatt was cited as "corporal of Marines, for conspicious good conduct at their [his] guns." Pges. 451–52 contain a report from Alden to Farragut asking that these brave men be conferred with the Medal of Honor, once again naming Oviatt. Both letters are dated Mobile Bay, August 6, 1864, and contain all names so cited. The Medal of Honor was awarded to Oviatt on December 31, 1864, but was not sent to him until June 17, 1865. [See copy of citation.] He received $2.11 as his share of the prize money for capturing the *Tennessee* in Mobile Bay, paid in 1867.

21. U.S.S. *BROOKLYN* TO BOSTON — ORN, Series I, Vol. 21, Pg. 629 contains a letter to Gideon Welles from Admiral Farragut, dated September 8, 1864, Dispatch 399 regarding orders to the *Brooklyn* to return to Boston for repairs as the Pensacola Navy Yard was too taxed with repairs.

22. PORTER'S SQUADRON — Admiral Farragut had declined this post due to ill-health. Rear Admiral David Porter was selected due to his successful cooperation with the army in opening up the Mississippi.

23. FLEET — The largest fleet ever assembled in the history of the American navy was to engage in the battle of Fort Fisher; nearly 60 vessels of which five were ironclads.

24. CITY POINT — Headquarters of General Grant and supply base, on the James River, Va.

25. EXPLOSION — An old gunboat no longer serviceable, the *Louisiana*, served as a booby trap in the first attempt to blow up Fort Fisher. Commander A.C. Rhind and a crew of volunteers floated the boat to a location near the fort and beat a hasty retreat to the waiting swift gunboat *Wilderness*. The ignited powder blew up as planned, but the morning light brought the grim result of failure, as the fort still stood with its flag flying defiantly. *B. & L.*, Vol. IV, Pg. 655.

26. DECEMBER 24TH BATTLE — This account agrees with Captain Alden's report to Rear Admiral David Porter, Commander of North Atlantic Squadron. ORN, Series I, Vol. 11, Pges. 317–18.

27. REEMBARK — Captain Alden, in his report of December 30, 1864, to Admiral Porter, states that when ordered to reembark to the ships, the soldiers and officers registered great dissatisfaction and loudly denounced the order. They said they had gone there to take the fort and they were going to do it before they left. [See reference, Note No. 26.]

Seven hundred men were left onshore overnight, the sea being too rough to get them off. The enemy, suffering losses, did not attack them. *B. & L.* Vol. IV, Pg. 657. ORN contain a small order from Porter to Alden of the *Brooklyn.* It says in part: "We must get those poor devils of soldiers off today, or we will lose them; they are starving for want of provisions and water...rig a large raft out of spars...or lash two boats together....I know the sailors are not all dead on board the Brooklyn and you can do it....won't I be glad to get rid of them; ain't a soldier troublesome?"

28. CASWELL — Fort Caswell is located at the eastern tip of a peninsula to the west of Smith Island where Cape Fear is located.

29. AMMUNITION — The *Brooklyn* filled up with shell from the *Aries*, part of the reserve 1st Division.

30. ATTACK BY NAVAL FORCES — Ensign Douglas Cassel commanded assaulting party from the U.S.S. *Brooklyn* and was assigned under Lieutenant Commander Thomas Selfridge to attack Fort Fisher in this raid. His report is contained in ORN, Series I, Vol. 11, Pg. 469. Records show three men wounded, their names and injuries. A complete report of the Battle of Fort Fisher can be found in *B. & L.*, Vol. IV, Pges. 655–62, written by Thomas O. Selfridge, Jr., Captain, USN.

31. EXPLOSION — Confederate Colonel William Lamb writes in his official report, "The Defense of Fort Fisher," that his reserve magazine containing 13,000 pounds of powder blew up, killing and wounding several hundred of the enemy and some of his own wounded officers and men. He attributes the unfortunate incident to two sailors from the Union Fleet, "stupified by liquor found in the hospital," and looking for booty with candles in the magazine. He refutes the allegation that the explosion had been triggered along telegraph wires connected to the opposite shore. *B. & L.*, Vol. IV, Pg. 654.

32. ARMSTRONG RIFLE — Colonel Lamb, Commander of Fort Fisher, C.S.A., mentions this as "the most effective gun in the work, the 150-pounder Armstrong." The Confederate side of the battle can be seen in his report found in *B. & L.*, Vol.IV, Pges. 642–54.

33. BLOCKADER — Colonel Lamb, in his aforementioned report, states that a Southern flat-bottomed steam-transport approached Craig's landing within enemy (Union) lines; did not respond to warning shots and fell captive to the enemy. This was Lamb's first indication that he and his men were deserted.

34. ORDERS — Admiral Porter's order to Captain Alden advises the *Brooklyn* to return to Hampton Roads for examination, due to her long time at sea and the damages incurred in several battles; to report immediately to the Secretary of the Navy stating her full condition. ORN, Series I, Vol. 11, Pg. 607.

Bibliography

Battle Chronicles of the Civil War, Vols. 1–6, indexed, James M. McPherson, Editor; New York: MacMillan Publishing Co., 1989.

Battles and Leaders of the Civil War, Vols. 1–4, 1884–1887, Reprint I.

Beyer, W.F., and O.F. Keydel, Editors. *Deeds of Valor.* Vol. II, Detroit, Mich.: Perrien-Keydel Co., 1905; Page 72 list of U.S.S. *Brooklyn* Medal of Honor Recipients.

Blakeney, Jane. *Heroes—U.S. Marine Corps 1861–1955.* Washington, D.C.: Guthrie Lithograph Co., Inc.; Pge 6–Description of Honorable Action of Miles M. Oviatt.

Bradlee, Francis B.C. *Blockade Running During the Civil War.* Philadelphia, Pa.: Porcupine Press, 1974.

Brininstool, E.A. *Fighting Indian Warriors.* Bonanza Books, Division of Crown Publ., Inc., 1953.

Buckman, Peter. *Lafayette, A Biography.* New York: Paddington Press, Ltd., 1977.

Cavanah, Frances. *Jenny Lind's America.* New York: Chilton Book Co., 1969.

Civil War Naval Chronology 1861–1865; compiled by Naval History Division; Washington: Navy Dept., 1971; Original 1961–1966 in six paperbacks.

Civil War Times Illustrated, Harrisburg, Pa.: Cowles Magazine, bi-monthly.

Commanger, Henry Steele, Editor. *The Blue and the Grey*, Vols. I & II, New American Library, 1950–1973; Indianapolis, Ind.: The Bobbs-Merrill Co., Inc.

Diary of Gideon Welles, Secretary of the Navy under Lincoln and Johnson. Vols. 1–3, New York, 1911.

DiPerna, Paula. *Complete Travel Guide to Cuba*. New York: St. Martin's Press, 1979.

Encyclopedia Americana. International Edition; Danbury, Conn.: Grolier, Inc., 1991.

Fodor's Complete Guide of 27 Caribbean Islands. New York: Fodor's Travel Publ. subs. of Random House, Inc., 1990.

Fuson, Robert H. *The Log of Christopher Columbus*. Camden, Maine: International Marine Pub. Co., 1987.

Gibbons, Tony. *Warships and Naval Battles of the Civil War*. New York: Gallery Books, W. H. Smith, 1989; 176 pages, colored drawings and documentation of major ships of Civil War conflicts.

Jones, Virgil Carrington. *The Civil War at Sea;* Farragut at Mobile Bay, Pg. 159. New York: Holt, Rinehart, Winston, 1960–1962.

Medal of Honor 1861–1949, the Navy. Bureau of Naval Personnel, Pges. 43, 297.

Meriwether, Colver. *Raphael Semmes*. 367 pages, indexed, American Crises Biographies; Philadelphia, Pa.: Geo. W. Jacobs & Co., 1913.

Milhallen, Hirst Dillon, and James Ralph Johnson. *Best Photos of the Civil War*. New York: Arco Publishing Co., Inc., 1961.

Military History Magazine, December 1991, Pges. 72–76; Leesburg, Va.: Empire Press, bi-monthly.

Myers, Elizabeh P. *Jenny Lind, Songbird from Sweden*. Champaign, Ill.: Garrard Publ. Co., 1968.

Naval Battles and Heroes. Indexed, illustrated. New York: American Heritage Publishing Co., Inc., 1960.

Rouse, Irving. *The Tainos: Rise & Decline of the People Who Greeted Columbus*. Yale University Press, 1992; See *Scientific American*, October 1992 issue.

U.S. Navy Department Official Records of the Union and Confederate Navies in the War of the Rebellion, 1895:

    Series I: Vol. 1 "Operations of the Cruisers, January 19, 1861 to December 31, 1862."

    Series I: Vol. 2 "Operations of the Cruisers, January 1, 1863 to March 31, 1864."

    Series I: Vol. 11 "Operations of North Atlantic Blockade Aquadron, October 28, 1864 to February 1, 1865."

    Series I: Vol. 21 "West Gulf Blockade Squadron, January 1, 1864 to December 31, 1864."

Webster's Ninth New Collegiate Dictionary, geographical and biographical sketches.

Who Was Who in America. Historical Vol. 1607–1896; Chicago, Ill.: Marquis' Who's Who, 1963.

Listing of Crew Members

Effort has been made to list all crew members of U.S.S. *Vanderbilt* and U.S.S. *Brooklyn* whether mentioned in this diary or not.

Explanatory notes: Marg Nts = Margin Notes found at beginning and end of diaries. Ships are italicized.

179

Barstow, Haviland, 2nd Asst. Eng. (*Brooklyn*)

Beldon (*Vanderbilt*)—25Sep63, 10Dec63

Bell (*Brooklyn*)—List Bk3

Bennet, Frank, 1st Cls. Boy (*Brooklyn*) Wounded Mobile Bay

Berger (*Brooklyn*)—Lists Bk3

Blagden, William, Ship's Cook USN (*Brooklyn*) Cong. Medal of Honor, Mobile Bay (Born 1832 England)

Blake, Charles F., Lieut. (*Brooklyn*) Wounded Mobile Bay

Bogart, Robert D., Capt's. Clerk (*Brooklyn*)

Bradford, William, Pvt. USMC (*Brooklyn*)—2Aug64, Watch lists Bk3

Bragdon, Charles A., Boatswain (*Brooklyn*)—14May64

Branagan, John, Pvt. USMC (*Brooklyn*)—Watch lists Bk3

Bray (*Brooklyn*)—2Aug64, Watch lists Bk3

Brayton, Daniel C., Sailmaker (*Brooklyn*) Wounded Mobile Bay

Brean [Brian] (*Brooklyn*)—Marg Nts end Bk3, Watch lists Bk3

Brierton, Patrick, Landsman (*Brooklyn*) Wounded Mobile Bay

Brittell, Rufus, Landsman (*Brooklyn*) Wounded Mobile Bay

Brooks (*Brooklyn*)—List Bk3

Brother, Charles Pvt. USMC (*Vanderbilt*)—25Feb63, Marg Nts end Bk1B (See his diary in CIVIL WAR NAVAL CHRONOLOGY 1861–1865)

Brown, Bernard, Ord. Seaman (*Brooklyn*) Wounded Mobile Bay

Brown, John, Capt. Forecastle USN (*Brooklyn*) Cong. Medal of Honor, Mobile Bay (Born 1826, Scotland)

Brown, Joseph, Quartrmstr (*Brooklyn*) Cong. Medal of Honor, Mobile Bay

Brown, William H., Landsman USN (*Brooklyn*) Wounded Mobile Bay, Cong. Medal of Honor, Mobile Bay (Born 1836, Baltimore, Md.)

Bryant, John, Armorer's Mate (*Brooklyn*) Wounded Mobile Bay

Bryson (*Brooklyn*)—List Bk3

Bullard, J.A., 3rd Asst. Eng. (*Brooklyn*)

Burdick (*Brooklyn*)—Watch lists Bk3

Burke, Richard, Coal Heaver (*Brooklyn*) Killed Mobile Bay

Burst (*Brooklyn*)—Watch lists Bk3

Bushby, Joseph, Pvt. USMC (*Brooklyn*)—Watch list Bk3

Byrnes (*Brooklyn*)—Marg Nts end Bk3, Watch list Bk3

Cameron (*Vanderbilt*)—9Dec62

Capell (*Brooklyn*)—List Bk3

Carberry (*Vanderbilt*)—11Apr63, Marg Nts end Bk1B

Carman (*Brooklyn*)—List Bk3

Carter, Alvin A., Ord. Seaman (*Brooklyn*) Wounded Mobile Bay

Cassell, Douglas, Ensign (*Brooklyn*) Wounded Mobile Bay

Cassidy, Thomas S., Gunner (*Brooklyn*)

Cavendy, Edward, Act. Vol. Lieut. Comm. (*Gemsbok*)—1Mar63

Chester, Henry, Seaman, Wounded Mobile Bay (*Seminole*)—25Aug64

Clark, Roland M., Ord. Seaman (*Brooklyn*) Wounded Mobile Bay—List Bk3

Coffey, Daniel, Pvt. USMC (*Brooklyn*)—Marg Nts end Bk3, Watch lists Bk3

Cole, Abel, Seaman (*Brooklyn*) Wounded Fort Fisher Battle

Collins, Napoleon, Commander (*Octorara*)—17Apr63

Cook, W.H., Master's Mate (*Brooklyn*) Killed Mobile Bay—List Bk3

Cooper, John, Coxswain (*Brooklyn*) Cong. Medal of Honor, Mobile Bay

Cooperman, George P., Pvt. USMC (*Brooklyn*)—Watch lists Bk3

Cornell, James D., Act. Master's Mate (*Vanderbilt*)—1Nov63

Cotter (*Brooklyn*)—List Bk3

Cummings, Simeon W., 3rd Asst. Eng. (C.S.S. *Alabama*)—6Sep63

Cushley, Robert, Drummer Boy, Wash. D.C. (*Brooklyn*)—4Sep64, Lists Bk3

Dailey (*Brooklyn*)—List Bk3

Danenhower [Dehenhon], Charles, Act Master's Mate (*Vanderbilt*)—1Nov63

Daniels, Joseph P.[D.], Act. 1st Lieut. Ex. Off. (*Vanderbilt*)—4Nov62, 14Dec62, 26Apr63, Marg Nts end of Bk1B, 2Jul63, 5Jul63, 28Jul63

Darling, V.P. (*Vanderbilt*)—16Dec62, Marg Nts end Bk1B

Davidson (*Brooklyn*)—Watch lists Bk3

Davis, E.M. (*Vanderbilt*)—21Oct63

Davis, George W., Pvt. USMC (*Brooklyn*)—2Aug64, 4Sep64, Marg Nts end Bk3, Watch lists Bk3

Davis, Samuel (*Brooklyn*) Cong. Medal of Honor, Mobile Bay

DeHart, W.H., 3rd Asst. Eng. (*Brooklyn*)

Deitz (*Brooklyn*)—List Bk3

De Lawrence, Guillaume, Fifer—Marg Nts begin Bk3

Denig, J. Henry, Sgt. USMC (*Brooklyn*) Cong. Medal of Honor, Mobile Bay (Born 1839 York, Pa.)

Dennis, Richard, Boatswain's Mate USN (*Brooklyn*) Cong. Medal of Honor, Mobile Bay (Born 1826, Mass.)

Dennison, Thomas, Landsman (*Brooklyn*) Wounded Mobile Bay

Deslin (*Vanderbilt*)—Marg Nts end Bk1B

Devine [Divine] (*Brooklyn*)—Watch lists Bk3

Devlan (*Brooklyn*)—Watch lists Bk3

Dixon (*Brooklyn*)—Marg Nts end Bk3, Watch lists Bk3

Doolan (*Brooklyn*)—Watch lists Bk3

Dorrington, Hugh, Pvt. USMC (*Brooklyn*)—2Aug64, Watch lists Bk3

Duffy (*Brooklyn*)—List Bk3

Duggin, Patrick, Landsman (*Brooklyn*) Wounded Mobile Bay

Duncan, Fred C., Master's Mate (*Brooklyn*)

Dunn, Anthony, 1st Cls. Fireman (*Brooklyn*) Killed Mobile Bay

Dunn, John, Coal Heaver (*Brooklyn*) Wounded Mobile Bay

Edwards (*Brooklyn*)—Marg Nts end Bk3, Watch lists Bk3

Evans (*Brooklyn*)—List Bk3

Fellmann, Charles, Seaman (*Brooklyn*) Wounded, Fort Fisher Battle

Ferguson, Alexander, Pvt. USMC (*Brooklyn*)—2Aug64, Watch lists Bk3

Flynn, Maurice P. (*Brooklyn*)—Marg Nts beg Bk3, Watch lists Bk3

Follett (*Brooklyn*)—Watch lists Bk3

Freeman, Martin, Pilot, Wounded Mobile Bay (*Hartford*)—25Aug64

Frick, William, Ord. Seaman (*Brooklyn*) Wounded Mobile Bay

Frisbee, Captain (*Jacob Bell*)—20Feb63

Gans (*Brooklyn*)—List Bk3

Gardner, J. (*Cumberland*)—5Apr63

Germain, John, Chf. Eng. (*Vanderbilt*)—4Nov62, Marg Nts end of Bk1B, 8Jan64

Gilligan, Peter, Pvt. USMC (*Brooklyn*)—2Aug64, Watch lists Bk3

Glisson, Oliver S., Captain (*Mohican*)—28Jul63

Golden, William H., 1st Assist. Engr. (*Vanderbilt*)—4Nov62

Goodwin, F.C., 3rd Asst. Engr. (*Brooklyn*)

Gray, James 1st Mate [native of Aberdeen Scotland, shot during capture of *Saxon*] (*Saxon*)—1Nov63

Green (*Brooklyn*)—Marg Nts end Bk3, Watch lists Bk3

Gregg, Josiah C., Pvt. USMC (*Vanderbilt*)—Marg Nts end Bk1B; (*Brooklyn*)—Marg Nts beg Bk3, Watch lists Bk3

Grimes (*Brooklyn*)—Watch list Bk3

Griswold, George R., Act. Master's Mate (*Vanderbilt*)—21Mar63, 7Apr63

Halstead, William, Coxswain USN (*Brooklyn*) Cong. Medal of Honor, Mobile Bay (Born 1837, N.Y.)

Hamilton, 1st Surgeon (*Vanderbilt*)—4Nov62

Hanson, Frank, Seaman (*Brooklyn*) Wounded Mobile Bay

Happy, Louis, Pvt. USMC (*Brooklyn*)—Watch lists Bk3

Hardie, David, 2nd Asst. Eng. (*Brooklyn*)

Haresk, Lewis, Ord. Seaman (*Brooklyn*) Wounded Mobile Bay

Harmon (*Brooklyn*)—Watch list Bk3

Harper [Hooper], Music Dir (*Vanderbilt*)—Marg Nts end Bk1B

Harris, Theodore R., Pvt. USMC (*Vanderbilt*)—Marg Nts end Bk1B; (*Brooklyn*)—Marg Nts beg Bk3, Watch lists Bk3, 2Aug64

Harrison, William A., Ord. Seaman (*Brooklyn*) Wounded Mobile Bay

Harwood, Eli, Capt's. Cook (*Brooklyn*) Killed Mobile Bay

Havlin, Michael, Pvt. USMC (*Brooklyn*)—Watch lists Bk3

Hawkins, Off. of the Deck (*Vanderbilt*)—27Jul63

Hawkins, William, Seaman (killed in the destruction of blockade runner *Ivanhoe*)—9Jul64

Henry, Jim (*Vanderbilt*)—30Mar63

Hersey, George W., Seaman (*Brooklyn*) Wounded Mobile Bay

Hill, Austin A., Pvt. USMC (*Brooklyn*)—2Aug64, Watch lists Bk3

Hopkins, T.G. (*Vanderbilt*)—Marg Nts end Bk2

Housel, John K.[R.], Coal Heaver (*Brooklyn*) Wounded Mobile Bay

Houston, G. Porter, Capt. of Marines (*Brooklyn*)—1Oct 64, letter 29Oct64 end Bk3, photo 97

Howard, William, Landsman, Wounded Mobile Bay (*Metacomet*)—25Aug64

Hudson, Michael, Orderly Sgt. USMC (*Brooklyn*)—1Oct64, Lists Bk3, Cong. Medal of Honor, Mobile Bay (Born 1834 Sligo County, Ireland)

Ingersol, Will, Pvt. USMC (*Vanderbilt*)—Marg Nts end Bk1B; (*Brooklyn*)—Watch lists Bk3

Irlam, John, Seaman USN (*Brooklyn*) Cong. Medal of Honor, Mobile Bay (Born 1840, England)

Irving, John, Coxswain USN (*Brooklyn*) Cong. Medal of Honor, Mobile Bay (Born 1839, East Brooklyn, N.Y.)

Irwin, Nicholas, Seaman USN (*Brooklyn*) Cong. Medal of Honor, Mobile Bay (Born 1833, Denmark)

Jackson, Charles, Surgeon's Steward (*Brooklyn*)

Madden, William, Coal Heaver USN (*Brooklyn*) Cong. Medal of Honor, Mobile Bay (Born 1843, England)

Maher (*Brooklyn*)—Watch lists Bk3

Mali(o)ry (*Vanderbilt*)—26Apr63

Mann, Edward, Ord. Seaman, Wounded Mobile Bay (*Seminole*)—25Aug64

Mathews, Sailing Master (*Vanderbilt*)—4Nov62, 28Jan63, 29Jan63, 4Jul63

Maulsby, George, Surgeon (*Brooklyn*)

Maxwell, John, Coal Heaver (*Brooklyn*) Wounded Mobile Bay

McBench, Patrick, Pvt. USMC (*Brooklyn*)—14Apr64, 2Aug64, Marg Nts end Bk3, Watch lists Bk3

McCafrey, William, Seaman (*Brooklyn*) Wounded Mobile Bay

McCandless, Robert, Corp. USMC (*Vanderbilt*)—Marg Nts end Bk1B

McCarren, William, Landsman (*Brooklyn*) Wounded Mobile Bay

McCarthy, Daniel, Landsman (*Brooklyn*) Wounded Mobile Bay

McDermott, James, Landsman (*Brooklyn*) Killed Mobile Bay

McDonald, Edward, Pvt. USMC (*Brooklyn*)—Watch list Bk3

McDonald, James, Seaman, Wounded Mobile Bay (*Metacomet*)—25Aug64

McGloin, William, Act. Master (*Vanderbilt*)—4Nov62, 16Apr63, Marg Nts end Bk1B

McGlone, James, Pvt. (*Brooklyn*)—Watch lists Bk3

McGowan, Patrick, Coal Heaver (*Brooklyn*) Wounded Mobile Bay

McKee, Edwin, Pvt. USMC (*Vanderbilt*)—30Oct62, 30Dec62, 15Feb63, Marg Nts end Bk1B, Marg Nts end Bk3

McKennon, John, Ord. Seaman (*Brooklyn*) Wounded Mobile Bay

McPherson, John, Seaman (*Brooklyn*) Wounded Mobile Bay

McQuaid, Patrick, Pvt. USMC (*Brooklyn*)—14Apr64, Marg Nts end Bk3, Watch lists Bk3

Megary (*Brooklyn*)—Watch lists Bk3

Mifflin, James, Engnr's. Cook USN (*Brooklyn*) Cong. Medal of Honor, Mobile Bay (Born 1839, Richmond, Va.)

Miller, Charles, Boatswain (*Seminole*) Wounded Mobile Bay—25Aug64

Miller, John, Seaman, Wounded & Died, Mobile Bay (*Seminole*)—25Aug64

Milliken, Charles E., Ord. Seaman, Killed Mobile Bay (*Seminole*)—25Aug64

Miner, Charles, Landsman (*Brooklyn*) Wounded Mobile Bay

Morgan, Patrick, Orderly Sgt. USMC (*Vanderbilt*)—5Dec62, 10Mar63, Marg Nts end Bk1B

Motts, Charles, Pvt. USMC (*Brooklyn*)—Watch lists Bk3

Regan (*Brooklyn*)—Watch lists Bk3

Remington (*Vanderbilt*)—9Dec62

Richards, Lewis, Seaman (*Brooklyn*) Killed Mobile Bay

Roache, Lawrence, Pvt. USMC (*Brooklyn*)—Watch lists Bk3

Roache, Thomas, Pvt. USMC (*Brooklyn*)

Robinson, William, Capt'n. Foretop (*Brooklyn*) Wounded Mobile Bay, Cong. Medal of Honor, Mobile Bay

Rowland (*Brooklyn*)—Watch lists Bk3

Ryan, James, Pvt. USMC (*Brooklyn*)—2Aug64, Watch lists Bk3

Ryan, John, Landsman (*Brooklyn*) Killed Mobile Bay

Sanders, James, Pvt. USMC (*Brooklyn*)—Watch lists Bk3

Searles, W. (*Prince Edward*) [Buried Angra Pequina Bay]—2Nov63

Semmes, Raphael, Capt. (*Alabama*)—5Feb63, 5Oct63, photo 80

Seymour, Charles B., Seaman (*Brooklyn*) Killed Mobile Bay

Shea, James, Quarter Gunner (*Brooklyn*) Wounded Mobile Bay

Shean (*Brooklyn*)—Watch lists Bk3

Sheppard, Stephen, Master Captain (*Saxon*)—2Nov63

Sigsbee, Charles D., Ensign (*Brooklyn*)

Smith, Heber, Asst. Surgeon (*Brooklyn*)

Smith, Willard Moon, Corp. USMC (*Vanderbilt*)—3Nov62, 21Feb63, 29Mar63, Marg Nts end Bk1B; (*Brooklyn*)—Marg Nts beg Bk3, Watch lists Bk3, Cong. Medal of Honor, Mobile Bay (Born 1840, Allegany, N.Y.), photo 3

Smith, William, Pvt. USMC (*Brooklyn*) Killed Mobile Bay—Lists Bk3

Somace, 2nd (*Vanderbilt*)—9Dec62

Stauffer (*Brooklyn*)—Watch lists Bk3

Steinbeck, Charles, Ord. Seaman (*Brooklyn*) Wounded Mobile Bay

Sterling, James E., Coal Heaver USN (*Brooklyn*) Wounded Mobile Bay, Cong. Medal of Honor, Mobile Bay (Born 1838, Maine)

Stevens, Abraham L., Master's Mate (*Brooklyn*) Wounded Mobile Bay

Stewart, John, Pvt. USMC (*Brooklyn*)—Lists Bk3, Marg Nts beg Bk3

Sullivan (*Brooklyn*)—Watch lists Bk3

Swann, Thomas L., Lieut., Ordn'c. Off. Exec. (*Brooklyn*)—24Dec64

Taylor, Benjamin K., Landsman (*Brooklyn*) Wounded Mobile Bay

Thomas, Robert G., Carpenter (*Brooklyn*)

Thompson, George, Seaman, Wounded & Died, Mobile Bay (*Seminole*)—25Aug64

Thompson, John, Ord. Seaman (*Brooklyn*) Wounded Mobile Bay

Thornton, G.E., Paymaster (*Brooklyn*)

Todd, Henry D., Lieut. (*Vanderbilt* Flag Lieut.)—19Mar63

Todd, Samuel, Quartrmstr USN (*Brooklyn*) Cong. Medal of Honor, Mobile Bay (Born 1815, Portsmouth, N.Y.)

Tolfree, James E., Act. Ass't. Paymaster (*Vanderbilt*)—4Nov62, 22Jan63, 26Apr63, Marg Nts end Bk1B, 17Sep63, 25Sep63

Topley, William, Orderly Sgt. USMC (*Brooklyn*)—4Sep64

Toppin, John D., 2nd Asst. Eng. (*Brooklyn*)

Tower, George E., 2nd Asst. Eng. (*Brooklyn*)

Towle, P.S. (*Vanderbilt*)—30Dec62, Marg Nts end Bk1B; (*Brooklyn*)—Asst. Paymaster, USN—29May64

Troutman, Daniel, Pvt. USMC (*Brooklyn*)—Watch lists Bk3

Utter, John, Act. Ensign (*Brooklyn*)

Wann (*Brooklyn*)—List Bk3

Webb, Henry, Master's Mate (*Brooklyn*)

Webster, Thomas, Landsman, Wounded Mobile Bay (*Seminole*)—25Aug64

Whaling, Thomas, Pvt. USMC (*Brooklyn*)—Watch lists Bk3

Wheaton, Pvt. USMC? (*Brooklyn*)—2Aug64, Watch lists Bk3

White, Charles, Boatswain, Wounded Mobile Bay (*Seminole*)—25Aug64

White, John, Act. Ensign, Wounded Mobile Bay (*Metacomet*)—25Aug64

White, Robert G., Seaman, Wounded & Died, Mobile Bay (*Seminole*)—25Aug64

William, Thomas, Seaman (*Brooklyn*) Killed Mobile Bay

Williams, William, Pvt. USMC (*Brooklyn*)—Marg Nts end Bk3, Watch lists Bk3

Williard, Act. Assist. Surgeon (*Vanderbilt*)—4Nov62

Wilson, James, Act. Corp. USMC (*Brooklyn*)—Watch lists Bk3

Wrand (*Brooklyn*)—Watch lists Bk3

Wyman, Henry, Act. Master's Mate (*Vanderbilt*)—1Nov63

Young, Isaac, Ordinary Seaman, Wounded & Died, Mobile Bay (*Seminole*)—25Aug64

Listing of Ships

Cadmus [British frigate]—26Jan63, 30Jan63

Caleb Cushing [schooner]—26Sep63

Chas. H. Foster [brig of Phila.]—12May63

Chickasaw [ironclad monitor]—5Aug64, 24Aug64

City of Bath [American cargo ship]—6Jul63, 22Jul63

City of Cape Town—30Aug63

Clyde of London [sidewheel cargo steamer]—14Feb63, 18Feb63, 13May63

Colorado [steam screw frigate]—1Oct62 Marg.Note, 24Dec64, 25Dec64

Columbia [ironclad steamer]—7Apr63, 11Apr63

Constitution [frigate]—6Jul63, 20Jul63

Conway of London [British mail steamer]—21Dec 63

Corsican [English steamer]—8Jan64

Cumberland [frigate]—5Apr63

D.B. Ende (*Double-Ender*) [gunboat]—14Jun64

Eastern Queen [troop transport]—3Dec62, 1Apr63

Egmond (*Egmont?*) [English]—1Aug63

Eleurie [French bark]—2Aug63

Eliza M. Strong [mail ship]—13May63

Fair Haven [US transport]—30Mar63

Fair West [brig]—19May63

Florida (*Oreto*) [screw sloop]—19Feb63, 7Apr63, 23Jul63, 26Sep63, 24Jan64

Frances Jane of Baltimore [American brig]—28Apr63, 29Apr63

Francis [British schooner]—27Feb63

Frank Boult (*Bolton*)—26Mar63

Fuchu (*Fuchsia?*) [cargo ship]—21Sep63

Galena [ironclad]—4Jul64, 2Aug64, 25Aug64

Gemsbok [bark]—1Mar63, 13May63, 16May63, 10Jun63

Genesee [sidewheel steamer]—4Jul64, 2Aug64

George Griswold [Clipper cargo ship]—15Jul63

Georgia [ironclad]—25June63, 1Jul63, 6Jul63, 10Jul63, 16Aug63, 30Aug63, 6Sep63, 1Oct63, 20Oct63, 6Dec63, 24Jan64

Gertrude [British screw steamer]—16Apr63, 17Apr63, Misc entries

Good Hope [British bark] 30Oct63

Hamlet of Boston [American ship]—20Oct63

Hampden of Liverpool [American ship]—26Sep63

Hartford [steam frigate]—1June64, 4Jul64, 9Jul64, 11Jul64, 2Aug64, 5Aug64, 6Aug64

Herald of Nassau [iron sidewheel cargo ship]—30Apr63

Hermona [French frigate]—8Oct63

Heymala (*Himalaya*?) [British steamer]—Marg. Notes after 24Jan64

Hudson of Bath, ME [American packet]—8Jan63

Illinois [steam sloop]—30Nov62, 3Dec62, 4Dec62, 26Jan63

Imortalite [English frigate]—19Dec63

Iriadley (*Ariadne*?) [English frigate]—19Dec63

Iroquois [steam sloop]—22Jan63, 23Jan63, 24Jan63, 30Mar63

Isabella M. A'Fransisia [ferry]—4Feb63

Itasca [screw steamer]—4Jul64, 2Aug64

Ivanhoe [blockader]—9Jul64

Jacob Bell [sidewheel steamer]—19Feb63, 20Feb63, 26Feb63, 7Apr63

Johanna Elizabeth [Dutch bark]—Marg. Notes end of Book 1, 31Aug63, 1Sep63, 3Sep63, 10Nov63

John Watt of Bath [American merchant ship]—30Aug63

Juniata [screw sloop]—30Apr63, 24Dec64

Kearsarge [screw steamer]—15Jul64

Kennebec [screw steamer]—4Jul64, 2Aug64

Lackawanna [screw sloop]—19Aug62 Marg. Note, 26Jan63, 27Jan63, 30Mar63, 12Jun64, 4Jul64, 10Jul64, 2Aug64, 5Aug64

Leander [English man of war]—15Jul63

Lucy Frances of Brookville [bark]—12May63

M. Sandford [troop transport]—3Dec62, 4Dec62

Magnolia [sidewheel steamer]—26Mar63

Manhattan [monitor]—9Jul64, 20Jul64, 28Jul64

Mattabesett [sidewheel steamer]—4Jul64, 2Aug64

May Queen [English schooner]—1May63

Mejico [Spanish mail steamer]—16Mar63, 21Apr63

Metacomet [sidewheel steamer]—8Jun64, 2Jul64, 4Jul64, 2Aug64, 5Aug64

Minna Ha Ha of Boston [clipper ship]—15Nov63

Minnesota [steam frigate]—18Jan63, 24Jan63, 24Dec64

Mohican [US steamer]—25Jun63, 1Jul63, 22Jul63, 23Jul63, 27Jul63, 28Jul63, 31Jul63, 24Dec64

Monongahela [screw sloop]—4Jul64, 10Jul64, 2Aug64, 5Aug64

Rising Sun of Providence [American whaling schooner]—28May63

Salvira (Salvor?) [troop transport steamer]—3Dec 62

San Jacinto [screw frigate]—4Feb63, 2May63, 21Oct63

Santiago de Cuba [sidewheel steamer]—17Mar63, 20Apr63, 26Sep63

Saxon of Cape Town [British bark]—30Oct63, 1Nov63, Misc entries

Scorio (Scotia?) [steamer]—8Nov62

Sea Bride—6Sep63

Sebago [sidewheel steamer]—24Aug64

Selma [sidewheel gunboat]—5Aug64

Seminole [screw steamer]—20Mar63, 4Jul64, 10Jul64, 2Aug64, 5Aug64

Sonomas [sidewheel steamer]—18Mar63, 5Apr63, 21Apr63

Shamrock [sidewheel steamer]—24Dec64

Shepherd Knapp [ship]—17Feb63, 19Feb63, 14May63, 29May63

St Lawrence [Man of War]—26Mar63

Sultanna [cargo ship]—29Oct63

Susquehanna [sidewheel steamer]—24Dec64

Tacony [bark]—26Sep63

Tecumseh [ironclad monitor]—2Aug64, 5Aug64, 25Aug64

Tennesee (Union) [sidewheel steamer]—2Jun64, 4Jul64, 11Jul64

Tennesee (Conf) [ironclad]—5Aug64

Thames [British mail steamer]—21Dec63

Ticonderoga [screw sloop]—30Mar63

Trent [steamer]—4Feb63, 13May63, 1Jan64, Marg. Notes after 24Jan64

Tug Union [ferry]—4Feb63

Tuscaloosa (formerly Conrad) [bark]—6Sep63, 29Oct63, 30Oct63

Tuscarora [steam sloop]—23Dec62, 27Dec62

Union of Provincetown [American whaling schooner]—28May63

Univ. of Watterford [prize taken by Union ship Alabama]—14Feb63

Vanderbilt [sidewheel steamer, 3360 Tonnage, 2 100-pdr Parrott rifles, 12 9-in Dahlgren guns]—19Aug62, 4Nov62, 26Feb63, 3Mar63, 18Mar63, 7May63 Marg. Notes end of Book 1, 14Jul63, 6Dec63, 24Jan64, 2Jun64, 24Dec64

Victoria of Nassau [schooner]—14Apr63

Wabash [screw frigate]—24Dec64

Wachusetts [screw sloop]—25Feb63, 26Feb63, 9Mar63, 14Mar63, 13May63, 15May63, 16May63, 18May63, 23May63

INDEX III

General

This index also contains persons mentioned in the diaries by position or title only. Their names are included here, some in parentheses, because of their significance to the period of the Civil War and have been extracted from Official Documents of the U.S. Navy.
(First names are included where known.)

A

Abaco, 27, 44, 46, 88, 107
Algoa Bay, Vice Consul of, 81
Allen, U.S. Consul, Bermuda, 8
Amerigo Island, 64
Angra Pequena Bay, South Africa, 83–85, 93

B

Bahia, 81, 85
Barbados, 38, 51, 64, 87
Bassa Terra, 34, 38, 39, 49, 50
Beaufort, North Carolina, 128, 130
Bennet, James G., 127
Bermuda, 8, 79
Birche, Governor of St. Thomas, 32, 40
Bird Key, 34
Blue Beard, the Pirate, 31, 32
Bonaire, Island of, 55
Borbon, Island of, 80
Boston, Massachusetts, Charlestown Navy Yard, 125, 127, 132; Marine Barracks, 125
Bragg, Braxton, Confederate General, 129
Brazilian Frigate Admiral, 86
Bridgetown, 38, 51
Brooklyn Marine Barracks, 1, 2, 99, 102
Buchanan, James, U.S. President, 124
Burnside, Major General Ambrose E., 10, 15, 72
Butler, Major General Benjamin F., 125, 129, 130

C

Caicos, Island of, 88
Calvin, John B., 64
Cameron, Secretary of War Simon, 6
Cape Fria, Brazil, 68
Cape Hatteras, 27
Cape of Good Hope, South Africa, 9, 73, 74, 86
Cape Town, South Africa, 75, 76, 81, 89, (Walter Graham, Esq., U.S. Consul)
Caracas, Venezuela, 54
Castel Morro, Cuba, 28, 45
Cat Island, 47
Cattaraugus County, New York, 73
Chancellorsville, Virginia, 55
Charleston, South Carolina, 46
Chronologies of Voyages, U.S.S. *Vanderbilt*, 58–60, 90–92; U.S.S. B*rooklyn*, 124, 136
City Point, Virginia, 125
Corcoran, General of Irish Legion, 12
Corrie, First Lieutenant Frederick Hamilton, 2
Crauford, Captain Fred A.B., H.M.S. *Egmont*, 72
Curacao, Island of, 55

D

Dahlgren, Rear Admiral John A., 72
Dominica, 33, 38, 51
Don Pedro, Emperor of Brazil, 70, 72
Dupont, Rear Admiral Samuel F., 72